D0128107

Using the *Teach Yourself in 24 Hours* Series

Welcome to the *Teach Yourself in 24 Hours* series! You're probably thinking, "What, they want me to stay up all night and learn this stuff?" Well, no, not exactly. This series introduces a new way to teach you about exciting new products: 24 one-hour lessons, designed to keep your interest and keep you learning. Because the learning process is broken into small units, you will not be overwhelmed by the complexity of some of the new technologies that are emerging in today's market. Each hourly lesson has a number of special items, some old, some new, to help you along.

Minutes

The first 10 minutes of each hour lists the topics and skills that you will learn about by the time you finish the hour. You will know exactly what the hour will bring with no surprises.

Minutes

Twenty minutes into the lesson, you will have been introduced to many of the newest features of the software application. In the constantly evolving computer arena, knowing everything a program can do will aid you enormously now and in the future.

Minutes

Before 30 minutes have passed, you will have learned at least one useful task. Many of these tasks take advantage of the newest features of the application. These tasks use a hands-on approach, telling you exactly which menus and commands you need to use to accomplish the goal. This approach is found in each lesson of the *24 Hours* series.

Minutes

You will see after 40 minutes that many of the tools you have come to expect from the *Teach Yourself* series are found in the *24 Hours* series as well. Notes and Tips offer special tricks of the trade to make your work faster and more productive. Warnings help you avoid those nasty time-consuming errors.

Minutes

By the time you're 50 minutes in, you'll probably run across terms you haven't seen before. Never before has technology thrown so many new words and acronyms into the language, and the New Terms elements found in this series will carefully explain each and every one of them.

Minutes

At the end of the hour, you may still have questions that need answered. You know the kind—questions on skills or tasks that come up every day for you, but that weren't directly addressed during the lesson. That's where the Q&A section can help. By answering the most frequently asked questions about the topics discussed in the hour, Q&A not only answers your specific question, it provides a succinct review of all that you have learned in the hour.

Teach
Yourself
THE
INTERNET
in 24 Hours

Teach Yourself

THE
INTERNET

in 24 Hours

Noel Estabrook
with Bill Vernon

201 West 103rd Street
Indianapolis, Indiana 46290

Publisher and President   Richard K. Swadley
Publishing Manager   Mark Taber
Director of Editorial Services   Cindy Morrow
Acquisitions Manager   Beverly M. Eppink
Assistant Marketing Managers   Kristina Perry, Rachel Wolfe

Acquisitions Editor
Beverly M. Eppink

Development Editor
Scott D. Meyers

Editors
Charles A. Hutchinson
Katherine Stuart Ewing
Marla Reece
Kris Simmons
Tonya R. Simpson

Indexer
Johnna L. VanHoose

Technical Reviewers
Bill Vernon
Robert Bogue

Editorial Coordinator
Katie Wise

Technical Edit Coordinator
Lorraine E. Schaffer

Resource Coordinator
Deborah Frisby

Editorial Assistants
Carol Ackerman
Andi Richter
Rhonda Tinch-Mize

Cover Designer
Tim Amrhein

Book Designer
Gary Adair

Copy Writer
Peter Fuller

Production Team Supervisors
Brad Chinn
Charlotte Clapp

Production
Rick Bond
Betsy Deeter
Paula Lowell
Janet Seib

Overview

Contents

Acknowledgments

I would first and foremost like to acknowledge The Author, Jesus Christ, for blessing me with the ability and perseverance to do a little authoring myself. For some reason, He keeps giving me strength to meet these insane deadlines book after book. Second, I would like to thank my wife, Anita. I hope that one day I can repay her in sacrifice half as much as she has sacrificed for me. I would also like to give a big "thank you" to Beverly Eppink at Sams.net. Even though she's the one who holds me to those insane deadlines I mentioned earlier, it's hard to imagine working for anyone else. We have worked on project after project together, and all of them have been successful in large part to her cooperation and flexibility. I'd also like to thank Stacy Gregg, Matthew Ferguson, and Matthew Lindgren for their contributions. These three added significantly to the quality of this book. Finally, I'd like to thank Grandpa and Uncle John and…wait a minute, sorry, wrong speech. I guess that's about it, after all.

—*Noel Estabrook*

About the Authors

Main Author

Noel Estabrook (noel@oesystems.com) is currently a faculty member of the College of Education at Michigan State University after having obtained degrees in Psychology, Education, and Instructional Technology. He is heavily involved in delivering Internet training and technical support to educators, professionals, and laymen, particularly those in the disabled community. He also runs his own training and Web consulting business part-time in addition to writing. He has been a contributing author on more than 10 Internet books for Macmillan Publishing and for some strange reason plans on doing even more in the future. You can find out a little more about him by visiting his Web page at `http://noel.educ.msu.edu/`.

Contributing Author

Bill Vernon (`oemga@midlink.com`) holds a Bachelor's Degree in Physics from Purdue University. He's a member of the Internet Services Group at Eli Lilly and Company where he helps maintain Lilly's intranet, ELVIS. Bill owns Omega Design, an Indianapolis-based company that develops Web sites for corporate and commercial clients. He enjoys mountain biking, skiing, snowboarding, soccer, and inline hockey. Bill spends the remainder of his time with his new wife Karly (whom he adores) and his Siberian Husky Kivi.

Tell Us What You Think!

As a reader, you are the most important critic and commentator of our books. We value your opinion and want to know what we're doing right, what we could do better, what areas you'd like to see us publish in, and any other words of wisdom you're willing to pass our way. You can help us make strong books that meet your needs and give you the computer guidance you require.

Do you have access to CompuServe or the World Wide Web? Then check out our CompuServe forum by typing **GO SAMS** at any prompt. If you prefer the World Wide Web, check out our site at http://www.mcp.com.

> **Note**
>
> If you have a technical question about this book, call the technical support line at (317) 581-3833.

As the publishing manager of the group that created this book, I welcome your comments. You can fax, e-mail, or write me directly to let me know what you did or didn't like about this book—as well as what we can do to make our books stronger. Here's the information:

Fax: 317/581-4669

E-mail: newtech_mge@sams.mcp.com

Mail: Mark Taber
        Sams Publishing
        201 W. 103rd Street
        Indianapolis, IN 46290

Introduction

My favorite television commercial of all time has to be one that aired several years ago. To be honest, I can't even remember what company it was for, but the images have stayed with me for a long time.

Imagine the scene: a high school classroom, crowded with adults, attending what is obviously some kind of introductory summer computer class. There's no air conditioning, all of the students are sweating in their business suits, ties loosened about the neck. In front of the class is the stereotypical computer geek—pocket protector, glasses, disheveled hair, the whole bit.

With sweat dripping into the students' vacant eyes, the instructor drones on, "one…more…time…repeat after me: MEGAbytes…GIGAbytes…TERAbytes." The class, mustering what is left of its fading energy manages to repeat a smattering of "…megabytes…gigabytes…terabytes…".

Does learning anything about computers have to be like this? No way! With all the new interfaces, easy-to-use software, and helpful guides like this one available, learning can be almost pain-free. Learning the Internet is no exception.

This book intends to help you make sense of ISPs, clients, servers, FTP, UseNet, and all those other words you might have heard. You will be taken step by step through those tasks that you will most often use on the Internet. You will know how to navigate the Internet from the time you get connected until the time you hang up.

Oh, one more thing: you don't *have* to finish this book in 24 hours. If you do, you'd better have a BIG cup of coffee!

What This Book Is

To begin, the key to learning anything is motivation. You've already got that one licked: you've bought this book, so it's obvious you want to learn.

The next key to learning is to consume information in small, easily understood chunks. Typical computer books of this size are often divided into a dozen or so chapters. You will find that this book contains twice that number. Why? Because we understand that most people like to learn a little information, get some practice, digest it, maybe take a little breather, and then move on.

Last, it's important that instructional material is just that: instructional. Many computer and Internet-related books today are nothing more than fancy user's manuals. Again, we've taken a different approach.

Each chapter is actually a lesson that offers you a chance to follow along with exercises. In addition, there is a Q & A section at the end of each lesson as well as a short self-quiz and an activity that you can complete on your own to reinforce what you have learned.

Here is a quick preview of what you'll find in this book:

- [ ] Part I, "The Basics," takes you through some of the things you'll need to know before you start. You'll get a clear explanation of what the Internet is really like, learn how you can actually use the Internet in real life, find tips on Internet Service Providers, and receive an introduction to the World Wide Web.

- [ ] Part II, "E-Mail: The Great Communicator," teaches you all you'll need to know about e-mail. Learn basics like reading and sending e-mail, as well as more advanced functions such as attaching documents, creating aliases, and more. You'll also find out all about listservs and how to use them to your advantage.

- [ ] Part III, "News and Real-Time Communication," shows you many of the things that make the Internet an outstanding tool for communication. You'll learn about newsgroups and how to communicate with thousands of people by clicking your mouse. You'll also learn how to carry on live, real-time conversations over the Internet, as well as get information on some of the hottest new technology such as Net Phones.

- [ ] Part IV, "The World Wide Web," shows you what is now the most exciting part of the Internet. Learn which browser is best for you, get the basics of Web navigation, and find out how to help your browser with plug-ins. Finally, you'll discover the most powerful tool on the Web today—the search engine—and more importantly, how to use it.

- [ ] Part V, "Finding Information on the Net," explains some of the other useful functions of the Net. You'll learn how to transfer files and use Gopher. You'll also learn how to access libraries and other resources by using Telnet. Finally, this section will show you how to use the Internet to locate people, places, and things that might not be available directly through the Web.

- [ ] Part VI, "Getting the Most Out of the Internet," shows you practical ways to use the Internet. You can find resources and techniques on how to get information about entertainment, education, and business. Finally, learn how to use the Internet just to have fun.

PART

I

The Basics

Hour

Hour 1

The Internet: What's It Really Like?

Information superhighway. Cyberspace. The Virtual World. You would have to be a hermit not to hear these terms on an almost daily basis. But what do they all mean? If VRML, HTML, plug-ins, and other terms related to the Internet make you want to throw down your phaser and meekly run away to where no one's run before, stick around.

This is the place where it all begins; in this book, the Internet starts to make sense. You can now put many of these terms together and make sense of them all. In this lesson, you can find answers to the following questions:

- ☐ How does the Internet really work?
- ☐ How is the Internet put together?
- ☐ What different types of things does the Internet enable you to do?
- ☐ What in the world is an Internet client?
- ☐ How are elements identified on the Internet?

If you think you already know the answer to these questions, you can skip ahead to the next lessons. You may want to read on anyway, however, because you might see the Internet presented in a way you've never seen before.

More Than a Highway

You don't need to be around the Internet for long to realize that the term *Information Superhighway* doesn't really explain the wonderful world of the Internet adequately. Using this term is kind of like using an ancient pulley system as an analogy for quantum physics.

What you need is a picture of the Internet that comes complete with whizzing electrons, fiber-optic cables, data transmissions at the speed of light, and all the other bells and whistles that are part and parcel of a miraculous system like the Internet.

Sounds sort of like the phone system, doesn't it? After all, because most Internet traffic basically travels over phone lines, such an analogy makes a lot of sense. Not convinced? A quick peek at Table 1.1 showing the similarities might win you over, as well as give you a more detailed preview of the rest of the lesson.

Table 1.1. The Internet and the phone system.

The Internet	The Phone System
Transmits data such as pictures, text, sound, and video via different types of transmission lines	Transmits data such as voice, video, text, and sound via different types of transmission lines
Is composed of a system of complex, interlocking parts	Is composed of a system of complex, interlocking parts
Requires that each participant system have a unique ID, i.e., e-mail address	Requires that each participant in the in the system have a unique ID, i.e., phone number
Uses various types of equipment to perform many functions—computers, routers, modems, and so on	Uses various types of equipment to perform many functions—phones, switches, and so on

1

When you begin to really think about these systems, the similarities are striking. While you're going through this beginning lesson, continually make note of more specific similarities between the two systems to help you understand even better how the Internet works.

A System of Systems

One of the biggest misconceptions most people have about the Internet is that it is a "thing." They want to put it in a box and try to describe it as if it were a single mechanism instead of a collection of different parts.

Most people, however, have no such misconceptions about the phone system. In fact, talking about the phone system *without* using the word "system" would be almost impossible. In the same way, you should try to always think of the Internet as the "Internet system." This further highlights how very similar the Internet is to the phone system.

Making the Complex Simple

Imagine what type of system can connect and enable literally billions of people to communicate with each other worldwide almost instantaneously. Well, such a thing exists in the phone system and to a slightly but still lesser degree, the Internet.

How does a phone call (or a piece of e-mail) get from Hang-Gin Tien in California to Rhea LaStayt in New York? It is accomplished through a complex series of transmissions through many different stations. Figure 1.1 shows how such a transmission might occur for a typical phone call.

Figure 1.1.

A typical phone call can actually "stop" at dozens of relay stations before reaching its destination.

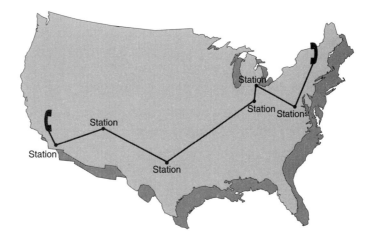

Of course, Figure 1.1 represents a vast simplification of what really happens during a phone call. Each of the points shown as a station in the figure performs a number of functions. Tasks such as deciding which station the current call will go to next, logging the call for record-keeping, and determining what type of call is being transmitted are performed at each station. These functions are completed by a number of wires, relays, and yes, computers, at each station a call passes through.

It's hard to imagine that all this work can happen in the same amount of time that a baseball player takes to swing his bat, but it does.

Now take a look at Figure 1.2. Not a lot of differences in the two, are there? Generally, the computer (or computers) at each routing station on the Internet are referred to as *nodes*.

Figure 1.2.

The methods of transmission for phone calls and e-mail messages are almost identical in nature.

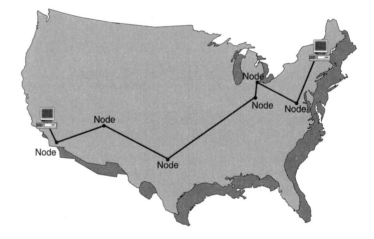

These nodes perform many of the same functions that phone routing stations do. What type of data is being transmitted? Where is it going? Which node will the data go to next? Is all the data here? These questions are some of the many that an Internet node asks and answers with every transmission.

All Those 0s and 1s

One difference does exist in the way data is transferred over these vast networks of computers and wires, and it is in the form that the data takes. A typical phone call transmits analog data in a steady stream, whereas a typical computer transmission is carried out as *digital* data in short bursts. You can think of a digital data transmission as a series of bullets being fired from a gun.

1

NEW TERM **Digital:** All digital data is made up of a series of 0s and 1s that are grouped in unique sequences. Each sequence of 0s and 1s can mean an infinite number of things to the computers translating them into what you see on your screen.

Any ballistics expert can tell you that every bullet has its own distinct fingerprint. Well, so does every "bullet" (referred to as a *packet*) of information sent over the Internet.

NEW TERM **Packet:** A packet is a single sequence of digital data. As each packet of data is sent through the various networks, it has a distinct digital "marker" that tells the routing computer which "gun" it belongs to, as you can see in Figure 1.3.

Sending data in packets offers enormous advantages during transfer. If an interruption occurs in transmission, for example, a computer can simply hold all the packets with identical markers until all the packets have arrived and then put them back together again, as illustrated in Figure 1.3. Sending data this way also means that multiple computers can send packets through the same wire at the same time (because they can be reconstructed at the other end according to their markers). Both of these factors contribute to faster and more reliable data transmission.

Figure 1.3.

No matter how packets get mixed up in transmission, they usually can be put back together again by a computer.

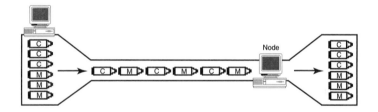

This method of handling data does, of course, begin to blur the lines between all types of data transfer. Even today, many phone calls are digitally switched to allow faster and more reliable transmission than ever before. Soon, phone and Internet data transmission will be handled the same way.

You Just Can't Stop It

You should make note of one last point before moving on to the next item. Because the Internet, like the phone system, is a *system*, you can't "take it down." If a tornado comes out of the sky and destroys a call routing station in Detroit, the system as a whole really isn't affected. That area may see a temporary lapse in service, but calls will be rerouted and the system will continue to run relatively smoothly.

On the Internet, the same is true. One computer, or even a whole set of computers, going offline may affect some users, but it won't damage the integrity of the system. As an example, America Online's computers recently went down for 19 hours, leaving 2 million users without Internet access. Users of other systems didn't even know about the situation until they read it in the paper the next day.

This happens because each computer or computer system on the Internet is, in a manner of speaking, self-sufficient. Of course, much as planes are often rerouted through different airports because of bad weather, so too can Internet traffic be rerouted. In the end, just remember that the Internet functions as an organism, not an organ.

A Variety of Functions

The first apparent benefit of any system is that it has allowances for a variety of functions. The body is a system: It can talk, it can walk, it can hold objects, and it can process information and a million other tasks.

The phone system, of course, works the same way. You can perform more than one task with it. Obviously, you can make phone calls. You also can send faxes and transmit videos using a video phone. If you're hearing-impaired, you can use a TTY machine and make phone calls from a typewriter. In addition, a host of other services are conducted over the phone system: fax-back, 800 and 900 services, and voice-mail messaging systems, to name just a few.

The same is true of the Internet. Because it is a system, you can perform a myriad of different tasks with it. You can send e-mail (Lessons 5–8), read and distribute news (Lessons 9 and 10), participate in real-time communication (Lessons 11 and 12), use the World Wide Web (Lessons 13–16), transfer files (Lesson 18), and more.

CAUTION

Remember that no analogy is perfect. You may think that the Internet seems a lot like the phone system. It is. Remember, however, a lot of differences exist between the two of them as well. One of the biggest is difficulty level. You probably don't need a 300-page book to place a phone call and send a fax; however, you might need such a book for using fax-back and complicated voice-mail systems. Similarly, you need a book that not only lays a foundation for understanding the Internet, but gives you the extra knowledge to handle more complex parts, as well.

1

The Client/Server Relationship

So far, you've learned that the Internet is a system that can perform a variety of functions. So what is the next step? Let me answer this question with yet another question: What do you normally need to perform any function? Answer: Equipment. In the following sections, I describe the standard and functional equipment you need to use the Internet.

It's Standard

If someone were to ask you what equipment you need to conduct business on the Internet, you would probably say, "A computer, a modem, and some type of connection." You'd be right, of course. But what you've really described is just the standard basic equipment needed to cruise the Internet. Although you do need these things, they aren't really the key "equipment" used on the Internet.

To explain, let me go back to the phone system again. Imagine that you have just moved into a brand new house. You're sitting on your nice new furniture, you've had the phone company give you a phone number, and your wall jacks are installed with a phone cord dangling from them. Is all this equipment sufficient for you to place a phone call? No. Obviously, you need a phone. You need that last piece of equipment necessary to "complete the circuit," so to speak. In this instance, the wall jack, cords, and phone number service are just basic prerequisites you need before you can actually start placing calls. The same is true of the Internet: Computers, modems, Internet service providers, and a telephone connection are just the basics.

TIME SAVER

Just because the equipment I just mentioned is basic doesn't mean it's not important. Generally, the more RAM you have, the faster you can go—16MB is almost a minimum now. The more *megahertz* on your PC, the faster you can go; Pentiums running at 100, 133, and even 166 megahertz are now common. The higher your modem speed, the faster you can go—28.8Kbps modems are now standard. Rule of thumb? The faster, the better.

NEW TERM **Megahertz (MHz):** One hertz represents a single cycle of current per second in a circuit. A *cycle* is merely the time it takes an electron to make a "trip" between two points in a circuit. A megahertz represents 1,000 cycles per second. PC speed is usually gauged in megahertz, so a 66MHz processor can complete 66,000 cycles in one second.

Getting the Job Done

Now that you know the basics, you're ready for the functional equipment I talked about earlier. On a phone system, the functional equipment is a phone, a TTY machine, a video phone, or a fax machine.

On the Internet, however, the functional equipment you use isn't a piece of hardware that you can touch or feel, like a phone is. Rather, the functional equipment on the Internet takes the form of a piece of software. This piece of software, which is possibly the most important piece of all, is called a *client*.

NEW TERM   **Client:** All the computers and software that make up the Internet are either clients (which receive and translate data) or servers (which provide and translate data). Thus, by using client software, you can get information from the Internet.

Suppose that you go into a restaurant and order a meal. Several minutes later, a "server" delivers food to your table and you begin to eat. You have just entered into a client/server relationship. You requested food, this request was communicated to a server, and the server fulfilled your request, at which point you consumed the food.

The Internet works exactly the same way. The difference is that, instead of ordering food from a restaurant, you order information from a computer. And just as you can order steaks, salads, desserts, or drinks from a restaurant, you can order e-mail, Gopher sites, World Wide Web pages, and more from Internet servers. Simple, huh?

The Final Piece to the Puzzle

In a restaurant, you order the food, whereas on the Internet, you need to have a piece of software do it for you. Why is that? Well, return to the restaurant example again.

Suppose that you walk into a Japanese restaurant where the menus are written in Japanese and the servers don't speak English. What would you do? You would either have to leave or ask an interpreter to order for you. If you ask an interpreter, you can tell him or her what you want and then he or she can place the order for you.

Because you already know that you don't speak "Internet" (all those 0s and 1s sent in packets), you need an interpreter (Interneterpreter?) to help you. Enter the software client.

Let's See Some ID

The last piece of the puzzle is how the Internet keeps track of all the different client and server computers on the Internet. Once again, using the phone system as an example helps. What one thing do you need more than anything else to call another person on the phone? Easy, the person's phone number. Without it, you're lost.

1

And Your Address Is...

As many phone numbers exist as do phone lines in the world; each one different, each one unique. Every computer on the Internet also has a unique number, and it's called the *IP address.*

NEW TERM **IP address:** This address is used by Internet Protocol (IP) to identify each computer on the Internet. An IP address consists of four numbers between 0 and 255, each separated by a period. A typical IP address might be 35.8.7.92.

But how do computers get IP addresses? An organization called InterNIC gives them to various Internet service providers, or ISPs. (See InterNIC's home page in Figure 1.4.) These ISPs then distribute the addresses to computers on their networks.

Figure 1.4.

InterNIC is responsible for registering all computers on the Internet with IP addresses.

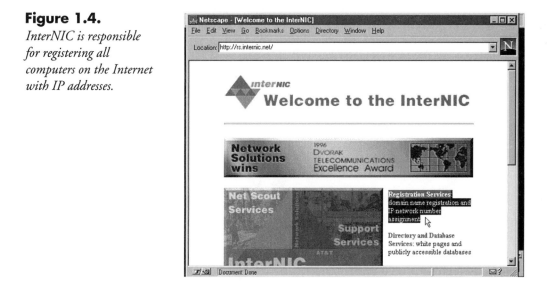

Just as a particular neighborhood might have all its phone numbers begin with 555, so too might all the computers connecting to a particular ISP start with 35.8. In fact, InterNIC usually gives out IP addresses in bundles. Company X, for example, might buy all the IP addresses beginning with 192.63.7 so that it can assign 255 different IP addresses, either permanently or temporarily.

Master of Your Domain

One more point and then you're done for now. If you've watched any TV lately, you may have seen statements like "Find us on the Internet at www.companyx.com." Given these weird-looking addresses, you might be wondering what happened to Company X's IP address.

Let me assure you that it's still there. Just like the SliceNDice Diceit Kitchen Knife Company tells you that its phone number is 1.800.SLICEIT so that you can remember it, the Internet uses *domain names* to "hide" the hard-to-remember IP addresses. After all, would you rather remember `192.63.7.45` or `www.companyx.com`?

NEW TERM **Domain name:** Also registered by InterNIC, the domain name is an "English version" of an IP address. Some computers (called Domain Name Servers) even translate domain names into IP addresses for fast access on the Internet.

Summary

Congratulations! Now you know more about how the Internet really works than a majority of the American population. Beyond the cold facts, you should have a grasp of what is really happening when you send that e-mail message or download that Web page.

You know that the Internet is a system and not a "thing." You should realize that data is transmitted through this system via a complex network of wires, computers, and nodes and that this transmission requires certain equipment, both standard and functional, in order to work properly.

Internet equipment consists of both hardware and software, and software clients translate the language of the Internet into a form you can read on your screen. You also know that, as a result of this complex system, you can perform a variety of different tasks on the Internet, from sending e-mail messages to cruising the World Wide Web.

Finally, you now know that every computer on the Internet has a unique ID called an IP address. You also see that domain names are put in place so that you don't have to remember all the IP addresses.

To further help you understand these concepts, you should go through the following workshop.

Workshop

The following workshop helps solidify the skills that you learned in this lesson.

Q&A

Q What are the basic building blocks of packets?

A Packets are made up of a number of 0s and 1s in a unique sequence that conveys certain information. A portion of these 0s and 1s makes up a marker that identifies a packet as belonging with all other similar packets.

Q Why is InterNIC responsible for assigning IP addresses and domain names?

A Basically, to avoid a lot of confusion. Can you imagine what would happen if every local phone company got to pass out phone numbers? They would have no way to avoid duplication of numbers and no way to route calls to unique numbers. The same is true of IP addresses. InterNIC acts as the administrator to make sure that the Internet runs smoothly.

Q Can clients and servers be either software or hardware?

A Yes. Server computers are generally loaded with server software to help them "serve" their information better. When you use the Internet, not only are you using client software to give you the information you need, but your PC also acts as a client computer at the same time.

Quiz

Take the following quiz to see how much you've learned.

Questions

1. Of the two computers listed below, which one would likely enable you to navigate the Internet more effectively?
    (a) A 386SX 66MHz PC with 4MB of RAM and a 14.4Kbps modem
    (b) A Pentium 100MHz PC with 16MB of RAM and a 28.8Kbps modem
2. How many cycles per second are processed by a 75MHz processor?
3. Is the Netscape Navigator Web browser software a client or a server?
4. On the Internet, which of the following is analogous to a telephone?
    (a) A modem
    (b) A computer
    (c) An e-mail client

Answers

1. (b) Remember: the faster, the better.
2. 75,000; a megahertz is 1,000 cycles per second.
3. A client.
4. An e-mail client. Keep in mind that, on the Internet, software can be considered equipment, too.

Activities

The next time you sit down to watch TV, grab a pencil and paper. Then stick around during commercials. Make note of how many companies have a domain name. Jot down some of them so that you can explore them in a later lesson. As an added activity, see whether you can figure out how many possible IP addresses exist on the Internet. (The answer is in the first section of the next lesson.)

Hour 2

Internet Uses in the Modern World

If one constant exists on the Internet, it is that the Internet is going to continue to grow. Since its inception in the early 70s (that's right, the Net has been around almost 25 years), the Internet's user base has grown from a handful to over 20 million!

To what can this phenomenal growth be attributed? This lesson answers that question, as well as the following:

☐ How did the Internet start?

☐ How has the Internet developed over the last quarter century?

☐ What is the most popular use of the Internet?

☐ How else can the Internet be useful?

In the preceding lesson, I promised you some of the cold, hard facts about the Internet. Well, hold on to your hat because you're about to get...

A 15-Minute Overview of the Internet

Certainly, something that has grown as popular as the Internet must prove useful for both its users and providers. Throughout the rest of this lesson and throughout this book, you will discover just why the Internet has grown so popular. You'll also learn about using the Net for communication and searching, but I'll discuss these topics later. First, here's the history lesson.

The Internet began as a project in 1973 by the U.S. Defense Advanced Research Projects Agency (DARPA). At that time, DARPA wanted to initiate a research program to investigate techniques and technologies for connecting packet networks of various kinds. DARPA ultimately wanted to develop communication *protocols* that would allow networked computers to talk freely across different platforms and networks. And so ARPAnet was born.

NEW TERM | **Protocol:** A protocol is nothing more than a set of rules. On the Internet, it is a set of rules computers use to communicate across networks. As long as everyone follows the rules, communication can occur freely.

ARPAnet, which came to be known simply as the Internet, developed a set of protocols known as Transmission Control Protocol/Internet Protocol, or TCP/IP. You should recognize "IP" from the discussion of IP addresses in Lesson 1, "The Internet: What's It Really Like?" An IP address is, in fact, an Internet protocol address.

JUST A MINUTE

> Did you figure out the answer to the IP address question from the "Activities" section in Lesson 1? The survey says that 4,294,967,296 possible IP addresses are available on the Internet.

The Internet continued to support a few hundred government scientists for over a decade until, in 1986, the U.S. National Science Foundation (NSF) initiated the development of the NSFnet, which even now provides a major *backbone* communication service for the Internet, as you can see in Figure 2.1. Today, the NSFnet backbone carries over 12 billion packets of information per month.

NEW TERM | **Backbone:** A backbone is nothing more than a major cable that carries network traffic. Although thousands of regional private and public networks exist, most Internet traffic spends most of its trip on one of the major backbones.

Although the entrance of NSF onto the scene was a major factor in the development of the Internet, possibly the biggest turning point came in 1991, when NSF dropped its funding of the Internet and lifted the ban on commercial traffic on its backbone. Up until 1991, all NSF traffic came from government and educational institutions.

2

Figure 2.1.

A look at the major U.S. NSF backbone as it appears today from a World Wide Web view.

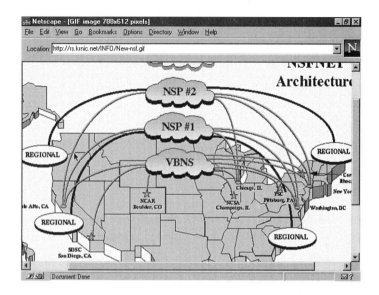

After 1991, however, the Internet was never quite the same. Commercial enterprises could respond more quickly to the market and to demand for information. New commercial backbones sprang up almost overnight. With them, of course, came the marketing and popularization of the Internet. The Net started to move away from UNIX and other science application languages to Windows-based interfaces that were easy for the public to use.

Soon after that came America Online, CompuServe, and other Internet service providers who went after Joe Enduser instead of Dr. Egghead. As the Internet became more accessible, companies began to see the enormous potential for business on the Internet. In addition, users also began to see some of the incredible applications for which they could use the Internet.

In this book, I will help you discover these uses. In the rest of this lesson, though, I give you a quick tour of the ways you can benefit from the Internet.

Using the Internet for Communication

With all the publicity and television commercials, you might conclude that the most popular use of the Internet is the World Wide Web, hands down. Well, here's a surprise. The most popular use, even today, is electronic mail, or e-mail. That's right, good old person-to-person, "let's talk"-type communication. It is almost fitting that one of the original uses of the Internet would still be the most popular.

You can, of course, communicate in other ways on the Net. In the following sections, you look at a few ways people are using the Internet to communicate with one another.

Personal Communication

E-mail provides you with more than just a way to write Aunt Jane a note about how things are going. Of course, many people can and do use e-mail for this very task, and it is very effective when used this way. But you also can find some more practical reasons for personal communication.

Have you ever tried to get in touch with someone and ended up playing phone tag for two days before finally getting hold of them? If you have, you know how frustrating this situation can be. Fortunately, e-mail eliminates this problem.

Using e-mail, you can quite often get hold of people who might otherwise take hours or days to get in touch with. Not only that, but by using e-mail, you can contact them on your time—no more waiting on hold or wondering whether you've been disconnected. Just send some e-mail, go about your other business, and wait for a response to pop in your mailbox. Which, by the way, points to e-mail's biggest advantage: It's fast!

It's in the Mail

Faxes are nice, but over long distances, the costs can add up. What if you had a quick and easy way to transmit instantly any type of file, document, or computer program electronically? Well, you do. With most e-mail programs, you can encode and "attach" documents to e-mail messages, as you can see in Figure 2.2.

Figure 2.2.

Why bother with wasted paper and time at the fax machine? E-mail your message!

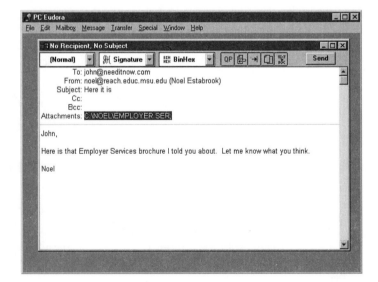

These documents can be computer programs, word processing files, or just about anything else you can create on a computer. All that is required of the recipient is that he or she also has an e-mail program or helper application that can "decode" these attachments.

A Public Forum

Wouldn't it be great if you could have access to hundreds of other people through one e-mail address? The *listserv* is just such a vehicle (see Lesson 8, "Communicating with the World: Using Mailing Lists," for detailed information on listservs). By signing up, or "subscribing," to a listserv, you then gain instant access to everyone else who subscribes to that listserv.

NEW TERM **Listserv:** A listserv is basically an e-mail address that is configured to forward every message it receives to the e-mail addresses of the users who have "subscribed" to it. You can think of a listserv as an electronic interactive newspaper. These are often commonly referred to as *mailing lists.*

Listservs are available on literally thousands of topics. Everybody from dachsund lovers to zoologists can find a listserv. If more than one person is interested in a particular topic, you can almost certainly find a listserv for it.

CAUTION

Listservs are great, no doubt about it. They do, however, pose a downside. Some of them are large and can sometimes dump hundreds of e-mail messages a day into your mailbox, so be careful out there.

More Public Forums

Using listservs isn't the only way to reach out and talk to large groups of people on the Internet. Using newsgroups, you can accomplish the same task in a different way.

The first difference between a listserv and a newsgroup is in the way messages are received. With listservs, messages are sent directly to your mailbox, where you have to sort them out and decide what to read. Newsgroup messages, on the other hand, are posted to something like a public electronic bulletin board, where you have to go to read the messages.

Another difference is one of access. Anybody with an e-mail address can subscribe to a listserv. To read newsgroups, however, your Internet service provider must provide you with access.

If your service provider does carry newsgroups, they are easy to subscribe to and are full of excellent information. Anything you can get from a listserv (and more), you can get from a newsgroup, as you can see in Figure 2.3. For more in-depth coverage of newsgroups, see Lessons 9, "Basic Journalism: Introduction to Newsgroups," and 10, "Getting the Scoop: Using Newsgroups."

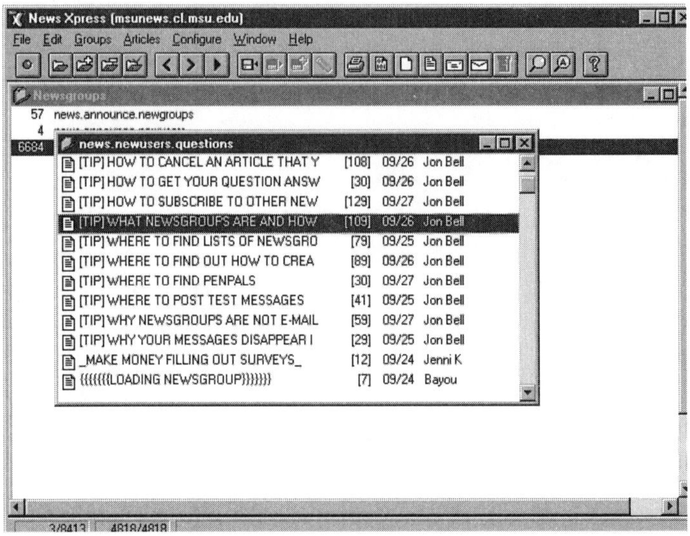

Figure 2.3.

New to newsgroups? You can find lots of tips.

Communicate in Real Time

In the last few years, the Internet has been hit by a wave of real-time communication (see Lessons 11, "Chatting Live on the Internet," and 12, "Internet Phone and Video," for more details). The processes of getting information, talking to others, and collaborating with colleagues no longer require a waiting period.

Perhaps a couple of examples would help explain these capabilities. I recently found myself in a position in which I had to work on a project at my computer. The problem was that the NBA finals were being played, and my office doesn't have a radio. Because I'm a huge basketball fan, this was a problem. Well, actually it wasn't because the NBA's Web site was broadcasting the game over RealAudio (a plug-in you'll read about in Lesson 15, "Helping Your Browser with Plug-Ins"), and I had a RealAudio player. So, I was able to work and listen to the game at the same time.

Care for a little more useful example? How about video conferencing? With the help of a small, inexpensive camera, like the one shown in Figure 2.4, and the right software on your computer, you can conduct face-to-face business and personal meetings right over the Internet. For an organization or individual who has contacts spread out over a large geographic area but who needs face-to-face contact with them on a regular basis, video conferencing is very useful.

Figure 2.4.

Connectix QuickCam can introduce you to the world of face-to-face communication on the Internet.

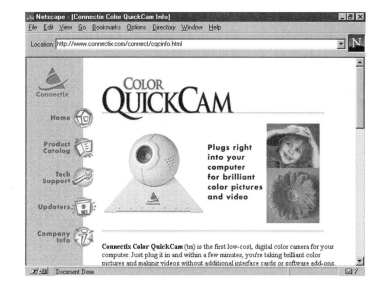

CAUTION

Audio and video transmissions take up a lot of room on the Internet. Though simple video and audio transmissions are reasonably reliable over a 14.4Kbps or 28.8Kbps modem connection, to use these capabilities to their full extent, you need a network connection to the Internet.

Find Anything on the Internet

The Internet isn't called the Information Superhighway for nothing. The Internet *is* information. Sometimes unfiltered, many times even useless, more information is available on the Internet than any one person could ever deal with.

Fortunately, some powerful search tools can help you find just about anything you want (see Lesson 20, "Finding People, Places, and Things on the Internet," for more details). In the final analysis, whether you find the Internet useful depends to a large degree on whether you can find the information you want and need. With some practice, and the help of this book, you should find great success.

Finding People

Because everyone on the Internet has an e-mail address, you should be able to find anyone, right? Well, think about it. How easy would it be to publish a telephone book with every phone number in the world? Not very easy at all. Even if you could gather all the numbers, by the time you published it, 10 percent of them would be wrong, disconnected, or changed.

The same challenge faces the Internet, and to be honest, sometimes the best way to find a friend's e-mail address is to just pick up the phone, call, and ask. With some tools, however, you can, with a little perseverance, locate e-mail addresses, as you can see in Figure 2.5.

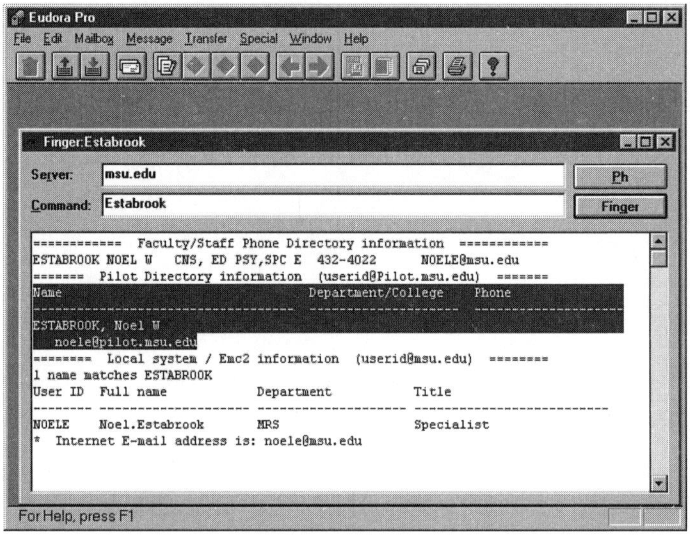

Figure 2.5.

Even a simple e-mail client can help you locate that elusive e-mail address.

Finding Places

One of the newest crazes on the Internet is locator services. Many Internet sites help you plan trips, find locations, take you through tours on maps, and more. See the example in Figure 2.6.

All these services start with a *search engine*, which enables you to search a database for information you want. In this case, the database consists of locations, highway routes, and other geographical information.

NEW TERM   **Search engine:** A search engine does exactly what its name says. It is really a computer program that indexes a database and then enables users to search it for relevant information.

Finding Things

You can search for billions of things on the Internet. Searching is an integral part of anyone's Internet use today. Covering every different type of search and information search is, of course, impossible, but in this book, I will point you to many of them.

Figure 2.6.

Planning a trip to New Zealand? The Internet can help.

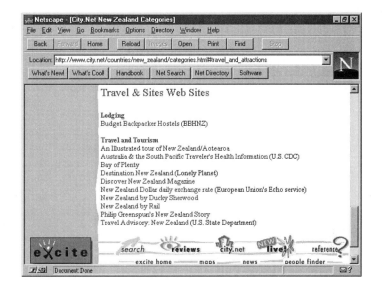

At this point, you've seen a few examples of things you can find on the Internet, and you'll see lots more by the time you're done with the last lesson. Whether you're looking for a classic car or the recipe for perfect stroganoff, chances are you can find it on the Internet. See the example in Figure 2.7.

Figure 2.7.

For a rare car collector, the Internet is a boon.

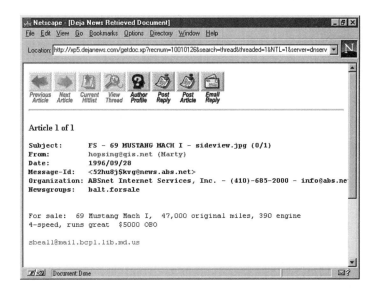

The Internet for Fun and Entertainment

Face it; if you don't enjoy doing something, you're not very likely to do it again. The same is true of using the Internet. You need something to pique your interest or give you a laugh once in a while.

Without a doubt, the Internet is full of weird, wacky, and just plain fun stuff (see Lesson 24, "The Internet Just for Fun" for some examples). Read a new joke every day on the Web, find a newsgroup dedicated to "The Far Side," or spend some time downloading space pictures from NASA. Whatever your taste, you can find something on the Internet. Figure 2.8 shows a fun example.

Figure 2.8.

You can find political spin with a twist at The Capitol Steps Web site.

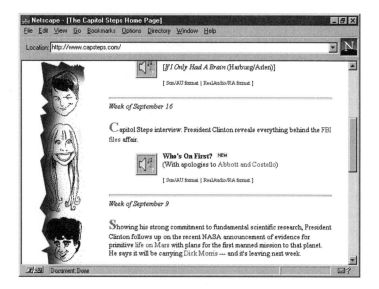

Summary

In this lesson, you learned some history behind the Internet. You discovered the Internet's humble beginnings as a small network for government scientists, as well as its phenomenal explosion in 1991.

Next, you learned how people are using the Internet to communicate by using e-mail to talk to individuals and groups, send files, and converse in real time. You also got a taste of how much information is available on the Internet and how to find it. Finally, you discovered that the Internet is also a place where you can have fun and enjoy yourself.

Workshop

The following workshop helps solidify the skills that you learned in this lesson.

Q&A

Q Has the Internet really been around 25 years?

A Well, yes and no. The Internet as you know it has really emerged only in the last five years or so, even though TCP/IP-based networks have been around much longer.

Q Does a difference exist between the Internet and the World Wide Web?

A The World Wide Web is just a part of the Internet, much like e-mail and newsgroups. Granted, it's a rather large part, but it isn't the same thing as the Internet any more than the telephone in your bedroom is the same as the phone system.

Q Is it really reasonable to expect to find good and useful information on the Internet?

A Absolutely. As you'll discover as you read this book, a myriad of online libraries, news sources, and other rich pockets of information are just waiting for you to tap into them.

Quiz

Take the following quiz to see how much you've learned.

Questions

1. What is TCP/IP protocol?

2. Because computer networks are simply connected with phone lines, it doesn't really matter what protocols are used for effective communications across these networks. True or False?

3. Which of the following delivers communications from a large group of people right to your mailbox?

   (a) A newsgroup

   (b) A listserv

   (c) Video-conferencing software

Answers

1. Transmission Control Protocol/Internet Protocol.
2. False. Without a common "language" or protocol such as TCP/IP, networks can never talk to each other.
3. (b) A listserv.

Activity

If you're already connected to the Internet and have started to look at Web pages, point your Web browser to `http://saturn.math.uaa.alaska.edu/~royce/biblio.html` to find out more about the history and growth of the Internet. If you aren't connected yet, save this activity for a future time.

2

Hour 3

Introduction to the World Wide Web

The World Wide Web is the fastest growing part of the Internet, as well as the most exciting. With the click of a mouse, you can start on the adventure of a lifetime, going to places you never dreamed of and gathering information otherwise unattainable.

In this lesson, you can find answers to the following questions:

- ☐ What is the history of the World Wide Web?
- ☐ What terminology do I need to know to navigate through the World Wide Web?
- ☐ What are some practical uses of the World Wide Web?
- ☐ What does the World Wide Web look like?

No matter where your travels through the World Wide Web lead the information in this lesson forms a foundation on which to build a strong knowledge base that will take you anywhere you want to go.

The History Behind the World Wide Web

Once upon a time (1980 to be exact), at a place called CERN (European Laboratory for Particle Physics), a man named Tim Berners-Lee envisioned the development of a worldwide computer interconnection that would provide access to all sorts of information and files for the physics community. In 1989, after years of toying around with his vision of a more interactive world, he submitted a proposal that was to be the beginning of the World Wide Web.

Soon people realized that the application of this "interconnected community" could reach far beyond those involved with physics. After the phrase "World Wide Web" was born, organizations began feverishly to assemble the hardware and know-how to develop this expansive network.

The first World Wide Web computers were created at CERN, which you can see in Figure 3.1. The visible success and ease of creating and employing these types of computers facilitated the ensuing explosion of the World Wide Web and its utilization.

Figure 3.1.

CERN, located on the Web at `http://www.cern.ch`, *is the place where the World Wide Web began.*

JUST A MINUTE

On many World Wide Web sites, including CERN's home page, you can find more extensive details and a more complete listing of actual events than the brief history of the World Wide Web given here. This introduction to the World Wide Web history aims at providing only a brief overview of events involved in its creation.

3

At first, the World Wide Web contained only a few *server* and *client* machines. Within a period of a couple years, however, the computing population caught onto the benefits and excitement of this new development, and the World Wide Web population growth exploded.

NEW TERM **Server** and **client:** These computers are the basis for the entire Internet. In a general sense, a server is any computer that "serves" or delivers information and data. A client is any computer that requests or receives the information and data.

In 1993, the Web had only about 50 servers. Within 18 months, this number increased by over 3,000 percent. Within the last few years, this number has grown into the millions, and today you can find information and files on the Web from practically anywhere in the world.

The World Wide Web was truly a visionary undertaking. The future seems to hold no limits. In time, most daily activities may very well take place through the World Wide Web. Almost every home, school, company, and organization will be connected, and with the click of a mouse, the world will exist at your fingertips.

The Web Encyclopedia of Terms

In your travels through the World Wide Web (and this book), you are bound to encounter some technical terms and phrases that you don't know. Much of this terminology relates to common activities and components present on the World Wide Web.

In an attempt to clear the path for some smooth "surfing" through the World Wide Web, several of the most common terms and phrases you'll encounter are provided here for you to learn and refer to. Specific examples of many of these elements are provided later in the lesson.

JUST A MINUTE

> The terminology presented here may have many variations in meaning, depending on whom you ask. I've tried to stick to the most basic definitions to help you easily understand some of what you'll see on the Web.

Web Site Terminology

The most important parts of the World Wide Web are the elements, such as servers, pages, hot links, and more—all of which comprise the bulk of the World Wide Web. The following are some related terms you may see:

☐ Web site: A collection of World Wide Web documents, usually consisting of a home page and several related pages. You might think of a Web site as an interactive electronic book.

☐ Home page: Frequently, the "cover" of a particular Web site. The home page is the main, or first, page displayed for an organization's or person's World Wide Web site.

☐ Link: Short for "hypertext link." A link provides a path that connects you from one part of a World Wide Web document to another part of the same document, a different document, or another resource. A link usually appears as a uniquely colored word that you can click to be transported to another Web page.

☐ Anchor: A link that takes you to a different part of the same Web page.

☐ Image map: A feature available on the World Wide Web that enables you to click various locations in an graphic image to link to different documents.

☐ Frame: A feature available on the World Wide Web that presents text, links, graphics, and other media in separate portions of the browser display. Some sections remain unchanging, whereas others serve as an exhibit of linked documents.

☐ Table: A feature available on the World Wide Web that presents document text, links, graphics, and other media in row and column format. Table borders may be visible in some documents but invisible in others.

The "Guts" of the Web

Now that you know about the surface elements of the Web, what goes on beneath the surface? What are some of the elements that actually create the foundation for what you see on the Web? Read on to find out.

☐ HTML: Hypertext Markup Language. HTML is the coding language for the World Wide Web that informs browsers how to display a document's text, links, graphics, and other media. This language forms the foundation for all Web pages.

☐ Webmaster: The individual responsible for maintaining and updating the content of a World Wide Web document. Webmasters are the creative forces behind the World Wide Web.

☐ Domain name: The name given to any computer registered on the World Wide Web as an official provider of information and files. Domain names are usually two or more terms separated by periods. Some examples are aol.com or www.msu.edu.

☐ URL: Uniform Resource Locator. A URL (pronounced *You-Are-El*) serves as identification for all World Wide Web documents. The URL is sometimes referred to as a World Wide Web page address. Every site and page on the World Wide Web has a URL. Refer to Table 3.1 for a rundown of all the common types of URLs on the Internet.

3

Table 3.1. URL elements.

Service	Server Type and Domain Name (Complete URL)	Lesson
Web	`http://www.server.name`	13–16
Gopher	`gopher://gopher.server.name`	18
FTP	`ftp://ftp.server.name`	17
Telnet	`telnet://server.name`	19
E-mail	`mailto:address@server.name`	5–8

Terms for the Tools

In the following lessons, you'll learn a lot about the tools that you use to access the World Wide Web. The following are a few terms that you will see frequently:

- ☐ Browser: A software program that requests, interprets, and presents World Wide Web documents. Frequently used browsers include Internet Explorer, Netscape Navigator, Lynx, and Mosaic.

- ☐ Client: In addition to being a computer, a client also can be a software program that requests and acquires information from computers that store World Wide Web documents and files. World Wide Web browsers are also known as clients.

- ☐ Hotlist: An option available in most World Wide Web browsers that maintains a list of frequently accessed home pages. A hotlist also refers to a list of home pages related to a particular subject that is published on an organization's home page.

Practical Uses of the World Wide Web

Notice that many of the lessons in this book contain practical applications of the Internet. In particular, Part VI, "Getting the Most Out of the Internet," is dedicated to many specific examples. The following sections merely provide you with a brief overview of some of the features available on the Web.

Practically Entertaining

One of the most commonly used capabilities of the Web is its ability to help you locate just about anything. Planning to take a trip or need to locate a place somewhere in the world? Several Web sites are designed to help you do just that. One of the best, MapQuest, is featured in Lesson 21, "The Internet for Home: Entertainment, Travel, and More."

Is it time to sell your old, rusty car and purchase a new one? Good news! The World Wide Web contains sites for every automobile manufacturer in the world. Figure 3.2 shows one example. Current prices, lease programs, different models, various options, company information, dealership locations nearest you, and residuals are all available at these sites.

Figure 3.2.

The Jeep home page tells all about Jeep brand vehicles.

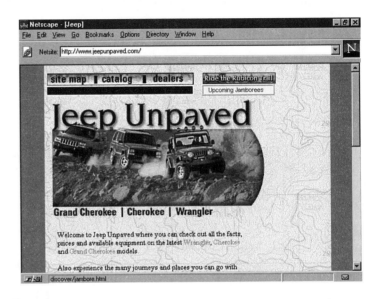

Practical Education

Suppose you want to attend a class next year at a local campus or university. Well, just about every educational institute maintains a site on the World Wide Web. Michigan State University, for example, provides an extensive site that offers information ranging from courses available to credit prices, degree program details, and career planning services, as you can see in Figure 3.3.

Many educational opportunities are available on the Web because many institutions offer for-credit courses and live lectures, right on the Internet. For more details, go to Lesson 22, "Education on the Internet."

Practical Business

Some of the most practical uses for the World Wide Web include activities in which you participate on a regular basis. If you're interested in owning stock (or if you already do), for example, you can find annual reports, current stock prices, and other pertinent information relating to just about any corporation or business, as shown in Figure 3.4. You can also buy and sell stock directly on the World Wide Web without leaving your home and without the cost of a stockbroker to trade for you.

Figure 3.3.

Michigan State University's home page offers a multitude of information on courses, faculty and staff, degree programs, and more.

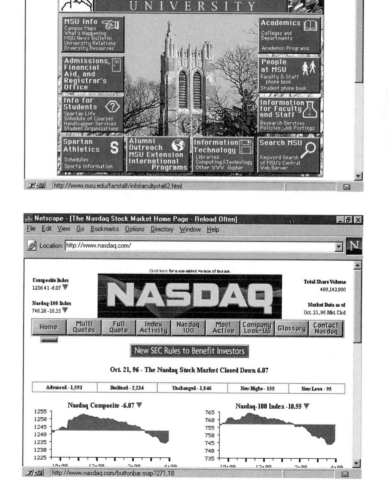

Figure 3.4.

Check out the Nasdaq home page on the World Wide Web for free.

The business-minded can find much more on the Web. Job searches, resume services, and so on are available on the Web. For more details, look at Lesson 23, "Taking Care of Business Using the Internet."

How Will It Look? Tables, Frames, and Animation

Okay, now that you know what's out there on the World Wide Web, you may want to know what it looks like. Again, the only limits to what you find are the imaginations of the Webmasters. The World Wide Web acts as the canvas for millions of undiscovered artists around the world.

Sites display text, graphic images, links, and attached media in a variety of styles, designs, and patterns. Many pages display these elements in a simple format that's easy to understand and navigate. Much of what appears on the Web, however, may use some special elements to add that extra bit of "zing" to a page. Several such features for designing sites include tables, image maps, frames, and animation. Webmasters use these features to design unique, effective, and attractive home pages.

Setting the Table

Tables involve the organization of information into a row and column format. This World Wide Web feature is particularly useful for charting and graphing text, graphic images, and links, as you can see in the example shown in Figure 3.5. Furthermore, if the desired appearance involves the arrangement of information into specific dimensions, tables provide the perfect format.

Figure 3.5.

ESPN's home page makes effective use of tables with borders you can see.

Interactive Images

On the World Wide Web, you will encounter image maps as well. This feature enables you to click various locations in an graphic image to link to different documents. Look back at Figure 3.3; notice that the MSU home page consists of an image map. Clicking the appropriate area links you to the section of the Web site you choose.

The Right Frame of Mind

Frames are a more advanced design tool for World Wide Web sites. The use of frames allows the division of the display screen into separate sections, each of which may contain text, graphic images, and links. Frames are especially useful if a site contains a list of links related to a certain subject, and the Webmaster wants the linked documents to appear on the screen while the list of links remains visible as well. Figure 3.6 shows a good example of this use.

Figure 3.6.

Andersen Consulting provides an excellent example of the use of frames on its World Wide Web home page.

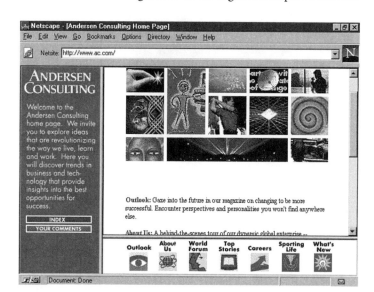

JUST A MINUTE

Being able to tell the difference between tables and frames might take you awhile because they often look the same. If you're confused, simply scroll down or across the page. If some of the information doesn't move, you know the page uses frames.

Action!

The features of World Wide Web design I've already talked about serve their duty as practical, organized, and attractive components of a site. However, nothing quite captivates the attention of users like animation does. Animation presents text, links, and graphic images in visibly moving action, as shown in Figure 3.7. Typically, the lively animation draws more attention, promises more excitement, and offers a more interesting display of information than the conventional presentations.

Figure 3.7.

On the Banking and Finance home page, a colorful fish swims horizontally across the screen, and a Pegasus flaps her wings in the upper-left corner.

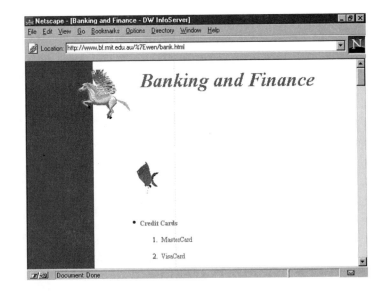

With the various tools available for constructing a World Wide Web site, you may encounter just about everything in your imagination during your travels. What is not available now will be shortly, as futuristic ideas for site development already live in the minds of designers.

Some futuristic plans for World Wide Web sites include 3-D and interactive displays. The technologies that facilitate this type of design now exist, and a few sites already show a glimpse of the future.

Summary

In this lesson, I delivered a brief introduction to the World Wide Web. You learned about the history behind the creation of the World Wide Web and found out about CERN and the phenomenal growth of the Web in the last 15 years. You also learned some of the terminology you may see in your travels. Furthermore, you discovered the practical uses of the Web and what you will see in your travels.

Finally, you got a quick view of some of the elements that will make the Web exciting for you and others, such as frames, tables, and animation.

Workshop

The following workshop helps solidify the skills that you learned in this lesson.

Q&A

Q **What is the difference between a World Wide Web site, a home page, and a page?**

A A World Wide Web site refers to the overall collection of documents and files present for a single organization or person. The home page usually denotes the first display of information you see when you visit a World Wide Web site. From that home page, any other related documents to which you can link at the same site are simply known as pages.

Q **Why would a site related to any given subject, no matter how ridiculous, be on the World Wide Web?**

A Well, you've heard of freedom of speech, right? The only regulations currently enforced for the World Wide Web are the limits of the imagination. So, if you think about it, and you have the time and money to create and maintain a site, you can put just about anything out there, no matter how absurd.

Q **Is knowing what formatting a World Wide Web site uses for displaying its information important for me?**

A Knowing the formatting is not important unless you plan to create your own World Wide Web site. Otherwise, tables, image maps, frames, and animation are just useful and attractive ways for displaying information that also make the Web a more interesting place to visit. Actually, the less you notice about how a site is actually put together, the better the designer has put it together.

Quiz

Take the following quiz to see how much you've learned.

Questions

1. Who first envisioned the creation of the World Wide Web?

    (a) Steve Jobs

    (b) Tim Berners-Lee

    (c) Bill Gates

2. What is a Webmaster?

    (a) A book containing a vast amount of information about the World Wide Web

    (b) The organization that maintains a directory of every Web site on the Internet

    (c) An individual responsible for maintaining and updating the content of a World Wide Web document

3. Which of the following would you be able to find on the World Wide Web?

    (a) Barney the Dinosaur

    (b) Travel agents

    (c) How to Prepare Sushi

Answers

1. (b) Tim Berners-Lee first envisioned the World Wide Web in 1980 while working for CERN.

2. (c) An individual responsible for maintaining and updating the content of a World Wide Web document.

3. (a), (b), and (c). Remember that your imagination is the only limit to what you will find on the World Wide Web. Almost everything from your daily life exists in some shape or form on the Web.

Activity

Write down several aspects of your daily life, such as what kind of car you drive, where you live, what you fix for dinner, and what movies you would like to see. Now take your notes and use them to bookmark Lesson 16, "Searching the Web for Virtually Anything." After you learn how to search the Web for information, try to find the things you're interested in.

Hour 4

Internet Service Provider Options and Pointers

Everyone seems to be talking about the Internet these days. Every television commercial points you to a Web site with more information. At this stage of the game, you should be considering how you want to connect to the Internet. Most users subscribe to an Internet service provider (ISP) for their dial-in access. An ISP serves to link you to the Internet when you need access, saving you from paying for a 24-hour connection.

In this lesson, you can find answers to the following questions:

- ☐ What features should I look for in an ISP?
- ☐ What is the average cost of an ISP?
- ☐ Should I use a national or local ISP?
- ☐ What questions should I ask if I want a Web site?

I'll try to answer these questions and more as you go in search of an Internet service provider.

Types of Connections

This section explains the different connection options available to you. The one you use—modem, ISDN, cable modem, T1 line, or T3 line—depends on many factors, with cost being one of the greatest determiners.

Modems

A *modem* is an electronic device that converts computer data into audio signals. These audio signals can then be transmitted over a normal phone line. At the receiving end, another modem converts the audio signals back into computer data.

Modems can be internal, part of the original computer system, or purchased as external components. On either configuration, you have a jack for connecting your phone line and the data line from your computer. You also have to install special software on the machine to dial out with the modem connection.

The speed of a current modem is measured in kilobits per second (kbps). The most common speeds are 14.4 and 28.8 kbps. Modems running at 33.6 kbps are currently available, although not many ISPs are capable of supporting this speed.

ISDN

ISDN stands for Integrated Services Digital Network. ISDN lines are connections that use ordinary phone lines to transmit digital instead of analog signals. With digital signals, data can be transmitted at a much faster rate than with a traditional modem.

ISDN converts audio signals—your voice, for example—into digital bits. Because bits can be transmitted very quickly, you can get much faster speed out of the same telephone line—four times faster than a 14.4 kbps modem, in fact. In addition, ISDN connections are made up of two different channels, allowing two simultaneous "conversations"; you therefore can speak on one channel and send a fax or connect to the Internet over the other channel. All these transactions occur on the same ordinary phone line currently plugged into your telephone. Your local telephone company can tell you if ISDN is available in your area.

ISDN is a powerful tool for Internet communications, but it is not available everywhere. Traditionally, it has been used in urban business zones and large corporate settings with special digital switching equipment, but residential ISDN service is expanding rapidly. If you're shopping for an Internet service provider that offers you ISDN, be sure to consider the equipment costs. An ISDN line can offer you inexpensive, high-bandwidth connections, but you may have to buy special hardware that will allow ISDN to communicate with your home or corporate machines.

4

Cable Modems

Cable modems may be the next great leap in "at-home" connection solutions. It would be great to have the speed of the T1 line you may have at work available to your home PC. Even if you dial in to your office you are still held to the speed of the modem connected to your computer using the normal phone lines.

Enter the cable modem. Your computer is hooked not to your phone line but to your coaxial television cable. Cable modems are targeted toward the Internet enthusiast with the need for speed. According to some accounts, the fastest cable modems will be capable of receiving data at 10 Mbps and sending it at 768 Kbps.

The suggested fee for that cable-modem service may fetch about $30 to $40 monthly. Including the $600 price tag on the modems themselves, this will be one substantial upgrade that many veteran Net surfers are willing to make.

Getting your hands on the hardware may be the easy part. Only certain areas are experimenting with the use of cable modems, but their use is rapidly expanding. Contact your local cable company to see whether it is planning to carry Internet access with cable modems.

T1 Line

A T1 line is a high-speed digital connection capable of transmitting data at a rate of approximately 1.5 million bits per second. A T1 line is typically used by small and medium-sized companies with heavy network traffic.

This line is large enough to send and receive large text files, graphics, sounds, and databases instantaneously, and it works at the fastest speed commonly used to connect networks to the Internet. Sometimes referred to as a *leased line*, a T1 line is basically too large and too expensive for individual home use.

T3 Line

A T3 line is a super high-speed connection capable of transmitting data at a rate of 45 million bits per second. This connection represents a bandwidth equal to about 672 regular voice-grade telephone lines. A T3 line is wide enough to transmit full-motion, real-time video and very large databases over a busy network.

A T3 line is typically installed as a major networking artery for large corporations and universities with high-volume network traffic. The backbones of the major Internet service providers, for example, are made up of T3 lines.

Ten Questions for Your ISP

If you're treading into an unknown area trying to find an ISP, arming yourself with some basic information is a good idea. The following questions should help you decide which ISP is going to get your business. If an ISP skirts the issue when you ask tough questions, strongly consider looking elsewhere. Just as in any other business, you can find good ISPs and bad ISPs.

1. What is the price structure?

   Some providers offer flat-rate fees for a certain number of hours online; for example, $15.00 for unlimited hours of connection time. Others structure their rates so that you pay $15.00 for the first 20 hours online and $1.50 an hour after that. Most ISPs charge your monthly subscription fee to a major credit card or even apply it to your local phone bill.

2. What type of connection does the ISP have to the Internet?

   Either a T3 or T1 high-speed line is great; two lines (in case one of them fails) are better. A T1 can accommodate 100 to 150 users logged on at any one time. Some providers may brag that they have a T1 connection, when in fact they share the line with another company or provider. This "partial" T1 can still support a large number of users, but your provider has only half of them.

   Some of the larger providers must handle the load of hundreds of users dialed in simultaneously. These providers may have multiple T1s or even a T3. Only very large providers need a direct link using a T3 line.

3. What speed are the modems used for dial-up access?

   Actually, two modems are involved in connecting your computer to the Internet. One is the modem at your home, and the other is at the ISP. The slower of these two modems determines your real connection speed to the Internet. The fastest modems now operate at 33.6 kbps. Some providers have modems that run at only 14.4 or 28.8 kbps.

   Another consideration if you want high-speed connections is whether the ISP offers ISDN connections. ISDN lines run at 64 kbps but cost more than $500 to establish with all the hardware and software requirements. Only consider this avenue if you have serious Internet access needs.

4. How many dial-up modems are available? How many customers use the service?

   Use this customers-to-modem ratio to determine the probability that you will have problems connecting to the ISP. Both the number of customers and number of modems are very important. Established ISPs (more than 150 customers) can run at about 10 customers to 1 modem with users facing a "reasonable" number of busy signals. If you don't ever want to receive a busy signal when you log on, look for an established ISP with a ratio of fewer than 10 customers per modem.

5. Is software included with the account?

   Some ISPs include a collection of basic software with your account. These basic programs may include a dial-up agent, Web browser, FTP client, compression agent, chat client, e-mail application, or a newsreader. Although most of this software is shareware, having it as part of the initial package makes working on the Internet a lot easier.

6. What kind of technical support is offered?

   Look for an ISP that provides support via e-mail and over the phone. Remember, e-mail support doesn't do much good if you can't log on in the first place. Ask your potential ISP what its telephone support number is (long-distance calls, of course, cost money) and what the hours are. Then call in—more than once, at different times—to see how long it takes to get a person on the line.

   Don't forget to ask how much tech support costs. Some ISPs (though not many locally) charge users for support. And make sure your ISP offers support for your type of computer and operating system.

7. Does the ISP offer onsite support?

   Some local ISPs send a service technician to your house if you're having problems installing their software or dialing in to their systems. This support may be a value-added service, but make sure you know the cost before the technician warms up the van.

8. Does the ISP have redundant equipment?

   Does the ISP have redundant equipment? That was worth repeating. Ask if the company has backups for all critical equipment, including a spare router and spare servers. With all the hardware necessary to run an ISP, the service provider has to be able to handle sudden problems. While you're at it, check to see whether the equipment runs on an *uninterruptible power supply (UPS)*.

   NEW TERM **Uninterruptible power supply (UPS):** A UPS is a short-term battery supply that kicks in when a system's power is lost. The battery, serving as an auxiliary power supply, gives you enough time to close your applications and save your files.

9. How often are tape backups performed?

   Having backups is most important if you have spent hours designing a fabulous Web site, but a hard drive crash at your ISP—and these drives occasionally do crash—can also mean that important e-mail is lost. Daily tape backups help prevent such catastrophes from causing serious problems with your work.

It's a good idea to back up your home machine on a regular schedule also.

10. How many newsgroups can I access?

Newsgroups enable users with similar interests to share their thoughts with each other. Star Trek fans, for example, can congregate in a specific newsgroup to discuss the characters, plots, and upcoming movies. Some ISPs offer limited newsgroup access; others have none at all.

Commercial Providers: AOL, CompuServe, MSN, and Prodigy

If you have recently bought a computer magazine, chances are it came with ads (and probably software) for one or more of the major national online services: America Online (AOL), CompuServe, Microsoft Network (MSN), or Prodigy.

Of these major online services, AOL is consistently rated best by magazines that compare the services. Figure 4.1 shows the AOL interface. CompuServe usually comes in second, with MSN, because it is still new and developing, in third place.

Figure 4.1.

For quick information, check AOL's Internet site.

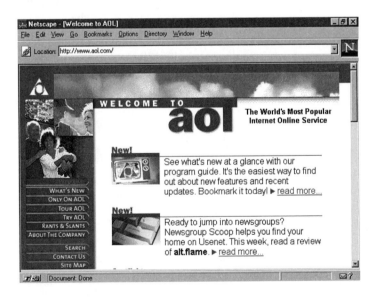

What Do These Services Offer?

One of the best selling points of these services is their sign-up process. Connecting to them is usually simple: You install the free software they provide, follow the onscreen instructions, and you're connected. In addition to the vast resources of the Internet, these services also give you access to certain content that is not available to people who don't use the services. These ISPs, for example, have their own chat rooms, newsgroups, online shopping, special-interest groups, and searchable references that only subscribers to the service can use.

What Do All These Services Cost?

Two drawbacks really stand out about using these services: cost and cost. The first cost to consider is the amount AOL, MSN, Prodigy, or CompuServe charges your credit card each month.

America Online (www.aol.com) now offers three pricing plans to better suit its users. The standard monthly package gives you unlimited Internet access for $19.95, with discounts down to $14.95 a month if you pay for two years in advance. Other offers include unlimited access to AOL's network through a local ISP for $9.95 a month, or the light-usage program at $4.95 for three hours of access.

MSN, (www.msn.com), not surprisingly, is running very similar deals: One month of unlimited access to the Internet and MSN for $19.95. MSN underbid AOL by offering access to MSN content for $6.95 a month when you use your own local ISP. The company also has hourly service at $6.95 for five hours of connection time.

Prodigy (www.prodigy.com) also offers an unlimited plan for $19.95. The company's secondary plan gets you 10 hours of online access for $10. To try out Prodigy's service you can sign up for one free month of unlimited access.

The price structure is changing regularly in response to an extremely competitive market. These charges were available at the time of this writing, but the deals will no doubt change and others will take their place as the competition gets stiffer.

The second factor that affects the cost of using one of these commercial online services is the dial-up access numbers. These national ISPs don't have local access numbers in all areas. If you live in an area not covered by a local access number, you may be forced to place a long-distance or local toll call whenever you log on.

4

National ISPs

One way many people use a national online service like AOL is to get their feet wet and to learn more about the Internet. When they feel comfortable, they move on to a local provider that gives more options and often better service.

National online services occasionally don't allow users with 28.8 kbps modems to run at 28.8 kbps. The modem banks they use may max out at 14.4 kbps, leaving those people with newer computers watching graphics download slowly as their wallets are being emptied. Be sure to check that the company offers at least 28.8 kbps connections in your area.

If you like the idea of working with a national company but don't want to pay per-hour prices, a number of national companies now offer direct access to the Internet at a flat rate. Netcom, as shown in Figure 4.2, offers a $19.95 package that gives you unlimited Internet access and 24-hour support.

Figure 4.2.

Netcom advertises its services and specials on its Web site.

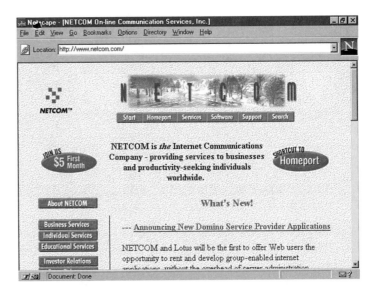

AT&T has started offering Internet access, and Bell Atlantic reportedly plans to do so soon. Even AOL and CompuServe are getting in on the act. AOL also owns GNN, which is a national ISP, and CompuServe is debuting its Wow! service, featuring "unlimited" Internet access for $18 per month.

Under such a price structure, you could theoretically log on to the Internet and never log off. Maybe you won't do that, but other people will—and when they do, that's one less modem available per person for all the other customers. Someone is losing out, and it's not the person who stays connected around the clock.

The Local Connection: How to Find a Local ISP

Finding a local ISP is getting easier all the time. Because ISPs are popping up all over the place, it's hard to talk to someone that hasn't done some of the work for you. Phone books, friends, coworkers, and local computer stores are all good sources of information for finding your local ISP.

I know this procedure will sound very low-tech, but the classics live: Tear your fingers from the keyboard and pick up the phone book. Check the yellow pages for Internet service providers, and you should find a good starting point. Because new ISPs are always beginning to offer services, some may not be included in the phone book.

The next source for finding a local ISP is as close as your local computer store. Odds are that the staff of the store can recommend a few good services. The computer store may also have special deals with some local providers and may be able to get you a trial subscription or a discounted rate. It never hurts to ask.

If you happen to be lucky enough to be investigating ISPs at the same time that a local computer club is having a computer show, you should know that providers flock to shows to have rate wars with the competition, and the winner is usually you. Here you have a collection of local ISPs in one area.

Spend some time talking to the people who work on the system. Ask them some of the questions from the beginning of this lesson. If they really know their system, they should have no problem answering your questions.

My final suggestion is to check *the List* (http://thelist.iworld.com), a Web site dedicated to listing many of the ISPs in the U.S. and Canada. This site, shown in Figure 4.3, even boasts a global ISP list categorized by country or country code.

4

Figure 4.3.

Use the List *to find a local ISP.*

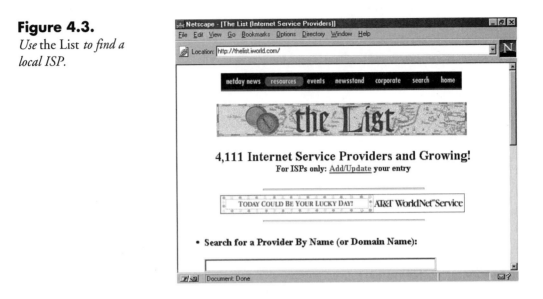

Web Sites at the Local ISP

Because most Web sites are developed on local ISPs, you need to be sure that your provider can support Web sites. You may find that, after surfing around on other companies' sites, you want to develop one of your own.

In addition to the questions you should ask any ISP before you sign up—and those questions really are the most important—here are a few to consider if you plan to design a Web site:

☐ Are any extra charges associated with planning a Web site?

Many ISPs include free Web pages in some subscription packages. Look for less obvious charges like "*x* cents per hit over 10,000" or "*x* cents per MB transferred over 100 MB." If your page becomes very popular or includes a good number of graphics, these charges can add up.

☐ How many hits can I expect to receive on a site like the one I plan to design?

The ISP can't give you a precise number but can probably make a reasonable estimate based on sites designed by its other users.

☐ How do I transfer the pages from my computer to the ISP's server?

Using a commonly available FTP (file transfer protocol) program, such as the shareware WS-FTP, is the easiest way to transfer pages. You should also be able to use your FTP program to update the pages, and no one should be able to modify your pages without your password.

4

☐ What will my URL (Web site address) be?

Addresses like `http://www.isp.net/~yourname/` are common, and they're easy for other people to remember. More complicated URLs aren't as good.

Summary

Picking an Internet service provider can be as much fun as picking a phone company. Unfortunately, ISPs don't pay you to switch back and forth like those other three-letter companies.

You have to consider rates, support, and accessibility before you can make a good decision. Choosing a national or local ISP depends on the features you want. National ISPs offer more perks than just Internet access. But if you can do without a special user's newsgroup and just want to get online, start looking for a local service provider.

Be sure to question your national or local provider about Web sites. Chances are putting up a small personal site doesn't cost you anything. If you plan to develop a business site, check rates and any hidden throughput charges that may be applicable.

Workshop

The following workshop helps solidify the skills you learned in this lesson.

Q&A

Q Is having an Internet service provider really necessary?

A Well, yes and no. You don't need an ISP to use your computer, but you do need one if you want to use the Internet. Unless you can afford the hefty $52,000 per year for a direct Internet connection, I suggest signing up with an ISP.

Q What are all the numbers associated with different types of modems?

A The numbers are the rates that the modem can transfer data across the connection. A 14.4 modem, for example, can transmit and receive data at a rate of 14.4 kilobits per second (kbps). The faster the transfer rate, the faster your connection to the Internet.

Q Can I find a local ISP in my area?

A Hard to tell. Local ISPs are popping up everywhere. You can turn to a number of sources. You can check with a local computer store or simply check your yellow pages. If a computer show is nearby, you might want to look there, too.

Q How much can I expect to spend?

A The answer to this question depends on how often you use the Internet and what special features you want. An account with a local ISP can run $15 for 150 hours of use per month. If you sign up with a national ISP, you can expect to pay about $20 for 5 hours of Internet use with access to its subscriber services.

Quiz

Take the following quiz to see how much you've learned.

Questions

1. Which connection can handle more users, T1 or T3?
2. How is the customers-to-modems ratio important?
3. Which is the fastest connection?
    - (a) 14.4 modem
    - (b) 28.8 modem
    - (c) 33.6 modem
    - (d) ISDN line

Answers

1. A T3 line can handle 3000+ users. A T1 line can support only about 100 to 150 simultaneous users.
2. The smaller the ratio, the easier it is to dial in each time and not get a busy signal.
3. (d) ISDN line

Activity

If you're currently using an ISP, reevaluate your provider. Find out how your ISP compares to other newer companies. Check out *the List* for any ISPs with Web sites in your area. Most ISPs advertise their rates and important info on their sites, so you might not have to do much more digging.

If you're looking for an ISP, check with your friends and neighbors for recommendations. Take a quick trip to the local bookstore or newsstand, and buy a computer magazine. Aim for one with a "Free Access" disk, and try it out.

4

PART

II

E-Mail: The Great Communicator

Hour

Hour 5

Understanding E-Mail

E-mail still makes up a majority of Internet traffic today because everyone with Internet access has an e-mail account, even though he or she may not have access to newsgroups, the World Wide Web, or other portions of the Internet. Undoubtedly, 20 million people can send a lot of e-mail!

In this lesson, you find the answers to the following questions:

- ☐ What is an e-mail address?
- ☐ Are all e-mail addresses the same?
- ☐ What are some examples of how to use e-mail?
- ☐ What are the basic parts of an e-mail message?
- ☐ Should I follow any rules or etiquette when using e-mail?

No matter what e-mail client you use, you will find the concepts and principles in this lesson universal.

The First Step: E-Mail Addresses

E-mail addresses are relatively easy to understand. In fact, if you read Lesson 1, "The Internet: What's It Really Like?" you're already halfway there. Every e-mail address has three necessary elements:

- ☐ User ID: Every person with an e-mail address has a user identification of some sort. It is usually something simple, like johndoe, but can be more complex.
- ☐ @: The "at" sign connects the user ID with the third element.
- ☐ Domain: You have already learned about domain names; every e-mail address has one.

CAUTION

E-mail addresses never contain spaces or commas. If you see an e-mail address with a comma or space in it, you know right away that it is invalid. This rule includes CompuServe addresses, which do contain commas. If you're e-mailing to a CompuServe address from an Internet e-mail account, replace the comma with a period.

So, to put it all together, a typical e-mail address contains all three of the preceding elements. One example of an e-mail address is johndoe@nomansland.com.

TIME SAVER

You might see some pretty strange addresses in your travels. If you see an e-mail address that you're really not sure about, simply reply to the message (as explained in Lesson 6) and make note of the e-mail address to which your client attempts to send the message. Your reply most often goes to the correct address.

Why Do You Use E-Mail?

I gave you some examples and reasons for using e-mail in Lesson 2, "Internet Uses in the Modern World," but you're ready for a little more detail now. The examples in the following sections are not meant to be exhaustive but should be enough to convince you that e-mail is a valuable tool.

"Let's Do E-Mail"

Our society is becoming increasingly interconnected. Networking, in the personal and societal sense of the word, is vital. The old maxim "It's not who you know, it's what you know" has never been truer. And you'll find no better networking tool than e-mail.

The following are some examples of how you can use e-mail to network with others:

- ☐ The mere act of having an e-mail address gives you an advantage for networking and collaboration. In how many people without a phone would you invest your time, business, and interest? E-mail is the phone number of today and the future. Simply having an e-mail address opens you up to a whole new avenue of connectivity.

- ☐ When you're working on a group project, either for business or personal purposes, you can e-mail ideas, feedback, and drafts of work to every member of the team. Often, without e-mail, these vital parts of collaboration have to be delayed until everyone can get together for a meeting.

- ☐ Join a listserv related to a project or personal interest of yours. You'll find no substitute for having access to experts and other interested parties all over the world.

Cheaper Than a Dime a Minute

Sorry, long-distance companies, you don't have the lowest rates; e-mail does. Even among commercial providers who charge hourly to use their service, you simply can't communicate less expensively than by sending e-mail.

For the $2.95 per hour a typical service provider might charge for access, you can send dozens of e-mail messages for the same price it would cost you to place a typical three-minute long-distance phone call. Of course, if you get Internet access through a provider that charges a flat fee with no hourly charges, you save even more.

In addition, using e-mail usually provides a big time savings. E-mail doesn't have to sit on hold, play phone tag, or deal with busy signals, even during the busiest times of day. You can sit down, type out your message, and move on, knowing that the person on the other end will get your message as soon as possible.

5

Don't kid yourself about using e-mail, though. You can't find a substitute for having an intimate dinner, hearing grandma's voice on the phone, or sealing a deal with a firm handshake. No one would suggest that you become an e-mail hermit by forgoing other, more personal forms of communication. Used with common sense, however, e-mail makes a lot of sense (and cents).

Anatomy of an E-Mail Message

The e-mail message is the cornerstone of all communications on the Internet. But what is in an e-mail message and how do the parts work together?

Every e-mail message contains two basic parts: the *header* and the *body*. To help you understand this description, think of any typical letter you write and mail to someone. You write your letter on paper, which then goes in an envelope, where you provide the recipient's name, address, city, state, and ZIP code. You can think of an e-mail message header as a digital envelope and the body as your electronic letter.

Message Headers

Because your e-mail message will go through dozens of high-speed computer networks on the way to its destination, an e-mail header is by necessity more complex than the name and address you put on an envelope. Figure 5.1, for example, shows a typical e-mail message header.

Fortunately, you don't need to know or worry about what all the different items in a message header are. Instead, slow down your racing heart by viewing what a typical message header looks like when you compose e-mail, as shown in Figure 5.2.

The following are the different headers you need to be concerned about when sending e-mail:

☐ To: The To: field contains the e-mail address of the person to whom you are sending e-mail. Often, if you're sending e-mail to someone in your own domain, you don't need to include @domain. If johndoe@nomansland.com sends e-mail to janedoe@nomansland.com, for example, he can probably just put janedoe in the To: field. Depending on what e-mail client you use, this field is sometimes called the Message To: or Mail To: field.

☐ From: This field includes your e-mail address. You almost never have to worry about this field because most e-mail clients automatically fill it in for you.

Figure 5.1.

Imagine if you had to put all this information on your next letter to Grandpa.

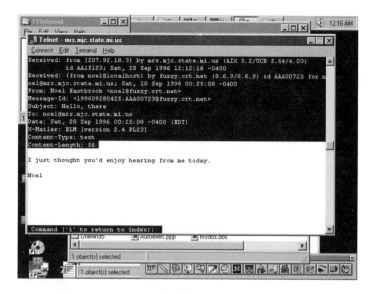

Figure 5.2.

Now this header is more like it. You really need to know only a few header elements.

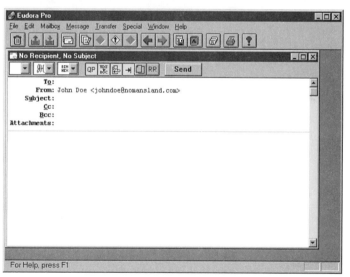

☐ Subject: The Subject: field should contain a very short (20–30 characters) description of what your message is about. This field can also be called Subject of Message: or simply Message:.

☐ CC: Most secretaries know that "CC" stands for Carbon Copy. This field contains the e-mail addresses of additional recipients. Most people put one e-mail address in the To: field and "copy" others by putting their addresses in the CC: field.

☐ BCC: Many e-mail clients either hide this field or don't give you quick access to it. This "black sheep" header field, which stands for Blind Carbon Copy, gives you a way of copying an e-mail message to another person without the first person you send the message knowing about it. Although this field has legitimate uses, people often use the BCC: field to send e-mail behind others' backs.

☐ Attachments: Some e-mail clients don't offer this field. Many clients, however, enable you to attach entire documents to e-mail messages. I will discuss this powerful tool in greater detail in Lesson 7, "Using E-Mail Like the Pros."

When all is said and done, a message header looks something like the one pictured in Figure 5.3.

Figure 5.3.

A typical e-mail header is simple and easy to understand.

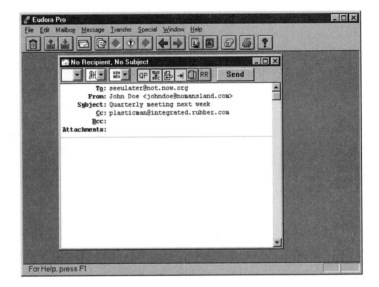

TIME SAVER

One header you don't see that you should know about is the Date: header. Although you usually never see it, many e-mail servers require it to process e-mail. If you use an e-mail client on a PC or Macintosh, make sure your Time and Date control panels are set to ensure that your e-mail has the appropriate time and date headers.

The Body

The body of an e-mail message is even easier to describe. It's simply the text that you want the person on the other end to see when he or she receives your message. In the next section, "E-Mail Etiquette and Conventions," I talk about some of the common rules to follow, but here are a few general rules:

☐ Try to keep messages short and to the point. With the exception of personal messages, you send e-mail to busy people (after all, you're a busy person too, right?). It is not uncommon for someone "on e-mail" to receive in excess of 100 messages a day.

☐ Make sure the Subject: field describes your message accurately. Many people who get lots of e-mail decide whether they're going to read a message based on the subject.

☐ Break up your message into short paragraphs. There is nothing worse than having to reply to a message that is one long paragraph. These messages are hard to read on a computer screen.

☐ Finally, don't be a pest. If you e-mail someone, assume that he or she received the message and will get back to you. If a couple of days go by, of course, you can send a reminder. Sending a message to someone every hour will only succeed in getting that person mad.

After all your hard work and diligence, you may end up with a short and concise message like the one shown in Figure 5.4.

Figure 5.4.

Often, a short e-mail message is effective.

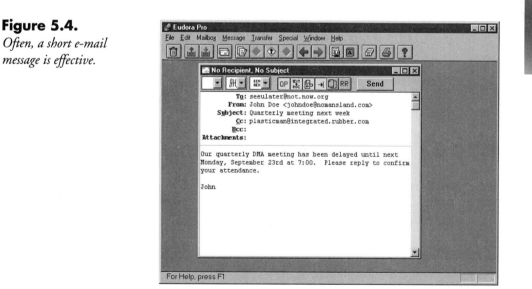

E-Mail Etiquette and Conventions

E-mail etiquette is one of those areas that could easily take up a whole book. In fact, you can find entire books about the etiquette and standards for e-mail use. In the following sections, I talk about only a few of the bigger areas involved in how to "make friends and influence people" through e-mail.

Mind Your Manners

Would you go to a foreign country for an extended visit without trying to learn about (and adapt to) that country's culture? If you did, you might end up getting funny stares because you refused an offer of food, or you might get kicked out of the country because you didn't realize that laughing out loud at someone's mistake is considered a grave insult.

Well, the same is true on the Internet. As I talked about earlier, the Internet culture has been around for 25 years. Typing a message in the wrong way might just get you *flamed.*

NEW TERM | **Flame:** On the Internet, a flame is a message that is, um, quite hot. Flames are messages that often contain profanity, question your heritage, and basically berate and belittle people. Flames can be either justified or unjustified.

Do	Don't

DO be as polite and courteous in e-mail as you would be face-to-face. People are more often inclined to be rude when they have a sense of anonymity.

DO exercise self-control. I use what I call the "24-hour rule." If I receive an e-mail message that offends me or makes me mad, I wait 24 hours before replying. More often than not, I realize the person who sent me the insulting message isn't worth my time. The rest of the time, I come to the conclusion that I have more important things to do.

DO try to be considerate by using proper grammar and punctuation so that the recipient can understand what you're saying. Lots of run-on sentences with oodles of spelling errors make for a bad reading experience.

DO use common sense. If you write a message for which you want a response, tell the recipient to please respond. If you're writing to someone you don't know for the first time, introduce yourself first. Courtesy and common sense are qualities to which almost everyone responds.

DON'T SCREAM. TYPING IN ALL CAPITALS IS CONSIDERED SCREAM-ING AND IS OFFENSIVE. Type as you would write a normal letter, using proper punctuation and syntax.

DON'T become a "leach." Leaches are people who go to others on the Internet for all their answers and can end up being really annoying. Most people on the Internet are more than willing to help someone who really needs it, but e-mailing someone to find out how to spell "ridiculous" is, well, ridiculous.

DON'T spam. *Spam* is any mass-mailed material meant for self-promotion, advertisement, or pure silliness. Spam, or electronic junk mail, is probably one of the most offensive acts on the Internet and, if you happen to send spam to an Internet veteran, you could find your e-mail account full of megabytes of junk until you apologize.

Tips for Brevity and Clarity

Believe it or not, you can shorten and clarify even when you're typing in simple text message. The following are some commonly used abbreviations on the Internet:

BTW	By The Way
FWIW	For What It's Worth
IMO	In My Opinion
IMHO	In My Humble Opinion/In My Honest Opinion
FAQ	Frequently Asked Question
RE:	Regarding
FYI	For Your Information
IRT	In Regards To
OTOH	On The Other Hand
YMMV	Your Mileage May Vary

To further help you clarify your point, you also can use a couple other accepted conventions:

underline	Underlines give emphasis without shouting. Because you can't usually underline a whole phrase, the custom is to put an underline mark in the first space preceding and following the text you want to be read as underlined.
asterisks	Same as underlining.

Emoticons

Conveying emotions in an e-mail message is tough. It is, in many people's opinions, one of the reasons that so much flaming and miscommunication occur on the Net. Face it, people interpret communication based not just on words, but on tone of voice, curvature of the lips, position of the body, and more. None of these factors are present in e-mail. It's just you, the text, and the reader. Using *emoticons* (short for *emotional icons*) is one way of trying to get across the emotion in what you say.

The following is a short list of but a few of the thousands of emoticons that you will see in your e-mail travels:

:)	Standard smiley face
;)	Winking smiley face
:>	Mischievous grin
:))	Big smile
:(	Standard sad face
:<	Angry/mad face

CAUTION

Just like anything, if overused, emoticons become useless and even annoying. Don't start using emoticons everywhere. Use them conservatively and where appropriate. When used appropriately, however, they can effectively connote sarcasm, humor, sadness, or any number of other emotions.

Look at the sample e-mail message in Figure 5.5. It incorporates many of the items listed in this section. Can you spot them all?

Figure 5.5.

This message has many elements of effective e-mail.

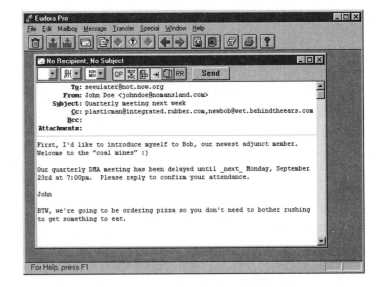

5

Summary

In this lesson, I took you through a quick tour to understanding e-mail. You learned that the user ID, an @ sign, and a domain name make up every e-mail address on the Internet. You also discovered some of the practical reasons you might want to use e-mail.

I then went on to explain the different parts of a message header (To:, From:, Subject:, CC:, BCC:, and Attachments:), as well as appropriate material for message bodies. Finally, I described some of the nuances of using e-mail, such as etiquette, proper ways to make your messages more concise and clear, and how to add emotion to what you write.

Workshop

The following workshop helps solidify the skills that you learned in this lesson.

Q&A

Q I've heard that emoticons can really annoy some people. If this is true, should I use them?

A Hey, some people get annoyed if you look at them. Should you stop looking at people? Yes, some people really dislike emoticons, but these people will usually tell you. For the most part, when you use emoticons appropriately, many people will appreciate your attempts to communicate more effectively.

Q I like to see all the little details. Can I see the entire header of all my messages?

A If you really want to see the entire header, most e-mail clients provide ways of viewing it. Look for preferences or options in your client that talk about how to "expand headers" or "display header information."

Q I have a friend who gave me an e-mail address that didn't look like any of your examples. Is it likely that this address is correct?

A If the address has a continuous string of characters, followed by an @ sign and then another continuous string of characters (some of which are usually periods), it is probably a valid address. Just make sure that no commas or spaces appear in the address, and give it a try.

Quiz

Take the following quiz to see how much you've learned.

5

Questions

1. Which e-mail address is likely invalid?

    (a) `example.no1@another.world.com`

    (b) `99%clx!!x%@uunet.net`

    (c) `example 3@another.galaxy.com`

2. Do e-mail messages contain a Date: header?

    (a) Yes

    (b) No

3. Read the following sentence:

    `IMO, _you_ are the one that's out to lunch, buddy. :)`

    Is this message likely a(n)

    (a) Friendly message

    (b) Flame

    (c) Inappropriate use of e-mail

Answers

1. (c) Remember, no matter how weird an e-mail address looks, you only know it's invalid if it has a space or a comma.

2. (a) Yes. Just because it doesn't show up doesn't mean it isn't a header.

3. (a) Notice the underscore marks for emphasis and not capital letters. Also note that the sender used a smiley emoticon at the end of the line.

Activity

Rent a movie or record a favorite TV show; then pick out a minute or two of dialogue you particularly like. See if you can transcribe the dialogue into acceptable "e-mailese." Show the dialogue to a friend or family member to see if he or she can tell you what emotions and feelings are being expressed. (You should pick someone who is familiar with e-mail to review your dialogue; otherwise, you'll have to explain what all your marks and abbreviations mean.)

5

Hour 6

Person-to-Person Communication with E-Mail

Now that you know all the elements that make up a good e-mail message, you're ready to actually get online and communicate. Once you're aware of the different elements of e-mail and have an easy-to-use e-mail client on your computer, using e-mail should be a breeze.

In this lesson, you can find the answers to the following questions:

- ☐ How do I send a basic e-mail message?
- ☐ How do I retrieve and read e-mail messages?
- ☐ How do I reply to e-mail messages?
- ☐ How do I forward an e-mail message to someone else?
- ☐ What else can I do with an e-mail message?
- ☐ What can I do to make sure that my message is easy for others to read?

You can easily find several good e-mail programs. Some Internet service providers, such as America Online, provide you with their own software for you to read e-mail. Many ISPs, however, either provide you with a third-party e-mail client or expect you to provide one of your own.

Far and away, the most popular e-mail program, which is used for all examples in this lesson, is Eudora. You can download a freeware version from `ftp://ftp.qualcomm.com/Eudora/ windows//1.5/eudor154.exe` for PCs or `ftp://ftp.qualcomm.com/quest/mac/Eudora/1.5/ eudora154.hqx` (or `eudora154fat.hqx` for PowerMacs) for Macintosh computers (refer to Lesson 17, "Getting Files with FTP," for more details on using FTP). Even if you don't use Eudora, your e-mail client probably uses many of the same features Eudora does.

Sending, Checking, and Reading E-Mail

Suppose you were to hire someone to retrieve your mail for you every day. What would you have to tell that person? Well, you would need to tell him or her who you are and where your mailbox is located, as well as where you would like your mail delivered in your house.

Your e-mail client works much like this person would. Your client gets your e-mail for you so that you can then read it, reply to it, file it, throw it away, or do anything else you want with it. This lesson covers all these elements, but you should start with the basics first.

Configuring Your E-Mail Client

Often, ISPs give you your e-mail client software already configured with the information you need to get going. If this is the case, you can skip this section. If you need to tell your e-mail client who you are (or even if you're just curious), however, read on.

Most e-mail clients need some basic information about you and your e-mail account before you can retrieve your mail. In Eudora, you can access your configuration settings by choosing Tools|Options (or Special|Settings on a Mac). In the resulting window, the following settings are organized by area.

Tools|Options|Getting Started

☐ Real Name: This setting provides your real name so that recipients of your messages will know who you are, much like a return address label on an envelope does.

☐ E-Mail Address: In this field, you enter your actual e-mail address. Eudora uses the term *POP account*. The POP account for `Tom who works at the Candlestick Company`, for example, might be `tom@candlestick.com`.

POP: This term stands for Post Office Protocol, which is the technical name for the way some e-mail servers deliver your mail.

Tools|Options|Personal Information

☐ Return Address: Most e-mail clients also require a return address, which in almost all cases is the same as your e-mail or POP account address. Figure 6.1 shows the Eudora Personal Information settings properly filled in.

Figure 6.1.

The personal information is probably among the most critical for your e-mail client.

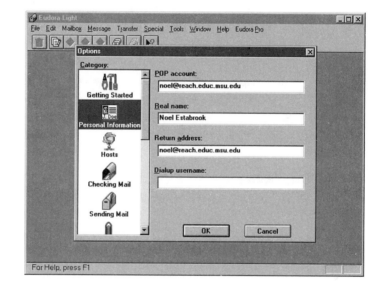

Tools|Options|Hosts

☐ SMTP Server: This setting is the domain portion of your e-mail address in most cases. In the previous example, `candlestick.com` would be a likely *SMTP* server for `tom@candlestick.com`. Your e-mail provider should tell you the name of your SMTP server when you set up your account.

 **SMTP:** This term stands for Simple Mail Transport Protocol, which is another technical name for the way e-mail messages are sent on the Internet. This represents the "language" or protocol used so that e-mail clients and servers can talk to each other.

After you enter all this information, you can click OK and then use your e-mail account to your heart's content.

Sending a Message

Before you can start reading e-mail, actually having something to read would be good! If you have already told several of your "connected" friends your e-mail address before looking at this lesson, perhaps you already have some messages to read. If you don't (or even if you do), sending a few messages out anyway might be a good idea.

To be safe, you should send an e-mail message to yourself first. This exercise serves two purposes. First, if you make a mistake, you'll be the only one who knows it. Second, if the process does work, you'll have at least one e-mail message to read for the next section.

JUST A MINUTE

You can access most of the common e-mail functions, such as sending, deleting, printing, replying to, and forwarding mail, from an easy-to-use toolbar at the top of your Eudora window. Simply put your cursor over each button, and a description of what it does automagically appears.

To Do: Sending an E-Mail Message to Yourself

1. Make sure that you are connected to the Internet.

2. Choose Message|New Message.

3. Put your e-mail address in the To: field, and press the Tab key or click in the next field to proceed.

4. Enter a subject for your message in the Subject: field, and press the Tab key several times until your cursor is blinking in the body of the message.

5. Type in a short message.

6. After your screen looks something like the one shown in Figure 6.2, click the Send button to mail your message to yourself.

TIME SAVER

In Figure 6.2, notice that the recipient's entire e-mail address isn't filled in. That's because Eudora and many other e-mail clients assume you're sending to a recipient in the same domain you're working in if you don't specify a full address. This knowledge can save you a few keystrokes.

You've just sent your first e-mail message. Want to see what it says (as if you don't already know)? Read on.

6

Figure 6.2.

Don't feel weird. Everybody sends mail to himself or herself once in a while!

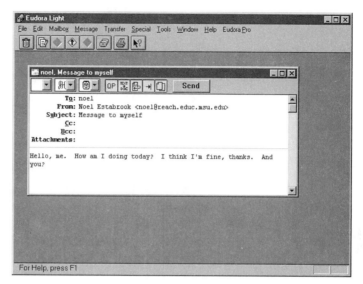

Checking Your Mail

Now that you know you have at least one message to read, you're ready to find out how. Make sure that you're still connected and follow these easy steps next.

To Do: Reading E-Mail Messages

1. Choose File|Check Mail. A window appears, prompting you for your password (though this prompt may appear when you first start up Eudora).

2. Type in your password, and click OK or press Enter. When your new mail is downloaded, a dialog box appears, telling you that new mail has arrived.

3. Press Enter. Your new mail then shows up in your In mailbox. Figure 6.3 shows the contents of a typical mailbox.

TIME SAVER

Make sure that Caps Lock is turned off before entering your password. Because most passwords are case sensitive (in other words, sensitive to whether the letters you use are capitalized or lowercase), having Caps Lock turned on could cause you to receive an "incorrect password" error message.

Figure 6.3.

This electronic "envelope" gives you information about messages in your mailbox.

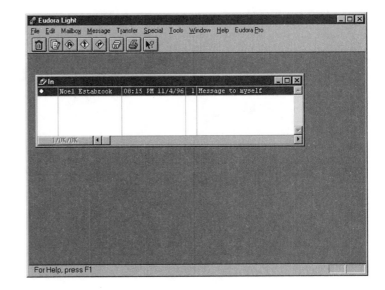

Notice that the message is presented on one line with various pieces of header information included. With most e-mail clients, this "envelope" includes the sender's name or e-mail address, the time the message was sent, and the subject of the message, as well as other information.

Reading Your Mail

If you thought sending and checking your mail was easy, you ain't seen nothin' yet. To read a message, simply double-click it. That's it. The message pops up on your screen for you to read. When you're done reading it, simply click the close box.

If you have more than one message in your mailbox, you also can use your up- and down-arrow keys to navigate your messages. When the message you want to read is highlighted, you can press Enter as an alternative to double-clicking to open the message.

Replying to and Forwarding Messages

With Eudora, like most e-mail clients, you can reply to and forward messages by simply clicking a toolbar button. You then see a window that looks almost identical to the New Message window. It does have a few differences, though, as you will soon see.

6

Replying

In the ultimate exercise of cyber-schizophrenia, go ahead and reply to the message you just sent yourself. You do so by choosing Message|Reply or by clicking the Reply button on the toolbar.

In the resulting window, you see both your and the recipient's e-mail address already filled in for you. Also notice that the entire content of the original message appears in the body of the message, with each line preceded with an *include mark*.

NEW TERM **Include marks:** These > characters are the quotation marks of the Internet. When you're reading or replying to an e-mail message, an include mark indicates a line of text that belonged to a previous message.

Why are these include marks here? The biggest reason is for you to lend context to your messages. First, you must realize that your e-mail client acts like a word processor while you are editing the body of the message you want to send. You therefore can select, cut, copy, paste, or type any text you want.

By using these editing techniques, you can "include" pieces of the message to which you're replying so that it's easier to read and understand. Find out more about how to use these techniques effectively in the section titled "The Easy-to-Read E-Mail Message" later in this lesson. For now, look at the sample message reply shown in Figure 6.4.

Figure 6.4.

A good reply generally includes portions of the original message to provide context.

Forwarding

When you have something good, being able to share it with someone is nice. E-mail enables you to do so with ease using the message forwarding feature.

To forward a highlighted message, choose Message|Forward or click the Forward button on the toolbar. You then see a window almost identical to the Message Reply window, except that the To: field isn't filled in for you.

A forwarded message, like a reply, cites the original message with include marks. Also as you can with a message reply, you can edit the message any way you like, although many people forward messages without any comments except for a possible "thought you might be interested in this" at the top of the message body, as you can see in Figure 6.5.

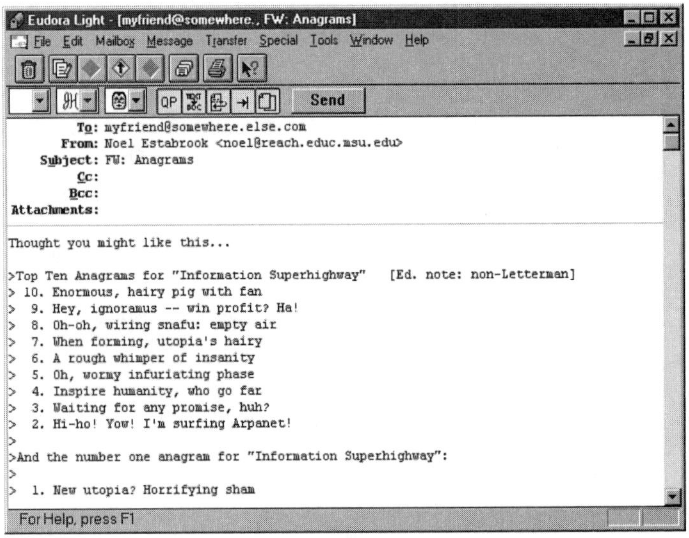

Figure 6.5.

Many people like to pass on a good joke to their friends.

```
Eudora Light - [myfriend@somewhere., FW: Anagrams]
File  Edit  Mailbox  Message  Transfer  Special  Tools  Window  Help

        To: myfriend@somewhere.else.com
      From: Noel Estabrook <noel@reach.educ.msu.edu>
   Subject: FW: Anagrams
        Cc:
       Bcc:
Attachments:

Thought you might like this...

>Top Ten Anagrams for "Information Superhighway"    [Ed. note: non-Letterman]
> 10. Enormous, hairy pig with fan
>  9. Hey, ignoramus -- win profit? Ha!
>  8. Oh-oh, wiring snafu: empty air
>  7. When forming, utopia's hairy
>  6. A rough whimper of insanity
>  5. Oh, wormy infuriating phase
>  4. Inspire humanity, who go far
>  3. Waiting for any promise, huh?
>  2. Hi-ho! Yow! I'm surfing Arpanet!
>
>And the number one anagram for "Information Superhighway":
>
>  1. New utopia? Horrifying sham

For Help, press F1
```

TIME SAVER

If you want to forward a message to someone else without all the include marks, simply choose Message|Redirect instead. This way, you can redirect a message without include marks to the recipient of your choice.

Other E-Mail Tasks

Of course, you can do many other things with e-mail messages. What you've learned so far covers about 75 percent of what you'll use e-mail for. Many of the advanced e-mail functions you'll need are covered in the next lesson.

You should know a couple other simple functions and shortcuts, however:

☐ Deleting mail: To delete a highlighted message, choose Transfer|Trash or Message|Delete. You also can click the Trash icon. Because this action only transfers your mail to your Trash mailbox, you also need to choose Special|Empty Trash to get rid of your messages for good.

☐ Printing mail: To print a highlighted message, choose File|Print or click the Print toolbar button.

☐ Saving mail: If you want to save an e-mail message as a non-mail text file, choose File|Save As.

TIME SAVER

Deal with it! Your e-mail, that is. When you get a message, read it and then reply, save, transfer, or do whatever you want with it when you get it. Putting off dealing with e-mail is easy. If you're an electronic procrastinator, though, your only reward will be a cluttered, outdated, and confusing mailbox.

The Easy-to-Read E-Mail Message

Follow these simple rules for creating an easy-to-read e-mail message, and you'll win friends and influence people:

☐ Cite the original message when you respond. Don't assume that the other person has any idea of what you're talking about. Quote the original message so that both of you know what's being said. Context is everything.

☐ Don't cite too much. Cut out material that isn't relevant to your reply. Much of knowing what to cut comes with experience, but always ask yourself if the original text you're including really adds context to your reply.

☐ Quote the original first. Citing an original message after your own comments is poor form. Often, people need to be reminded of what they said and to what you are replying. So quote the original message before your reply. After all, that's how normal conversation works (unless you're psychic!).

☐ Don't reply if a response isn't necessary. Nobody likes to receive several pages of an original message with a "me too" appended to the end.

☐ Space out. The text, not you. Always leave at least one blank line between included text and your reply. This way, you make the message easy on the eyes.

Figure 6.6 shows an e-mail reply that is properly edited and composed. Notice how easy to read the format is. By the way, after reading the message in this example, aren't you glad you don't have to deal with e-mail in UNIX?

Figure 6.6.

Though the content might look like Greek, the form is easy-to-read English.

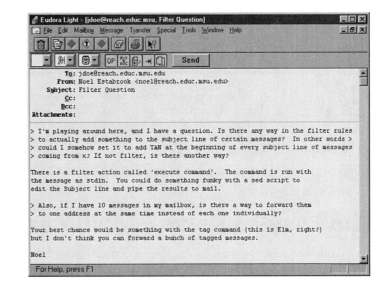

Summary

In this lesson, you learned how to configure your e-mail client to use your account effectively. You also found out how to send, retrieve, and read your e-mail. In addition, you learned how to reply to and forward a message.

After learning all these basics, you found out how to complete some miscellaneous e-mail tasks such as deleting and printing messages. Finally, you examined some rules to help you properly reply to and forward a message with consideration for your reader.

Workshop

The following workshop helps solidify the skills that you learned in this lesson.

Q&A

Q **I've seen some forwarded messages that indent and separate the original message instead of using include marks. Is this okay?**

A Include marks are a universal symbol of citation and are less likely to confuse your reader. E-mail correspondence is about communication. Err on the side of clarity, and use the include marks.

Q **I've heard that Eudora has some neat features like message filtering and spell checking. But I don't see those functions in Eudora Lite. What's up?**

A Remember, you're using the freeware version of Eudora. If you want to purchase the commercial version of Eudora, Eudora Pro, choose Help|About Eudora Pro|Request More Info, and Qualcomm will send you information on how to get the "beefed-up" version. Remember, though, for most of your tasks, Eudora Lite works very well.

Quiz

Take the following quiz to see how much you've learned.

Questions

1. Which of the following is the likely SMTP server for `bobw@late.night.org`?

    (a) `bobw@late.night.org`

    (b) `bobw`

    (c) `late.night.org`

2. Where should you put quoted text in a message reply?

    (a) At the end of the message

    (b) Just before your reply text

    (c) Just after your reply text

3. Including the entire message you're replying to is always a good idea so that the person receiving it will know exactly what you're replying to.

   (a) True

   (b) False

Answers

1. (c) `late.night.org`

2. (c) Always cite the original message first before your reply, just as you would in normal conversation.

3. (b) False. Include only what's necessary.

Activity

Practice makes perfect. Your activity for this lesson is simple: Send some e-mail! Find some friends or family with e-mail addresses, and let them know you're alive. You can even send me a message letting me know you (hopefully) liked my book if you want. After all, another 20,000 messages in my mailbox won't make a difference, right?

Hour 7

Using E-Mail Like the Pros

You should now be able to perform most of the basic functions of e-mail such as reading, sending, and replying. Coupled with the information you learned in Lesson 5, "Understanding E-Mail," you should now be able to complete a vast majority of e-mail tasks. But what about the rest? Surely, you can do more.

In this lesson, I tell you what you need to know to take e-mail to "the next level." In this lesson, you can find answers to the following questions:

- ☐ Can I attach documents to e-mail messages?
- ☐ Do I need to sign every e-mail message by hand?
- ☐ How can I remember everyone's e-mail address?
- ☐ Can I manage e-mail effectively?
- ☐ Do I always need to be online to use e-mail?

Many of the functions I discuss in this lesson are available in most e-mail client software. What the functions are called and how they are accessed can be quite different from package to package, but the concepts are similar.

TIME SAVER

If you can't find a particular function discussed here in your e-mail client, check out its Help menu. The Help menu can often help you locate a particular function within seconds.

Attaching Documents

As I discussed in Lessons 2, "Internet Uses in the Modern World," and 5, "Understanding E-Mail," most e-mail clients enable you to attach non-text documents to standard e-mail messages. This capability is very powerful. When you use it effectively, you can save lots of time and money over transmitting documents via fax or overnight mail.

As you'll see, attaching a document doesn't always make sense, but often it is a useful alternative to other, more traditional methods for file transfer.

What Can You Attach?

The first question to answer is an obvious one: What types of documents can you attach? The answer is simple: just about anything. If you can store a file on your computer, you can attach it to an e-mail message. Such files include word processing documents, spreadsheets, multimedia presentations, graphics, and software.

CAUTION

Just because you can attach anything, I'm not saying that you should. Be particularly careful about the size of the file you're sending. Many e-mail accounts have quotas that restrict the amount of e-mail they can have at any one time. Exceeding this quota can cause some problems. A good rule of thumb is to make sure that the files you attach are less than 500KB (1/2MB) in size.

Sending Attachments

Sending an attachment is really quite easy. For instance, the following section explains how to attach a message in Eudora.

7

To Do: Creating a Signature

1. Compose a new message as you normally would, filling in the To:, Subject:, and Message Body fields of your message.

2. Choose Message|Attach File to bring up a standard browser window.

3. Browse your hard drive until you locate the file you want to attach; double-click on that file.

4. Check the Attachments: field in your message to make sure that you selected the correct attachment.

Just about every e-mail client has either a toolbar button or menu item that you can use to attach a document. Choosing this option generally opens a standard browsing window, like the one shown in Figure 7.1, that enables you to locate the file you want to attach. After you find the file you want, just double-click and you should see the file path and name in your message header.

Figure 7.1.

Most e-mail clients enable you to find and attach any file on your computer.

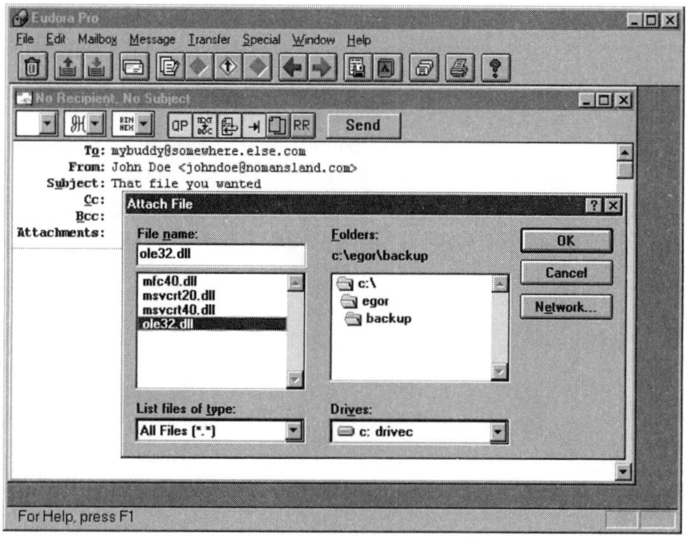

The following are a few more points to know before you go on. First, an e-mail message with an attached document takes longer to transmit because the entire file has to be sent as part of the message. Second, you need to make sure that the person to whom you're sending the file will be able to read it. Sending a Microsoft Excel file to someone without Excel doesn't do him or her a whole lot of good. Third, you need to make sure that the encoding scheme your client uses for attached documents can be read by the person to whom you're sending it. On this last point, let's take a coffee break, shall we?

COFFEE BREAK

As you may have already noticed, every e-mail message you send is composed of simple text. You type in a word, and that word is sent. Documents produced by other pieces of software, as well as the software itself, however, contain a lot of information that isn't simple text.

You now have a problem because you can't just copy and paste non-text characters into e-mail. Fortunately, you can encrypt, or encode, these non-text files in such a way that every non-text character is translated into a simple text character for transmission via e-mail protocol.

One downside of this great capability is the fact that, to "decode" your message, the e-mail client of the recipient must "understand" the encryption method your client uses to encode the message in the first place. Note that this type of "encryption" does not make your document secure, as it can be translated by any standard decoder out there.

Your e-mail client should enable you to choose which encoding method to use. If it doesn't have such an option, use the Help menu or your user's manual to find out what method your client uses. Three types of encryption are standard: BinHex (used on Macintoshes and the Eudora e-mail client), uuencode/uudecode (used by UNIX and some other e-mail clients), and MIME (used on the Web and by a few other e-mail clients).

Make sure that you "know the code" for your e-mail client and your recipient's e-mail client. Sending a small test attachment first is a good way to make sure that everything is working correctly before sending larger, more important files.

Receiving Attachments

Believe it or not, receiving attachments is even easier than sending them. Almost every e-mail client that can send attachments automatically decodes attachments from others and saves them to your hard drive, provided the client can understand the encoding scheme (see the preceding "Coffee Break").

The only thing you need to know is the place where the attachment is saved. Generally, you use an Option or Preference to tell your client where to save every attachment. Picking an empty directory is a good idea, so you can quickly locate attached documents. Usually, a line in the body of the message tells you that an attached document has been converted.

Creating (and Creative) Signatures

One of the most used (and most enjoyable) functions of e-mail is the *signature*. You can give information, make a joke, and so on by properly using a signature.

7

NEW TERM **Signature:** A signature is a small text file that contains information that your e-mail client automatically attaches to the bottom of every message you send. Most people also use their signature when sending messages to newsgroups.

Just Make It Up

Creating a signature is easy.

To Do: Creating a Signature

1. Within your e-mail client, find the option that enables you to create a new signature. It is important that you use a monospaced font, such as Courier, to create this signature.

2. Some clients require you to first create a signature file in a simple text editor and then locate the file created within that processor. If you have such a client, open a simple text editor such as Notepad or Wordpad (Windows) or SimpleText (Macintosh).

3. To begin, just type in your name, address, phone number, and e-mail address on separate lines.

4. Save the file and you're done. If you create this file in a text editor, you can now locate it from within your e-mail client to begin using it.

Now that you have finished creating a simple signature, every message you send will have this information attached to it. Figure 7.2 shows a basic signature attached to the bottom of a message.

What You Need to Know About Signatures

You need to know a few points about signatures before moving on. First, keeping your signatures to about four lines is generally good etiquette; you certainly should not use more than six or seven. By limiting the number of lines, you prevent others' mailboxes from filling up with a bunch of messages that have signatures that are longer than the message itself.

Second, create your signature in a fixed font such as Courier. This way, you can ensure that your signature will look the same on everyone's e-mail client. For this same reason, making sure that each line in your signature is no longer than about 75 characters is also a good idea.

Finally, don't be afraid to have a little fun. The following are two examples of what really creative people have done with simple text characters to create "ASCII Art" signatures. Notice that, although creative and humorous, they're both still within the four-line limit.

```
      ,,,    John Doe - Consultant
     (o-o)   Acme Computing, 555.4677
==-=-=-=— .oOo—(_)—OOo.—=-=-=-=-=-=-=-=-=-==
johndoe@acme.com   "    http://www.acme.com/~johndoe

The probability of forgetting something is              __o
directly proportional to...to...uh...                  -\<,
Rob Richman, robtrich@robin.hood.com_____(_)/(_)_____
663.555.6723 (v)   563.555.6721 (f)   1421 Sherwood Forest_____
```

Figure 7.2.

A standard signature usually contains important information about the sender.

TIME SAVER

With many e-mail clients, you can have two signatures. Having both a "business" and a "personal" signature to use in different situations is a good idea. Even if you don't have this option, you would be wise not to use your "make love, not war" signature when sending e-mail to a prospective employer.

Aliases: The Three-Letter E-Mail Address

After you've used the Internet for a while (or even if you haven't), you may find yourself having a hard time remembering everyone's e-mail address. Not only that, but you may also tire of typing in your friend's 43-character address. Oh, what to do?

The solution is to use an alias or nickname. With just about any e-mail client, you can create an alias that represents a real e-mail address. Doing so can save you lots of time and effort when sending e-mail.

7

TIME SAVER

Before you start creating aliases, decide upon a standard way of creating them. You may want to always use a person's first name and the first letter of his or her last name, for example, as an alias (johnd for John Doe, beckyt for Becky Thomas, and so on). Keeping to a standard may not seem important now, but after you create dozens of aliases, they can be just as hard to remember as the e-mail addresses if you don't follow a standard for creating them.

To Do: Creating an Alias

1. Within your e-mail client, find the option that enables you to create nicknames or aliases.

2. Choose the option to create a new alias.

3. Enter the nickname and the e-mail address for the alias.

4. With some clients, you can even put in additional information such as real name, address, and more. You can enter this information to use your e-mail client as an address book as well.

5. Save the nickname. Your window might look something like the one pictured in Figure 7.3.

Figure 7.3.

This window contains a small, standard set of nicknames.

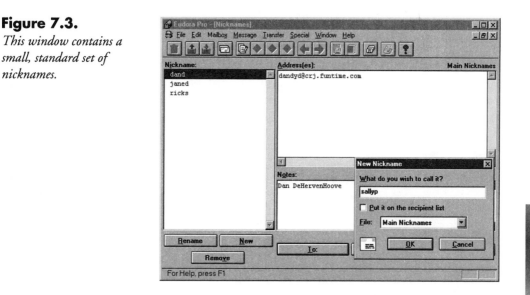

7

From now on, just type the nickname in the To: field of your e-mail message. Your client automatically knows to whom you want to send the message.

Managing Mailboxes

Before long, you'll start to realize that your mailbox can get awfully full awfully fast. When you start to feel overwhelmed, you can apply some of the techniques presented in the following sections to help you manage your e-mail more effectively.

Mailbox Lower-Level Management

You can take a few steps to make your life less complicated without using any additional features of your e-mail client. The following are a few simple, common sense methods you can implement to help reduce your mailbox clutter and confusion:

☐ Don't procrastinate. Sometimes you have to. If at all possible, though, read a message and reply to it, if necessary, as soon as you get it. Putting it off "until later" means that you'll add it to your collection of mail to get to, or you may even forget about it altogether.

☐ Do something. After you take care of the message, do something with it. Either store the message in another mailbox (which I cover in the mid-level management section) or delete the message. You can even print out important messages before deleting them.

☐ Don't be a packrat. E-mail messages can really stack up. Before keeping a message, make sure that you really need to first.

☐ Live and learn. Don't feel compelled to read every line of every e-mail message you get. If you're like most people, you may get a fair amount of junk mail, as well as other assorted mail that doesn't require a lot of attention. Learn to recognize this mail so that you don't waste time on it.

Mailbox Mid-Level Management

Your best mailbox management tool is the mailbox itself. More accurately, I should say *mailboxes*. With most e-mail clients, you can create and organize mailboxes to help you manage your messages better. Think of mailboxes as an electronic filing cabinet.

Many clients come preconfigured with a few standard mailboxes such as the In, Out, and Trash mailboxes. For basic mail management, they are okay, but soon you'll want more. When this time comes, you may want to develop a mailbox structure that lets you do even more. The following steps show you how to create a mailbox in Eudora.

7

To Do: Creating Mailboxes

1. Select Mailbox|New to bring up the New Mailbox Window.

2. Type **Personal** in the Name the new mailbox field.

3. If you want this mailbox to be a folder (which can then contain other mailboxes), choose the Make it a folder option.

4. Click OK to save the mailbox name.

You may need to experiment, but you will soon have a mailbox structure that works for you. Just as with other tools I've talked about, you should organize them well and not use too many of them. Figure 7.4 shows an example of a set of mailboxes that might be useful.

Figure 7.4.

This organization of mailboxes looks effective. Notice that each folder gives you the opportunity to create yet another new mailbox.

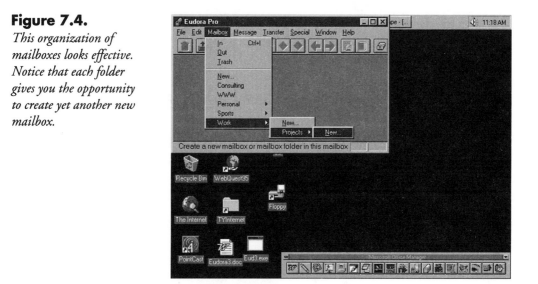

Mailbox Upper-Level Management

Some higher-end e-mail clients, such as Eudora Pro, make use of e-mail *filters*. Filtering e-mail messages can help save you the hassle of having to transfer many messages yourself. Keep in mind, however, that message filtering is really useful only if you generally have a high volume of mail or a large or complicated mailbox structure.

NEW TERM **Filter:** Filtering is really just a way any program can automatically screen data. An e-mail client looks at e-mail message header information to determine what to do with the message. A filter might, for example, put all messages with a certain domain name in the header into a certain mailbox.

If your client offers filtering, you probably can use a Filter Rules option to tell your client specifically how to filter e-mail. Rules for filtering usually fall into one of several different categories:

☐ Header Information: Most filters read the e-mail message's header information to determine what to do with it. With most filters, you can identify the To:, From:, Subject:, and Reply To: headers. Others filter by looking at any header, and still other filters search the body of a message for filtering information.

☐ Action: Most filters are intended to perform some action. The most common actions are to change the subject of a message or to raise or lower the priority of a message you receive.

☐ Transfer: This filtering rule is the most common. Most often, you want e-mail messages transferred to a particular mailbox based on who the message comes from. You might want all the e-mail you receive from your work's domain name, for example, in your Work mailbox. Figure 7.5 shows such an example.

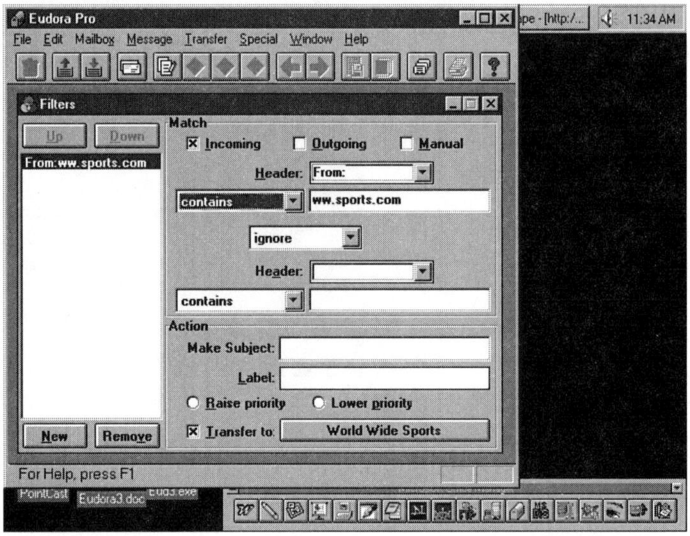

Figure 7.5.

This user wants to make sure that his sports mail goes to the right place.

Using E-Mail Offline

Unless you have a service provider that charges you a flat fee no matter how long you stay connected to the Internet, time is money. Fortunately, with most e-mail clients, you can read and compose messages without being connected. After you are ready to send and download new mail, simply connect, transmit all your messages, and then disconnect.

7

The process for working offline can vary widely from client to client. America Online, for example, has "Flash Sessions," whereby you can connect, download mail, send any composed messages waiting to be sent, and then disconnect. Another popular client, Eudora (both the shareware and commercial version), actually has a setting that enables you to use Eudora offline, as you can see in Figure 7.6. After you compose and read mail, you can simply connect, toggle this setting, and then check for and send your mail.

Figure 7.6.

Using e-mail clients offline can save you money.

As with several other aspects of e-mail I've covered, you may have to consult your client's Help menu or a user's manual for specifics. Usually, though, with just a little nosing around, you can find what you need.

Summary

In this lesson, you learned to use e-mail "like a pro." You learned how to send and receive e-mail attachments as well as some of the ins and outs of how to do so most effectively. You also learned how to avoid having to sign all your e-mail manually by using signatures.

I also gave you some handy management techniques such as how to create mailboxes and use filters to organize your mail better. Finally, you learned how to save money by using your e-mail client offline.

Workshop

The following workshop helps solidify the skills that you learned in this lesson.

Q&A

Q I've heard people say that using e-mail to attach documents really isn't worth the effort. Is it?

A Definitely, as long as you do it wisely. Again, make sure that your attachment encoding method is compatible with the person receiving or sending the message. Next, make sure that the file isn't too big. Finally, realize when a fax or other method might work better.

Q I have a dozen or so friends who I find myself sending messages to all the time. Can I send them mail without having to type in all those addresses every time?

A Certainly. You should use your client's Nickname function. Instead of creating an alias for a single name, create a group alias name (such as Friends). Then, when you're asked to provide the nickname's e-mail address, simply type in all the addresses, with each one separated by a comma. Save it and you're set. Just remember, no spaces!

Q When does using an e-mail client offline not make sense?

A If your Internet service provider charges a flat fee no matter how long you stay connected, using your e-mail client offline usually doesn't make a lot of sense.

Quiz

Take the following quiz to see how much you've learned.

Questions

1. Which method is best for managing e-mail messages?

   (a) Attaching documents

   (b) Using signatures

   (c) Creating different mailboxes

2. Which of the following is not a common file attachment encoding type?

   (a) Zip

   (b) BinHex

   (c) uudecode

7

3. Keeping e-mail messages for at least a week is a good idea in case you need to look at them again.

    (a) True

    (b) False

Answers

1. (c) The other two methods are useful but don't really help you manage e-mail.

2. (a) Zip. Zip is a method of compressing files, not encoding them.

3. (b) False. Don't be a packrat!

Activity

Your mission for this lesson is simple. Create at least four mailboxes to help you manage your e-mail. Think about the kind of e-mail you might receive when creating them. Write down this structure. Then, in a couple of months, compare it with your mailbox structure to see how it has expanded, shrunk, or changed.

7

Hour 8

Communicating with the World: Using Mailing Lists

By now, you know just about everything you need to know about what e-mail is and how to use it. But before you're done with e-mail, you need to know about one more powerful e-mail tool: mailing lists. Mailing lists, often called *listservs*, have been around for a long time. Using mailing lists, many people from all over can effectively communicate with each other.

By the end of this lesson, you should be able to answer the following questions about mailing lists:

☐ What is a mailing list?

☐ How do mailing lists work?

☐ How do I get onto a mailing list?

☐ How do I send and receive messages using listservs?

☐ Where can I find what listservs are available?

Using listservs is a great way to talk to other people in a "group" setting. Before you start looking for the right listserv, however, you need to find out more about listservs in general.

Mailing Lists Explained

After the advent of e-mail, users soon realized that being able to send e-mail to groups of people for collaboration and discussion would be very helpful. Thus, the first listserv was originally devised by the BITNET Information Center (BITNIC). This e-mail list "server" managed a large number of mailing lists, each one addressing a specific area of interest for network users and each having an independent set of list members. This service made the exchange of ideas and information among the members very convenient.

How Listservs Work

The functionality of a listserv is generally easy to understand. Remember that, by defining one word or phrase, you can create a nickname with your e-mail client to distribute e-mail to an individual or a group. Listservs work much the same way, only on a larger scale. A mailing list program runs on a computer and defines a unique e-mail address to distribute all e-mail sent to it. This listserv software automates the process of enabling people to add and remove their names from this giant "nickname" (called *subscribing* and *unsubscribing*), as well as a host of other functions.

After this listserv is set up, anyone who subscribes to the listserv can send e-mail to it; that e-mail is, in most cases, automatically distributed to everyone on the mailing list, as the diagram shows in Figure 8.1.

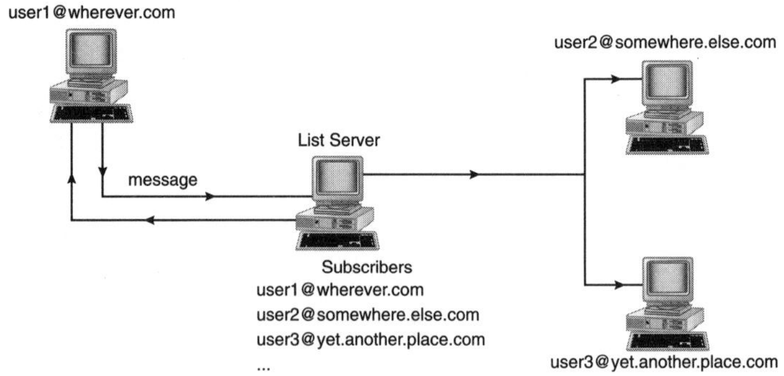

Figure 8.1.

A list server acts as the distribution point for messages to be sent to multiple subscribers.

user1@wherever.com

user2@somewhere.else.com

List Server

message

Subscribers
user1@wherever.com
user2@somewhere.else.com
user3@yet.another.place.com
...

user3@yet.another.place.com

Listserv Personality

So who maintains these listservs? How can one person keep track of hundreds or thousands of subscribers on one listserv? In fact, a person usually doesn't maintain the listserv. Many people don't realize that, for the most part, listservs are automated. After a listserv administrator sets up a listserv, he or she usually leaves it alone and lets it take care of itself.

Two exceptions to this rule are the *private* and *moderated listserv*. A private listserv is simply one which requires an administrator's approval to join the list. With a moderated listserv, a human being usually approves subscription additions and removals also, but in addition approves message submissions before they are finalized. Usually, listservs that deal with highly volatile issues are moderated.

NEW TERM **Moderated listserv:** Just as a debate has a moderator to make sure that both sides stick to the rules, so too do some listservs have a human moderator who makes sure that the rules of the listserv are being followed.

Finding the Right Listserv

Before using a listserv, you first need to actually find one that is of interest to you. You can find a listserv of interest in basically three ways:

☐ Word of mouth: Many people still find out about listservs from others who have similar interests. As you talk, e-mail each other, or surf the Web, you can usually find a listserv that interests you.

☐ E-mail: If your Internet access is limited to e-mail (or even if it isn't), you can order a list of the available listservs. Simply send a message to LISTSERV@waynest1.bitnet. Leave the Subject: field blank and, in the body of your message, type LIST GLOBAL. Although you will receive a list of quite a few listservs, it will by no means be exhaustive.

CAUTION

Many listservs are available. When you order the list of listservs, be prepared to read through a long document, like the one shown in Figure 8.2, to find the listserv you're looking for.

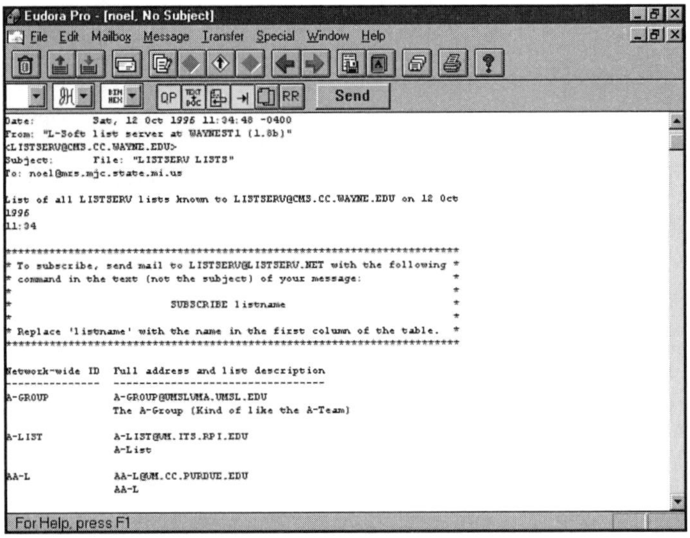

Figure 8.2.

The list tells you about hundreds of listservs from A to Z.

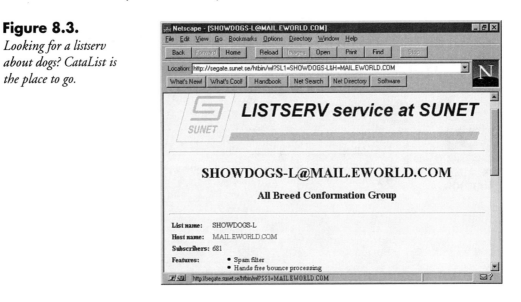

The Web: Some excellent listserv search engines are available on the World Wide Web. (If you haven't got on the Web yet, look at Lesson 13, "Navigating the Web.") A great place to start is CataList at `http://segate.sunet.se/lists/listref.html`. With CataList, shown in Figure 8.3, you can search in dozens of different ways for the listserv you want.

Figure 8.3.

Looking for a listserv about dogs? CataList is the place to go.

You cannot get an exhaustive list of every mailing list available with any of these three methods. Using them in combination, however, you are sure to find some listservs you can subscribe to.

Signing On and Signing Off

The most important procedures to know when using listservs is how to get onto them and then how to get off. If you know what you're doing, getting on and off is easy. You definitely need to know a few points, however, to make your access of listservs easier.

Easy On

After you find a listserv, you can subscribe to it. Most listservs are similar in how you can subscribe and unsubscribe. Depending on where you located the listserv you want to subscribe to, you should have specific instructions on where to subscribe. In general, though, you need to complete the same basic steps.

To Do: Signing On a Listserv

1. Send a new e-mail message to the address of the listserv or listserv administrator.
2. Leave the Subject: field blank.
3. In the body of the message, you usually type `subscribe Your Name`. Some lists require you to type `subscribe ListName Your Name`.
4. If you have a signature attached to your messages, you should turn it off when sending this message.

CAUTION

Always monitor your e-mail closely for several days after subscribing to a listserv. High-traffic listservs commonly deliver dozens of messages to your mailbox every day. You may want to think twice about staying subscribed to some of these listservs.

Here's one last note: If you subscribe to a moderated listserv, getting a message confirming that you're on may take a day or so. You may even get a message from the moderator to confirm that you really want on the list. Waiting at least three days for a response before resubmitting a request to subscribe to a moderated listserv is usually a good idea.

Easy Off

You may have many reasons for signing off a listserv. Maybe it isn't exactly what you thought, maybe you're tired of it, or maybe it has too much traffic for you to handle. Whatever the reason, you follow almost exactly the same steps to get off a listserv as you do to get on.

To Do: Signing Off a Listserv

1. Send a new e-mail message to the address of the listserv or listserv administrator.

2. Leave the Subject: field blank.

3. In the body of the message, you usually type unsubscribe `Your Name`. Some lists require you to type unsubscribe `ListName Your Name`.

4. If you have a signature attached to your messages, you should turn it off when sending this message.

CAUTION

When you're unsubscribing from a listserv, make sure that you send the message from the same e-mail account you used when subscribing. Most listservs search for an exact e-mail address match when removing a subscriber. If you have trouble getting unsubscribed, contact the listserv administrator immediately. In addition, make sure that you send your unsubscribe message to the listserv (the same address you sent your subscribe message to) and not to the entire mailing list.

Sending and Responding to Messages

Reading, sending, and replying to listserv messages involve the same basic steps as working with any other e-mail. You should know about a few differences, though. I describe these slight differences, along with a few handy rules, in the following sections.

Sending Messages to a List

Sending a message to an individual is really no different than sending one to a listserv. The only difference is in who receives your message. You can still fill in the To: and Subject: fields, as well as the body of the message. You should keep in mind a few points, however, when sending those messages.

8

To begin, after reading the listserv mail for a couple of days, start by sending a message of introduction to the listserv. Make this message brief, but include information about yourself that might be of interest to other subscribers. Remember, you are hopefully subscribing to the listserv to contribute information as well as get it. The only time you might not want to do this is if you have subscribed to a particularly large listserv with lots of traffic.

TIME SAVER

Make sure that you keep your contributions to the listserv reasonable. Remember, every time you send a message, you're sending it to everyone on the list. Don't dominate or flood a listserv with messages. You may find yourself on the receiving end of subtle (or not so subtle) hints to cease and desist.

You may receive a copy of your message shortly after sending it. When you subscribe to a listserv, you receive a copy of all mail sent to the list, including your own. Conversely, don't be alarmed if you don't receive a copy of your mail right away, especially if you belong to a moderated list. For your e-mail to show up back in your mailbox can take anywhere from a few minutes to a few days.

Responding to Listserv Messages

As with sending messages, responding to listserv messages is similar to replying to personal e-mail. You may need to pay special attention to one major difference, however.

When you reply to an e-mail message, you generally know that it is going to be returned to the person who sent it to you. With a listserv, however, this is not necessarily the case. Listservs are set up one of two ways:

☐ Replies are automatically sent to the list. Most listservs are set up this way. In this case, you use your client's Reply option to reply to the list and the Forward option to forward a reply to the individual.

☐ Some listservs are also set up to route replies automatically to the original sender. In this instance, you can use your client's Reply option to reply to the individual and the Forward option to forward a reply to the listserv.

So how do you tell which way the listserv you've subscribed to is set up? Easy. Simply compose a reply to a listserv message. When you do, look at the information your e-mail client puts in the To: field. If a reply goes to the listserv address, as in Figure 8.4, the listserv is set up in the standard way. If the reply goes to the individual, the second type of listserv setup is used.

Figure 8.4.

Most listservs are set up to have replies automatically sent to the entire listserv.

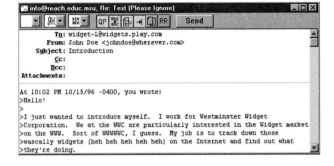

Listservs Helping Listsurfers

One of the best places to go for help in finding out what user options your listserv offers is the listserv itself. To get help, try the following steps with a listserv to which you are currently subscribed.

To Do: Finding Help

1. Send a new e-mail message to the address of the listserv or listserv administrator. This address is the same one you sent your subscription message to.
2. Leave the Subject: field blank.
3. In the body of the message, type help.
4. If you have a signature attached to your messages, you should turn it off when sending this message.
5. You should get a message after a few seconds; it should look something like Figure 8.5. Again, the amount of time it takes you to get this message back could vary.

Table 8.1 lists the most common listserv commands. You use these commands in the body of a message you send to the listserv administrator address.

Table 8.1. Common listserv commands.

SUBSCRIBE	Subscribes you to a list
UNSUBSCRIBE	Unsubscribes you from a list
LIST	Shows all listservs served from a particular server
REVIEW or WHO	Shows the list of users currently subscribed
HELP	Sends the HELP message
INFO	Sends information on the list
INDEX	Shows a list of documents available for GET

GET	Retrieves documents from the listserv
SET ACTIVE	Makes your subscription active
SET INACTIVE	Suspends your subscription until the next SET ACTIVE command
SET DIGEST	Sends you a digest of listserv messages once a day instead of individual messages

Figure 8.5.

Most listservs offer help online.

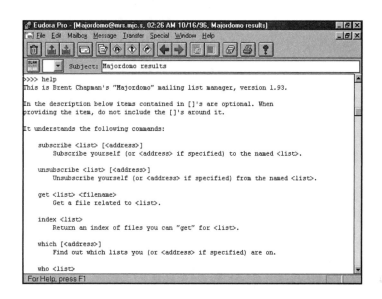

Depending on the listserv you use, other or different listserv commands may be available as well. The SET commands can be particularly useful, as can the GET command. Another important setting is the Digest option. When you first subscribe to a listserv, read the introductory message to learn whether you can get a digest of listserv postings once a day (as opposed to receiving each individual message in your mailbox). Getting a digest of a listserv—especially lists with high traffic—can save you a lot of time. Feel free to experiment with the different settings to see what style of listserv participation best fits your needs.

Summary

In this lesson, I gave you a lot of information about listservs. You should now understand that listservs are basically mass mailing lists that enable you to communicate with other people who are interested in the same things you are. You also learned many ways to find the right listserv for you.

In addition, you learned some of the ins and outs of sending and replying to listserv messages, including how to watch particular headers to see to whom replies to the listserv go. Finally, I gave you some pointers about how to actually get some help from the listservs themselves.

Workshop

The following workshop helps solidify the skills that you learned in this lesson.

Q&A

Q It seems that listservs are everywhere, and I could easily start getting hundreds of messages a day. Is this true?

A The simple answer is yes. You can easily get "oversubscribed," just as many people subscribe to too many magazines to read.

Q How do I avoid "oversubscribing"?

A You can avoid this situation in a couple of ways. First, make sure that you stay subscribed only to listservs that you really read. If you find yourself automatically deleting most listserv messages without reading them, you should unsubscribe. Second, go to Lessons 9, "Basic Journalism: Introduction to Newsgroups," and 10, "Getting the Scoop: Using Newsgroups," to find another alternative to listservs available on the Internet: newsgroups.

Q Does it really matter who gets a listserv reply? After all, you're sending it for all to read.

A Careful. What if someone sends an e-mail message to the listserv and you want to reply to the individual? Further assume that you say something unflattering about another listserv participant. What if you inadvertently send that message to the whole list? Could be embarrassing, no? Until you're used to how listservs work, always check the To: field before composing a reply to a listserv message.

Quiz

Take the following quiz to see how much you've learned.

Questions

1. One of the advantages of listservs is that they all work the same.

    (a) True

    (b) False

8

2. Which of the following is probably not a good source for finding a listserv?

   (a) Your local community library

   (b) The World Wide Web

   (c) Friends

3. Which listserv command retrieves a file listing for a listserv?

   (a) SEARCH

   (b) GET

   (c) INDEX

Answers

1. (b) False. Although they are all similar, you will find some important differences in how they work.

2. (a) Although the library is not a good example, the Web and friends are excellent sources to find out about listservs.

3. (c) INDEX

Activity

Go to at least two different sources to find at least three listservs. Subscribe to all three. Then find the one you use the least and unsubscribe to it. If you find them all wonderfully helpful, great! You've hit the jackpot!

PART

III

News and Real-Time Communication

Hour

Hour **9**

Basic Journalism: Introduction to Newsgroups

Explaining Usenet and newsgroups, like the Internet itself, is like explaining the phone system. Sure, all the phones in the world are connected by cables and wires and switches, as you read in Lesson 1, "The Internet: What's It Really Like?" But that's not what matters to the people who use it. What really matters about the phone system to users is communication—people talking to each other, people doing business, people exchanging documents and computer programs, and people just passing the time of day.

In this lesson, you'll be able to find the answers to the following questions about Usenet and newsgroups:

- [ ] What exactly is Usenet?
- [ ] How do newsgroups work?
- [ ] How are newsgroups organized?
- [ ] What type of information is on Usenet?
- [ ] Does Usenet have rules like e-mail does?

As with the lessons on e-mail, the principles I talk about here are universal, regardless of the specific newsgroup client you may use.

Usenet and Newsgroups Explained

Is Usenet wires and cables? Are newsgroups just data and commands traveling over these wires and cables? Or is it the people who use these computers? Well, someone once said, "Usenet is the set of people who know what Usenet is." This answer may seem circular, but it really isn't.

The participants in Usenet are what make up Usenet. In fact, these people, collectively, can answer almost any question you ask of them, entertain you, teach you, listen to what you have to say, and broaden your horizons in ways you never dreamed possible.

Usenet Defined

The first question most people ask is, "What does Usenet mean?" Well, the name is modeled after *Usenix*, the UNIX users' conference series. It was supposed to mean UNIX *Users Network*, because all the early sites were UNIX machines, and many of the early discussions were about the UNIX operating system.

New Term   **UNIX:** Believe it or not, UNIX is not an acronym for anything. UNIX is an operating system originally developed in 1969 by Ken Thompson and Dennis Ritchie (allegedly so they could play games!). UNIX, a powerful and portable operating system, expanded and became the foundational operating language of the Internet.

Of course, you may want to know a little about how Usenet actually works. Usenet is actually rather complicated, but perhaps a short explanation can make the essentials clear:

You can get "news" transferred across the Internet in basically two ways. The first is by means of listservs, which I discussed in Lesson 8, "Communicating with the World: Using Mailing Lists." The second way to get news is to have a machine that is dedicated solely to storing and serving news, as illustrated in Figure 9.1.

Using this second method, which is how Usenet works, you can read from and *post* to the news server using a news client. You then can read what you want, when you want—instead of having tons of listserv mail jamming up your mailbox. These news servers organize, distribute, and keep track of thousands of messages—a task that a listserv simply can't duplicate.

9

Figure 9.1.
With Usenet, you can go to the news instead of having the news come to you.

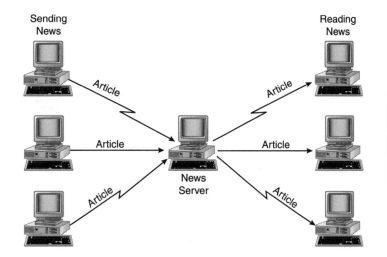

Sending News

Reading News

Article

Article

Article

Article

News Server

Article

Article

9

NEW TERM   **Post:** A message to a Usenet newsgroup is called a post. When you submit messages (also called articles) to newsgroups, you are posting.

Newsgroups Defined

Many people have a difficult time distinguishing between Usenet and newsgroups. To clarify, think about the publishing industry. You can talk of the *publishing industry* as an umbrella enterprise that is all-encompassing. When you start talking about *publications* such as *The Wall Street Journal*, however, you're talking about the actual "stuff" of which the industry is made.

You can think of Usenet, in this sense, as the structure, or umbrella, that encompasses the thousands of newsgroups that make up Usenet. The newsgroups themselves define this electronic "industry."

Trying to describe all the newsgroups available would be akin to trying to describe all the publications in the world—you couldn't. In short, you can find a newsgroup on just about every topic you can think of; Figure 9.2 shows some examples.

Figure 9.2.

This list shows just a few of the thousands of newsgroups available.

Newsgroups cover topics regarding recreation, society, culture, business, and computers (of course). Currently, over 12,000 newsgroups are available. How they are constructed and organized is covered in the next section.

CAUTION

> Just because thousands of newsgroups exist doesn't mean that you can get them all. Remember, you need to have access to a server that can handle every single article on every single newsgroup. Just like no bookstore carries every magazine, no Internet service provider carries every newsgroup. A service provider that carries 4,000 to 8,000 newsgroups is considered average.

Newsgroup Hierarchies

Now that you know that all these great groups are out there, you are ready to begin making sense of how they are organized. In the beginning, Usenet, like the Internet itself, was relatively small. Thus, no real need for a lot of organization existed. As traffic increased on the Net, however, the number of people (and issues) also began to rise. It soon became apparent that some structure was necessary, in order to prevent Usenet from becoming a runaway train.

9

Going to a Different Level

Out of this newfound need for structure, hierarchies were born. Everyone knows what a hierarchy is. In business, the CEO is at the top, followed by top-level managers, then middle-management, who are above supervisors, who are above the workers. Newsgroups are organized exactly this way also, as illustrated in Figure 9.3.

Figure 9.3.
Newsgroup hierarchies are much like any other structure composed of different levels.

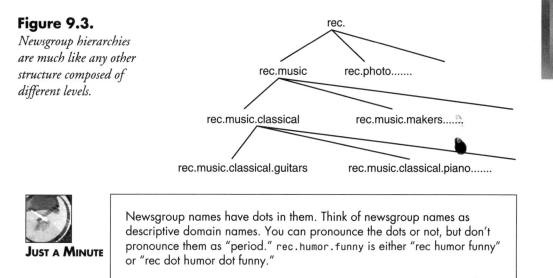

Newsgroup names have dots in them. Think of newsgroup names as descriptive domain names. You can pronounce the dots or not, but don't pronounce them as "period." `rec.humor.funny` is either "rec humor funny" or "rec dot humor dot funny."

JUST A MINUTE

The Big 7

The hierarchies established years ago are still in effect today and comprise what's known as the *Big 7* newsgroup hierarchies. The following 7 hierarchies contain a majority of all newsgroup traffic:

- ☐ `alt.`: This alternative hierarchy deals with almost any issue under the sun and is considered the "rebel" hierarchy.
- ☐ `comp.`: This hierarchy is composed of newsgroups having to do with computers.
- ☐ `misc.`: This is the catch-all miscellaneous newsgroup hierarchy.
- ☐ `news.`: The smallest hierarchy, `news.` contains only a handful of newsgroups dealing with issues surrounding Usenet and newsgroups themselves.
- ☐ `rec.`: These newsgroups cover recreation.
- ☐ `sci.`: This hierarchy contains newsgroups about various topics in science.
- ☐ `soc.`: The `soc.` hierarchy contains newsgroups that deal with social issues.
- ☐ `talk.`: In the newsgroups in this discussion hierarchy, you can talk about almost anything.

Wait a minute! I listed eight hierarchies, not seven. Am I trying to pull a fast one on you? No, not really. The `alt.` hierarchy wasn't actually a part of the original seven. Today, however, it is the biggest hierarchy on Usenet.

A little more explanation regarding this issue might be in order. In the seven standard hierarchies, proposed new newsgroups must be nominated and voted on by the Usenet community before they are carried by most news servers. Many people using Usenet didn't want to wait for the voting process, however, or simply wanted to deal with topics outside the realm or taste of the standard hierarchies. As a result, the `alt.` groups were born. In short, anyone can create an `alt.` newsgroup.

So why do you still need the Big 7? Simple; when everybody can start creating groups; you end up with topics such as `alt.american.automobile.breakdown.breakdown.break`. Therefore, many news server administrators don't even carry the `alt.` hierarchy because of the large amount of *noise* on these groups.

| NEW TERM | **Noise:** Sooner or later, you'll hear the term "signal-to-noise ratio." This expression is merely a way of describing how much useful material (signal) compared to useless material (noise) is on a given newsgroup. |

Today, dozens of legitimate hierarchies exist, many of them bigger than some of the original ones. Table 9.1 gives you a taste of some of the bigger ones.

Table 9.1. Additional newsgroup hierarchies.

Hierarchy	Description
`bionet.`	The Biology Network newsgroups.
`bit.listserv.`	Many listservs are also available on Usenet. This hierarchy represents the listservs that are also available as newsgroups.
`biz.`	This hierarchy, business, is a natural for the commercialization of the Internet.
`k12.`	The hierarchy for primary and secondary education.
`au., uk., tw.`	No `country.` hierarchy actually exists, but many countries do have their own, such as `au.` (Australia), `uk.` (United Kingdom), and `tw.` (Taiwan).

9

What's in the News?

By now, you should realize that you can probably find anything under the sun by cruising through the world of Usenet. In the following sections, you can see a few good examples of how Usenet can be extremely helpful.

To the Newbies

One of the first and best places to go if you're new to Usenet is to the news. hierarchy. Several groups—in particular, news.announce.newsgroups, news.announce.newusers, and news.answers—are helpful. In these groups, you can find out about proposed new groups, get announcements and explanations, and get general answers from people who have been on the Net awhile.

The best of these groups is most likely news.answers, because you can get the *FAQs* in this group. These helpful documents answer the most common questions asked by beginners on almost any topic under the sun. Figure 9.4 shows an example.

NEW TERM	**FAQ:** FAQ stands for Frequently Asked Questions. Many times, newcomers to a newsgroup ask questions that the old-timers have heard over and over again. So someone writes a FAQ and posts it periodically to reduce the number of redundant questions.

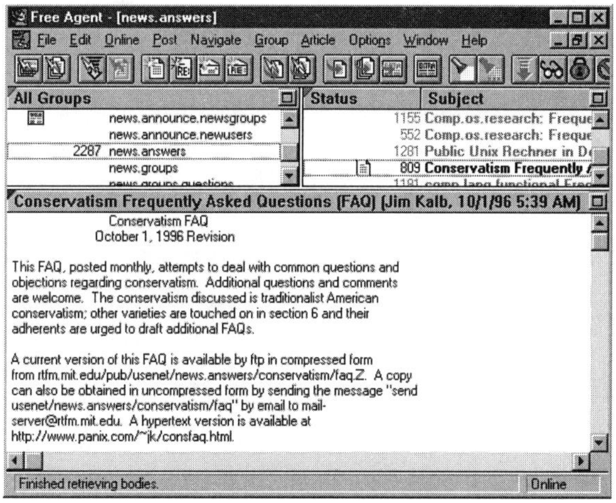

Figure 9.4.

The FAQs available on Usenet are almost as diverse as the newsgroups themselves.

World's Biggest Garage Sale

In addition to finding some really good information on Usenet, you might find that you can locate some really good stuff, too. For some examples, turn to the misc.forsale hierarchy. With a little patience and perseverance, you can buy just about anything.

TIME SAVER

You can find probably over 100 forsale newsgroups in all, not all of which are in the misc. hierarchy. In fact, many news servers carry their own hierarchy of local newsgroups, one of which is usually a forsale group.

Of course, most of these groups are under the misc.forsale.computers hierarchy, where you can buy modems, equipment for PCs or Macs, and a host of other items. You also can check out misc.forsale.non-computer, which has hundreds of postings a day, as you can see in Figure 9.5.

Figure 9.5.

Need to revitalize your music collection? Here's the place to do it.

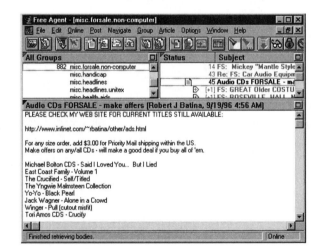

What Money Can't Buy

Not everyone on the Internet is looking to make a profit. In fact, a majority aren't. What better place to look than to the Internet if you're interested in working for the "public good."

If you're so inclined, look at soc.org.nonprofit, as shown in Figure 9.6, to find many useful resources (even a FAQ) if you're looking to serve the public. Get information on fund-raising, management tips, research tools, and more—all geared toward people interested in the public welfare.

Figure 9.6.

Usenet is a great place to go when you're in unfamiliar territory.

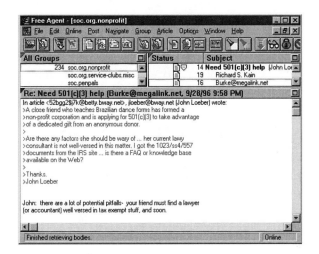

Usenetiquette

Usenet is, in many ways, a community. People who are "on the Net" have heard many of the same jokes, remember many of the same incidents, and have heard of many of the same people as the others. As with any other community or society, you need to figure out the rules everyone goes by. Of course, no matter what you do, learning is going to take a little time.

Many of the tips on etiquette I gave you in Lesson 5, "Understanding E-Mail," apply to Usenet, as well. In fact, you may want to go back and quickly read the end of that lesson again to refresh your memory. You can take several additional steps on Usenet to make your transition to the Net smoother.

Lurk Before You Leap

When I first got on the Net many years ago, a friend of mine told me to never post to a newsgroup until I had read it for two weeks first. Never was a better piece of advice given. Getting on a newsgroup and immediately posting is the same as barging in and interrupting a conversation in progress.

Caution

> Whatever you do, don't ever use the terms *bulletin board* or *bbs* to describe a newsgroup. This offense is tantamount to referring to a Harley Davidson motorcycle as a scooter.

The act of simply reading a newsgroup, also called *lurking*, is a great way to find out what is appropriate for that newsgroup. Lurking is the best way to get the "context" of the group before jumping in. Also, remember that not all groups are the same; lurking on one group for a while does not qualify you to jump in on another group. Read each group you want to post to for at least a few days before you begin to participate.

The War of the Newsgroups

No, this section isn't a rewrite of the H.G. Wells classic. Newsgroup wars can all too easily happen when tempers and emotions get out of control. Remember that a flame is a personal or otherwise derogatory attack. In e-mail, a flame can be relatively harmless. But let one fly in a group surrounding a particularly heated topic, and you've got a full-blown flame war on your hands.

In Usenet, perhaps more than anywhere else on the Internet, you must think carefully about what you're going to write before you write it. Senseless attacks on people and ideas rarely win over anyone and usually succeed only in producing lots of useless posts about nothing. If you're susceptible to a quick keyboard finger, you might want to stay away from groups such as alt.abortion and others that are just flame wars waiting to happen.

Newsgroup No-Nos

Posting the same article to hundreds or even thousands of newsgroups, either as individual postings or as a number of *cross-postings*, is possible. This act, called *spamming*, is not acceptable behavior. No topic is relevant to 20 or more newsgroups. If you choose to spam anyway, someone will cancel your posts, and chances are your site will revoke your Usenet access as well.

NEW TERM **Cross-posting:** Just as you can send e-mail to more than one person, you can post an article to more than one newsgroup, which is called cross-posting. You should always exercise extra caution when cross-posting, to make sure that you are sending articles only to appropriate groups.

Another way to bring yourself lots of grief is to shamelessly advertise your business on Usenet. Advertising is not the purpose of Usenet. More appropriate forums, such as the World Wide Web, are set up for business promotion. More often than not, advertising on Usenet brings a lot of unwanted e-mail into your mailbox.

Finally, most copyright laws do apply to Usenet and other electronic media. You may be tempted to post the text to John Grisham's latest thriller. Just be aware that, if you do, you are liable for the same consequences that any other copyright violator faces.

So what does happen when people start using a newsgroup inappropriately? Most newsgroups deal with this issue by using *moderation*. Quite simply, in a *moderated newsgroup*, each posting goes to an individual instead of directly to the group. This person, called the *moderator*, checks the message to make sure that it's appropriate and then sends it on to the group.

Some newcomers to Usenet are shocked to hear of moderated groups and think of moderation as a form of censorship. All a moderator can do is prevent a posting from appearing in one particular newsgroup; plenty of unmoderated newsgroups are around, so any rejected posting can easily be posted elsewhere.

On the other hand, some newcomers can't believe that some groups are unmoderated. These people expect some authority figure to remove offensive or obscene material. Because Usenet is a cooperative anarchy, however, and the vast majority of groups get along nicely without moderators, always having a moderator isn't likely to happen.

Summary

In this lesson, you learned exactly what Usenet and newsgroups are and where they came from. They work similarly to listservs but differ in that they are accessed by the user. This lesson taught you how newsgroups are arranged into hierarchies, as well as how these hierarchies help you find useful information.

In addition, you learned some of the ins and outs of newsgroup etiquette. You now know many of the most common mistakes to avoid, such as flaming, spamming, and advertising. At this point, you're ready to move on to the workshop to help extend your knowledge.

Workshop

The following workshop helps solidify the skills that you learned in this lesson.

Q&A

Q I'm not sure I understand why it's so terrible to do some advertising and cross-posting on Usenet. Can you explain a little more?

A Sure. First, a vehicle for disseminating commercial information already exists; it's called the World Wide Web. Second, a lot of newsgroups and a lot of articles appear in those newsgroups. Remember that someone is paying for all this traffic. Needless replication of posts and lots of useless posts only add to the costs a server administrator absorbs and then immediately passes on to you, the user.

Q What if I'm interested in a newsgroup but can't find it on my news server. What do I do?

A The best thing to do is to ask your Internet service provider if such a group exists. If it does, you can ask the ISP to add the group to its server. Another avenue is to find a related newsgroup, lurk awhile, and then ask if such a newsgroup exists.

Q I was fascinated by the concept of buying something through a newsgroup. Isn't there a lot of potential for getting ripped off?

A Yes, there is. A little common sense, however, can help. First, avoid deals that look too good to be true; they probably are. Next, lurk on the newsgroup to see if you can find any complaints about the person selling the item. Finally, when you're buying a big-ticket item, always use C.O.D. This way, you assure yourself that you'll at least receive the product before you buy it.

Quiz

Take the following quiz to see how much you've learned.

Questions

1. Which of the following newsgroups does not belong to the `soc.` hierarchy?

    (a) `comp.soc.women`

    (b) `soc.culture.indian`

    (c) `soc.penpals`

2. "Usenet" and "newsgroups" are two terms that mean the same thing and can be used interchangeably.

    (a) True

    (b) False

3. If you were trying to find out some information about a particular breed of hunting dog, would you

    (a) Find `rec.hunting.dogs` and immediately ask your question.

    (b) Lurk on a couple of dog groups and then cross-post your question to the entire `rec.pets.dogs` hierarchy.

    (c) Look on a few groups to try to find a FAQ on hunting dogs and then post your question to `rec.hunting.dogs` if you couldn't find anything.

Answers

1. (a) `comp.soc.women` belongs to the `comp.` hierarchy.
2. (b) False. Remember that Usenet is the overall structure, and newsgroups are the parts that make up Usenet.
3. (c) Looking a little on your own before jumping into a newsgroup is always a good idea.

Activity

Come up with at least five topics that you're interested in. Next, given what you know about newsgroup hierarchies, try to guess which hierarchy each one of your topics would fit into. For an added challenge, try to guess the actual newsgroup name your topic might have. When you learn how to search for newsgroups in the next lesson, you can see how well you did.

9

Hour **10**

Getting the Scoop:
Using Newsgroups

Now that you know a little bit about how newsgroups and Usenet work, you can dive in. Before continuing, you should have access to a news server through your Internet service provider and should be set up with one of the many newsgroup clients available. Keep in mind that Internet Explorer and Netscape Navigator have built-in newsreaders.

After you set up your client and complete this lesson, you'll be reading and posting like a pro. In this lesson, you discover the answers to these questions:

- ☐ How do I subscribe to newsgroups?
- ☐ What does a typical article look like?
- ☐ How are the articles in newsgroups organized?
- ☐ How do I post to newsgroups?
- ☐ What is a binary?

Most of the figures you see in this chapter feature a newsgroup client called WinVN. As you learn in Appendix B, "Shareware Products for Windows," several other good clients are available for both Windows and Macintosh. (Appendix C, "Shareware Products for the Macintosh," lists some products for Macintosh, as well.) Most of these clients operate basically the same way; slight differences in clients are generally easy to figure out.

TIME SAVER

> Most newsgroup clients have an accompanying help file. If you have trouble finding or using a particular option, go to the client's Help menu.

Subscribing to Newsgroups

Before you can begin participating in the wonderful world of Usenet, you actually have to subscribe to some newsgroups first. Once you have some newsgroups to look at, you can proceed. In the following sections, I describe how to sign up for some groups to read.

Who Are You?

No one calls up a magazine subscription service, tells the operator, "Give me a subscription starting next month, please," and then hangs up the phone. How would the publisher know who or where to send the magazine? The same is true of subscribing to newsgroups. You first have to tell the client a little bit about yourself before you proceed.

Most newsgroup clients have a menu option called Config, Configurations, Properties, or Preferences. From these configuration menus, you tell your client who you are. You need to provide several pieces of information to your client before you can continue. Depending on your service provider, some of this information may come preconfigured with your software:

- ☐ SMTP server: To post and reply via e-mail to posts on newsgroups, your client has to know your e-mail, or SMTP, server.
- ☐ E-mail address: You must also provide most clients with your e-mail address.
- ☐ NNTP server: This is the news domain name of the server that carries your news (for example, news.company.com).

NEW TERM   **NNTP server:** NNTP stands for Network News Transfer Protocol. An NNTP server transfers news to your client using the language of Usenet.

You also can define many other settings, such as your real name and other personal information and how many articles to download at a time. As a rule, sticking with the settings that come preconfigured with your client is usually safe.

10

Sign Me Up!

Your client is ready, you're ready, your server is ready—let's go! If your client doesn't automatically connect to your NNTP server, now is the time to do so. After connecting, you should be presented with a list of all the groups your server carries, as shown in Figure 10.1.

Figure 10.1.

Begin looking for groups in a full group listing.

CAUTION

If you're connecting to news over a modem, this process could take as long as 10 minutes or more. Many clients have an option disabling the retrieval of a server's listing every time you start up. After you subscribe to some groups, you should select this option.

Take a moment to scroll quickly through some of the groups. Quite a few of them, aren't there? At this point, you can simply double-click any group name to read it. After you close the group window, however, your client doesn't save any information about your actions on that group. This way, you can "test out" a group to see if you want to subscribe to it first. Opening up groups before subscribing to them gives you a "snap shot" of what the group is about.

You can quickly see that finding a group in which you're interested could take quite awhile if you simply scroll through the list. For this reason, all news clients have a Find option (which also works to find articles within a group). Using this option, you can search the entire newsgroup list for interesting groups. Locate your client's Find function (in WinVN, it's under the Group menu), and begin searching for topics. Figure 10.2 shows a search in progress.

Figure 10.2.

Searching for groups is the quickest way to start subscribing to groups.

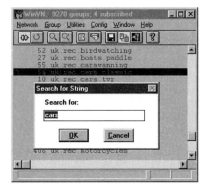

To Do: Searching for Groups

1. Get your list of topics from the "Activity" section in Lesson 9.

2. Use your client's Search or Find function to locate one group under each topic.

3. As you find a group or groups for each topic, locate the Subscribe to Group option (usually under the same menu as the Find option), and subscribe to each group.

4. Locate the option that enables you to display only groups to which you have subscribed. This option is usually a toolbar button or a menu option; you can generally toggle it on or off to get back to a full group listing at any time.

After you locate and subscribe to some groups, you should see a window that looks similar to the one pictured in Figure 10.3. Proceed to the next section to find out what the parts of this window actually mean.

Figure 10.3.

This typical group window is displayed in WinVN.

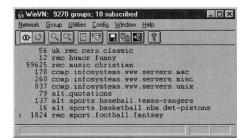

News Anatomy

You deal with several different windows when using newsgroups: the Group Listing window, the Article Listing window, and the Article window. The following sections help you discover how each one works.

The Group Listing Window

Figure 10.3 shows one example of what a Group Listing window might look like. Generally, this simple window contains two pieces of information: the name of the group and a number.

The number represents the number of unread articles in the group. So, the 56 next to uk.rec.cars.classic means that 56 articles appear in that group and haven't yet been seen by the user. As you can see from Figure 10.3, some groups have a lot of traffic (as indicated by a high number), and some groups have less traffic (as indicated by a lower number). Beware of very high traffic groups; keeping up with them can often take a lot of time and money.

The Article Listing Window

Now you're ready to take a close look at what's inside a newsgroup. What do all these articles look like? For an example, take a peek at Figure 10.4, which shows an Article Listing window. A little confused? Well, read on.

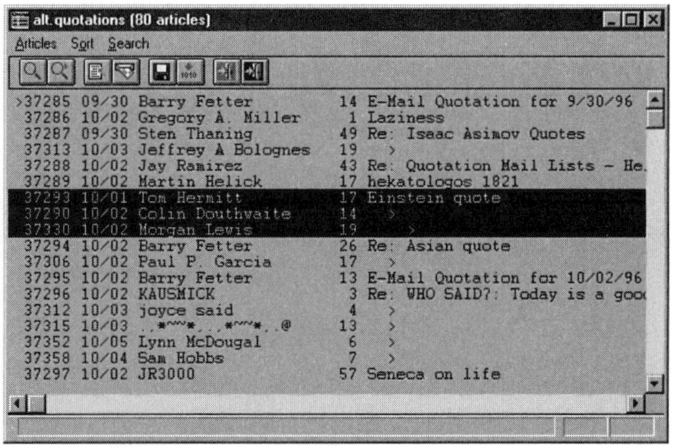

Figure 10.4.
This Article Listing window is typical, if initially confusing.

Most news clients display a lot of miscellaneous information about each article, such as the time and date it was posted, the sequential number of the article, and how many lines appear in the article. You really need to pay a lot of attention to only two pieces of information, however. First is the *poster*, which is usually a name (real or made up) of the person who posted the article. Second, you should see the subject of the article. With this second area, most confusion arises.

All newsgroup articles combine to make what is called a *thread*. A thread is basically nothing more than a number of articles that all deal with the same subject. Just like many cloth threads make up a piece of clothing, so too do many article threads make up a newsgroup.

NEW TERM **Thread:** A thread is a series of articles all dealing with the same topic. Someone replies to an article, and then someone else replies to the reply, and so on. This organization of original topic articles and replies makes up a newsgroup thread.

Notice that several articles are highlighted in Figure 10.4. The first article has a subject, whereas the other two articles simply have a > indented at various levels. This setup indicates a typical small thread. The article with the subject is the original available article in the thread. The article with the > indented once is a reply to the original posting, and the article with the > indented twice is a reply to the reply. Even though this example is simple, threads can get very complicated. With a little time and practice, you'll get used to them.

The Article Window

From the Article Listing window, you can double-click any message to read it. When you do, you see a window similar to the one pictured in Figure 10.5.

Figure 10.5.

The information in this newsgroup article should look familiar to you.

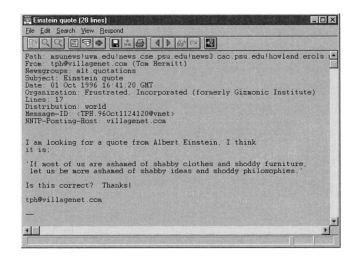

Experiencing a little deja vu? Well, you should be. Newsgroup articles are similar to e-mail messages. They both contain headers with lots of technical information about the article and bodies with the actual text of the article.

Much like e-mail headers, most news article headers can be ignored. You should, however, pay attention to several headers:

☐ From: This header generally supplies the name and e-mail address of the person posting the article.

- ☐ Subject: This header tells you what the article is about.
- ☐ Newsgroup: This header, which you haven't seen before, tells you to which newsgroup (or newsgroups) a particular article was posted. As you learn in the "Replying to Posts" section later in this lesson, paying attention to this header is very important.

Posting, Replying, and Managing News

I can hear you screaming, "Enough explanations already!" Okay, okay, you can post some news now. First, a piece of advice: Using your client's Find option, locate and subscribe to the newsgroup alt.test. This newsgroup is set up specifically to accept test messages. If you make a mistake posting or replying to articles in this group, no one cares. After you practice here awhile, you can post some real articles to those groups you've been lurking on.

Posting Articles

As a rule, with most news clients, you can post new articles from either the Group Listing or Article Listing windows. Generally, selecting the Post New Article option from within an Article window results in a reply to that article, which I talk about in the next section. For now, here's how you can post your first article.

To Do: Posting Articles

1. From either the Group Listing or Article Listing window, choose the New Message option for your client.
2. Type in a Subject: and which newsgroup (alt.test, in this case) to which you want the article posted.
3. Click in the body of the article composition window, and type a short message. It should look something like the message shown in Figure 10.6.
4. Finally, click the Post or Send button (or choose the corresponding option).

Congratulations! You have posted your first article to Usenet. Don't worry if it seems that you did not fill in a lot of the header information; your client provides such details to the news server automatically. The next time you retrieve the new articles for alt.test, search for your article; new articles generally appear on the group within several minutes.

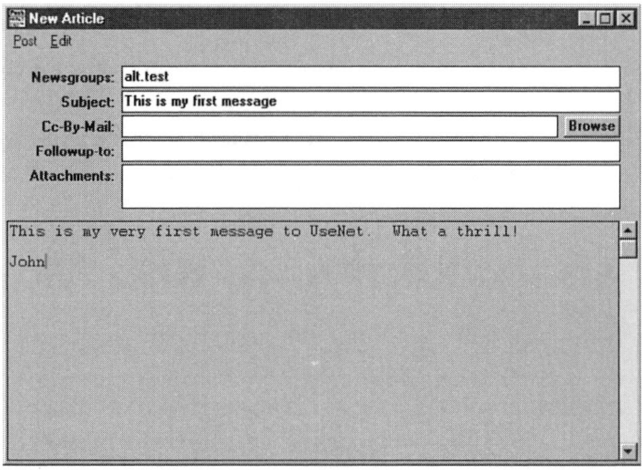

Figure 10.6.

A newsgroup article looks almost identical to an e-mail message.

New Article

Post Edit

Newsgroups: alt.test
Subject: This is my first message
Cc-By-Mail: [   ] Browse
Followup-to: [   ]
Attachments: [   ]

This is my very first message to UseNet. What a thrill!

John

Replying to Posts

Another type of post is the *reply*. Again, the similarities between replying to a post and replying to e-mail are striking. With the exception of the Newsgroup: header, the process is almost identical. You can generally reply to a post from either the Article Listing window (with the article you want to reply to selected) or from the Article window itself.

Look at the header for just a moment before replying to the article. Your client provides all the information you need to post your reply.

CAUTION

Before composing your reply, make sure that it will not be cross-posted to many groups. If you're replying to an article that has been cross-posted, select and delete the names of all but the newsgroups you want your reply to go to. This way, you can help eliminate a lot of the unwanted traffic on Usenet and become a more responsible poster.

In the body of the message, notice that, like e-mail, the original article is included, with each line preceded by an *include mark* (>). As with e-mail, you can select and edit the original article's text in any way you want. After your reply is complete, select the Post or Send option. The next time you read the group, you should find your reply in the list of articles.

Managing Newsgroups

As you have already seen, newsgroups can contain a lot of traffic and can get quite complicated at times. For this reason, you need to be able to manage newsgroups effectively. Most of your newsgroup management will consist of making sure that you keep your *.newsrc file* up-to-date. Failure to do so can result in a lot of wasted time and effort.

NEW TERM   **.newsrc file:** A .newsrc file contains information about your newsgroups, such as which groups you're subscribed to and how many articles (both read and unread) are in each group you subscribe to. Most other news clients have somehow managed to keep this term, which is actually used by UNIX newsreaders.

You maintain your .newsrc file by marking a group or article as read, which is also called "catching up" by some news clients. You can use the following procedure to manage your groups:

To Do: Managing Groups

1. Choose a group to read.
2. Browse the group until you have read, posted and replied all you want.
3. Find the Catches Up or Marks Articles As Read menu option or toolbar button, and select it.
4. Go to the next group and repeat this process.

Most people manage groups this way. Failure to catch up a group means that, the next time you read news, you'll have to sort through articles you have already read. Especially with high-traffic groups, having to re-sort can get messy really fast.

The following are a couple of final notes on group management:

☐ Most clients also offer an option to mark all articles as unread. This capability is handy if you want to go back and look for or reread an article after already catching up a group.

☐ Many clients include an option, usually at the Group Listing level, called something like Mark All Groups Read. Instead of catching up each group as you read it, you can wait until you're finished with all your groups and then select this option before you're done.

More 0s and 1s: Binaries

No discussion of news would be complete without talking about *binaries*. Dealing with newsgroup binaries could easily take up several chapters, but it may help you if I talk about them and point you in the right direction here.

NEW TERM   **Binary:** A binary is any non-text file, such as a picture or shareware program. For the purposes of e-mail and newsgroup messages, a binary file is encrypted and then attached to an e-mail message or newsgroup posting. Special utilities are usually required to decode these files for use.

First comes the task of determining which newsgroup articles are binaries. Fortunately for you, probably 95 percent of all binary articles on Usenet are posted to newsgroups with the term `binary.` or `binaries.` included. By searching for these groups, you can find most groups in which binaries are posted.

Next, you should know that most good Windows news clients, such as WinVN and NewsXpress, can handle binary files. They do this by either using an external application (which you'll never have to launch yourself) or by doing the decoding internally. The best Macintosh newsreader, Newswatcher, does require an external application to handle binaries (see Appendix B).

In general, you handle binaries from the Article Listing window. Follow these steps to handle a binary file while using a typical news client:

1. From the Article Listing window, click each article belonging to the same binary. Most binaries are too big for one article, so they are usually labeled `Binary Posting Subject (1/3)`, `Binary Posting Subject (2/3)`, and so on.

2. After you select the binary, find the Decode Articles option from the menu or toolbar and select it. Your client may ask you where and under what name you want to save the binary.

3. After the binary is downloaded to your hard drive and decoded, you should be able to use the file in the same way you use a file on a disk or CD.

Again, your client's Help menu may be of great assistance in figuring out the details. With most clients, however, you can handle binaries easily by following the simple steps outlined here.

Summary

This lesson provided you with a comprehensive tour of how to participate in newsgroups. You discovered what information your client needs to let you subscribe to groups. You now should know how to browse, find, and subscribe to newsgroups.

This chapter showed how similar newsgroup articles, postings, and replies are to e-mail. You also learned how to "catch up" newsgroups for effective management. Finally, you learned the basics of how to find and handle binary articles.

10

Workshop

The following workshop helps solidify the skills that you learned in this lesson.

Q&A

Q I have limited time and don't want to spend too much money online to access newsgroups. Do you have any advice for me?

A Yes. Begin by subscribing to a moderate number of groups (20 to 25), possibly including 2 or more groups dealing with each topic. Then browse each group for a week or so to weed out the groups that have too much traffic or information that isn't useful to you. Most people settle on 5 to 10 groups that they read on a regular basis.

Q Bottom line: Are binary newsgroups really worth reading?

A I'll answer that question with a qualified "No." Many of the binary newsgroups contain nothing but illegal and useless material. In addition, most useful files that you find on binary newsgroups are usually much more easily and readily available through other services such as the World Wide Web and FTP. Given that these files usually take a long time to locate and download, most people would be better off looking elsewhere.

10

Quiz

Take the following quiz to see how much you've learned.

Questions

1. In which window would you be able to view a thread?

    (a) The Group Listing window

    (b) The Article Listing window

    (c) The Article window

2. Most news clients include your vital header information when you reply to an article, so you don't need to pay attention to it.

    (a) True

    (b) False

3. The number 632 next to a newsgroup name in the Group Listing window indicates which of the following?

   (a) The number of articles a user has not yet read

   (b) The total number of articles on the news server

   (c) The number of articles you have read since subscribing to the group

Answers

1. (b) The Article Listing window.

2. (b) False. Always look at the Newsgroup: header to make sure that you don't needlessly cross-post.

3. (a) The number of articles a user has not yet read.

Activity

It's time for the rubber to meet the road. After lurking on some groups for a while, post an original article to a newsgroup and get involved in one additional thread by replying to an article. **Hint:** The `alt.quotations` newsgroup is a great place to start. In this group, people are always looking for the sources of quotations and discussing their origins and other interesting topics.

Hour 11

Chatting Live on the Internet

At some point, you may want to remove the time delay between sending and receiving e-mail. You may want to converse directly with another person or have the ability to address a group of people. This lesson covers many different ways to converse with people via your keyboard.

In this lesson, you can find answers to the following questions:

☐ What is IRC?

☐ Do I need any special software?

☐ Who is available to chat with?

☐ Can I play games?

☐ Should I follow any rules or etiquette when I use IRC or MUD?

Just like computers themselves are changing, so is Internet Relay Chat (IRC). What was once only a text-based system is evolving into a graphical interface. The blank text screen is becoming a new client, complete with Windows elements and 3-D virtual reality interfaces.

What Is IRC and How Does It Work?

Internet Relay Chat, or IRC, is a multiuser version of a program called *talk*. Talk allowed only one-to-one conversations, so it was pretty limited. Using IRC, large groups of people can simultaneously participate in discussion groups, called *channels*.

IRC was developed in the late 1980s by Jarkko Oikarinen. It consists of a network of chat servers located all over the globe. Each server is connected via the network, allowing users to have real-time communications. A user's message is instantly viewed by all the other guests in that channel.

IRC poses no restrictions to the number of users. Tens of thousands of people connect to IRC everyday to discuss everything from world news to what they had for dinner last night. If you can't find a channel for your topic of discussion, you can always start your own.

Although most conversations that take place on IRC are thought of as frivolous, some have notable value. During the 1991 Persian Gulf War, IRC was used to gather eyewitness accounts of military activities. A special channel was created so that users from all over the world could join and hear the latest news reports.

A similar application of IRC was used in September 1993 when the coup against Boris Yeltsin began. Again, users gathered on IRC channels to hear live reports of the situation. IRC gained U.S. appreciation when the 1994 California earthquake hit, downing phone lines and inhibiting news of what had happened. Within 20 minutes of the aftershocks, two new channels were created on the IRC to handle questions and accounts of the earthquake.

Actually, a few separate networks make up IRC. The two biggest are EFnet and Undernet. Some channels are shared by both, whereas other channels reside on only one of the networks. Because of the network connections to either EFnet or Undernet, you don't have to connect to the same server every time. Try connecting to the one that is geographically closest to you. Doing so may make your connection faster.

Clients

Now that you know a little about IRC, you should examine the software needed. IRC originally used only text-based clients developed on UNIX machines. Today, however, many users have traded in the text client for a more user-friendly Graphical User Interface (GUI) client.

GUI clients use buttons, pull-down menus, and selection tools to replace some of the frequently used commands within the IRC client. Buttons for emotions and actions can now replace the normal code syntax.

Later in this lesson, I describe three of the most-used clients to access IRC. Take the time to try out one of them. Many new users feel more comfortable using a GUI interface, so you might like it.

Channels

Channels on IRC are much like channels on a CB radio. Each channel has its set topic of discussion. All users on that channel can participate in any discussion that is being carried on. Generally, multiple discussions are carried out simultaneously across any given channel.

A channel has the image of a big party atmosphere—lots of people talking, everyone trying to hear the person next to him or her while picking up fragments of other conversations. After you enter a channel, you should wait until you gather an idea of what conversations are covered before you try to jump in.

Users find it rude for a new person to invite himself or herself into a conversation, so you may want to *lurk* (stand on the sidelines and watch) and wait to be invited to join the discussion. Take that chance to familiarize yourself with the topic and level of the dialogue.

Afraid no one will know that you entered the channel or room? Fear not! All the users are automatically notified if a new user enters and if someone leaves. How embarrassing to talk to someone who wasn't there anymore.

11

Commands

If you're going to use a text-based IRC client, you need to know a few of the common commands. For more help on IRC commands, try entering `/help newuser` or `/help intro` after you are logged on to the IRC.

Table 11.1 shows a list of basic commands that will get you started.

Table 11.1. Sample IRC commands.

Command	Use
`/List`	Lists all the current IRC channels, the number of users, and topic.
`/Names`	Shows the nicknames of all users on each channel.
`/Join <channel>`	Joins the named channel. All non-commands that you type go to everyone on that channel.

continues

Table 11.1. continued

Command	Use
/Msg <nick> <msg>	Sends a private message to the specified person. Only the person with the specified nickname can see this message. Sending a message this way is also known as *whispering*.
/Nick	Changes your nickname.
/Quit	Exits IRC.
/Help <topic>	Gets help on the IRC commands.
/Who <channel>	Shows who is on a given channel, including nickname, username and host, and real name.
/Whois <nick>	Shows the "true" identity of someone. This command is valuable to test whom you're talking to. Nicknames are not owned by one person.
/Part <channel>	Enables you to leave the specified channel; short for *depart*.

After you join a channel, you don't have to begin all your lines with a slash (/). Anything you type is simply distributed to all the users as a message from you. Only include the slash when you want to use a command or when you don't want the message to be seen by the entire group.

CAUTION

> The /Names and /List commands can produce massive amounts of text, especially on large IRC networks. Be prepared!

As with any graphical interface, some Windows and Mac clients can relieve you of having to memorize a list of commands by enabling you to use buttons and pull-down menus.

Finding, Plugging In, and Surfing IRC Channels

IRC servers make up the hardware for the IRC network. You have to connect to one of these servers to access the network, so finding one is very important. You also may want to use an IRC client. You can download clients from various FTP sites. Some of the coolest that I have found are listed in the following sections. You also should obey some general rules, as outlined later in this lesson, when using IRC.

11

IRC Servers

The following is a short list of some of the IRC servers available for use. If you downloaded an IRC client, you can probably find a much larger list of sites. Due to the constant change of the Internet, not all of these servers may be available by the time you read this lesson.

```
blacksburg.va.us.undernet.org:6667

pittsburgh.pa.us.undernet.org:6667

ann-arbor.mi.us.undernet.org:6667

auckland.nz.undernet.org:6667

luxembourg.lu.eu.undernet.org:6667
```

These servers are all within the Undernet network. Numerous other servers are connected to other networks. Find the one closest to you that you enjoy for the best effects.

FTP for the Client

You may want to download an IRC client to make connecting and communicating easier. The easiest way to find a client that you like is to check a search engine. Lycos (www.lycos.com) and Infoseek (www.infoseek.com) both have long lists of sites offering IRC clients, as well as complete information on installation.

You also may want to check with your Internet service provider about what software they recommend. You may be able to download a copy of a client from their site. They may also be able to offer you some support if you run into problems.

The following are some popular places to start looking for a client:

```
ftp://ftp.undernet.org/pub/irc/clients/windows/

ftp://cs-ftp.bu.edu/irc/clients/pc/windows/

ftp://papa.indstate.edu/winsock-l/winirc/

ftp://ftp.winsite.com/pub/pc/win3/winsock/

http://alf8.speech.cs.cmu.edu/~ircle/

http://www.ex.ac.uk/~jastaple/irc/irchelp.html
```

Etiquette

Just as you do with e-mail and newsgroups, you should follow some etiquette guidelines with IRC.

11

Do	**Don't**

DO admit that you are new and ask for help if you need it. No one likes to admit it, but everyone was a newbie once.

DO be tolerant of other users.

DO be friendly and talk to other people. Friendships will develop quickly and can be useful if you're playing in Internet combat games.

DO answer messages and public comments.

DO use "shorthand" whenever possible. The following abbreviations also relate to shorthand that you may see in e-mail:

brb	be right back
bbl	be back later
oic	Oh, I see!
imho	In my humble opinion
rotfl	rolling on the floor laughing

DON'T flood the channel with massive numbers of messages in a row. These messages may overflow some users' modems. Along those lines, don't send pages of information; keep your messages short and to the point.

DON'T use autogreets, or automatic messaging, to say "Hello" and "Goodbye" automatically as people enter or leave the channel. They get old, and you may not really mean what you say.

DON'T be offensive.

People also use *emoticons* in IRC. The smiley **:)**, for example, and all other sorts of characters are widely used to show emotion in an emotionless environment such as IRC. See Lesson 5, "Understanding E-Mail," for more emoticons.

Chatting on the Web

As I've said before, hordes of IRC clients are available for use on most platforms. In the following sections, I describe three that I have found the most useful and that will go to the next level in chat. The first, mIRC, is a great chat program that is the most-used IRC application in the Windows environment. The next is ichat, a browser plug-in that offers you the privilege of not having to learn how to use a chat program because it is integrated within the Web browser. The last is of the next generation of IRC clients; Worlds Chat uses 3-D graphics and virtual reality to go above text-based chat.

mIRC

mIRC, which is a shareware IRC client for Windows, was developed by Khaled Mardam-bay. mIRC includes all the functionality of the normal text-based IRC clients from the UNIX, Windows, and Mac platforms. With a user-friendly interface, it is the most-used Windows IRC client.

mIRC is highly configurable, enabling you to save settings for each connection. A toolbar with all the frequently used commands is displayed at the top of the screen. Tooltips are even included, in case you forget what the icons stand for.

User customization is one of the strong points of the mIRC client. mIRC offers colored text lines, aliases, and remote commands. World Wide Web and sound support round off this client. Figure 11.1 shows a sample session using mIRC.

Figure 11.1.

Using mIRC to chat with other users.

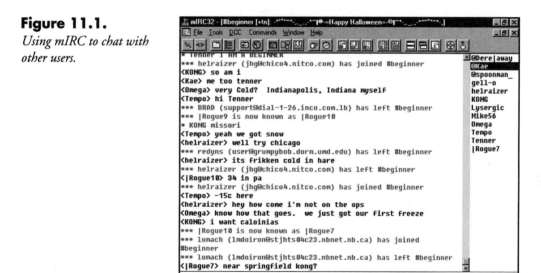

ichat

ichat is the first IRC plug-in for Netscape Navigator and Microsoft's Internet Explorer. Developed by ichat, inc. (www.ichat.com), the ichat plug-in integrates seamlessly with your browser to make access to IRC, MUD, and the ichat rooms as easy as viewing a Web page.

JUST A MINUTE

See Lesson 15, "Helping Your Browser with Plug-Ins," for more information on plug-ins and how they work.

When you visit a Web site that is chat-enabled, like the one shown in Figure 11.2, the ichat plug-in configures the browser window for a chat session. The top frame remains for Web browsing, and the bottom contains a real-time chat session of all the visitors to that Web page.

Figure 11.2.

A chat session using the ichat plug-in.

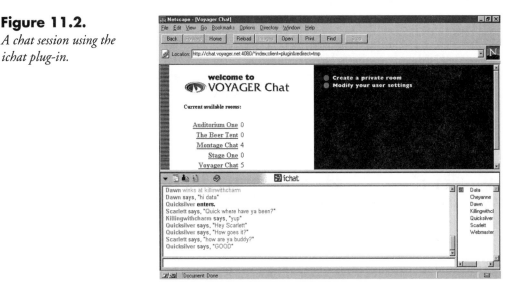

Remember, when you're visiting a Web site, you can assume that you are the only person reading the pages. Now you can chat with others as you explore a site. You don't have to memorize any special commands. You simply type your message if you want to address the entire group. You can also choose items from the menu bar for special responses as well as send a private message to one user.

For users without plug-in compatible browsers, you can configure the stand-alone client to run a helper application. The client is launched whenever an ichat, IRC, or MUD link is encountered on the Web.

The ichat Web site has a listing of major servers using the ichat software. A listing of special events that are moderated via the ichat plug-in also is included. Event moderation enables users to contribute to interviews with special guests. The lead moderator forwards questions from the online audience to the guest speaker. Replies to the questions go out on the chat line for all to see. Audio and video broadcasts may also be possible through the integration of a capable browser.

Worlds Chat

Virtual reality hits IRC, and Worlds Chat is born. Worlds Inc. (http://www.worlds.net) recently released the production version of their 3-D IRC client. Worlds Chat is just one of the new generation of IRC clients that use 3-D graphics and VRML to transport users to new arenas.

Imagine experiencing a leisurely stroll with your virtual friend, hearing the babbling of a nearby brook and the chirping of birds overhead. You converse about your recent metaphysics journey. At a moment's notice, you take flight over your three-dimensional world, leaving your friend as he watches you hover above.

Worlds Chat goes beyond the traditional flat screen of text and pictures to deliver a realistic experience. You can interact and "see" thousands of other real users in hundreds of different worlds.

You navigate through 3-D virtual worlds suited as your persona, or *avitar*. Worlds Chat offers over 40 different avitars for you to choose from. Your avitar represents you while you communicate to other users in the virtual world. These personas range from seven-foot tall penguins to four-headed aliens, whichever fits your spirit at the time. You can even provide your own custom avitar, as shown in Figure 11.3.

Figure 11.3.

Big Dave's avitar is a little more original than the seven-foot tall penguin in the background.

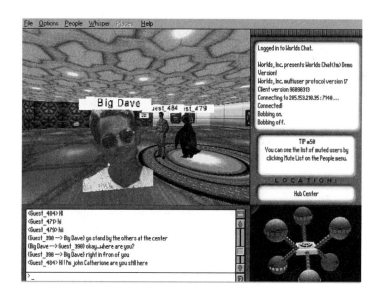

11

With the addition of sound effects and music to highlight the mood of the individual worlds, scenes take on a new excitement. The central space station, known as the Hub, connects you to the seven environments within the Worlds Chat arena.

The Worlds Chat Gold is currently in its 1.1 version. A trial version is available on the Internet. This version, however, does not have the full functionality of the Gold version but will provide you with the basic experience.

MUDs, MOOs, and Other Interactions

Multiuser Dungeons, or MUDs, could be considered computer adventure games. As the user, you are placed in a network of rooms and passages. These rooms contain other players, as well as valuable items to help you in your quest. The ultimate prize is to gain the class of wizard.

CAUTION

MUDs are extremely addictive. Students at colleges that provide free Internet access have been known to spend 16 hours connected to a MUD. Needless to say, their school work paid the price.

MOOs, MUCK, MUSE, and MUF are all variations of the MUD theme. These games, as well as some normal MUDs, have overall themes associated with them. One such game, for example, may be running on a *Star Trek* theme. Players in this game would be expected to act in the manner of a character from *Star Trek*. Not keeping with the theme of a MUD is grounds for being kicked off the MUD.

Starting a MUD session requires you to pick a MUD to connect to. Check out one of the MUD newsgroups—for example, `rec.games.mud.misc`—to find a MUD that you might be interested in trying. You can Telnet directly to that MUD to begin your quest if you have a Telnet client, or you can use a MUD client to make the connection easier.

You can do a search on your favorite search engine to find the best MUD client for your style. With the MUD client come instructions on connecting to the MUD, so I won't cover them here. Here's the URL for the MUD search on Yahoo! to help you get started:

```
(http://www.yahoo.com/Recreation/Games/Internet_Games/
MUDs__MUSHes__MOOs__etc_/)
```

Actions

Once you're in a MUD, you will probably want to move around to see what all lies ahead. Some of the commands to move are straightforward, so I won't get too involved. The commands I describe are just some of the basic actions. Each MUD has its own set of special commands that you will have to learn.

When you enter a room, probably the first thing you do is look around. Same with the MUD. When you first log in, you find yourself in a room. You have to find out whether anything valuable—food, water, or other people—is in the room, so look around. To look around or examine an object, you enter the following command:

```
look <object>
```

If the object resides in the room with you, a description of that object appears as the output. Otherwise, if you leave off the `<object>` portion of the command, you receive a description of the room itself. This command also lists the contents of the room.

The description of the room may hint to more than simply the contents. Sometimes the MUD gives you advice on how to proceed. To move about in the MUD, you use the go command, as follows:

```
go <object>
```

MUDs generally understand directions such as north, south, east, west, up, down, in, and out. So simply entering out takes you out of the present room. With some more complex MUDs, you can use complete commands like this one:

```
go through the north door
```

At this point, you leave the room and exit the north door. Upon entering a new room, you are given a brief description of the room and its contents.

If you encounter other players in the MUD, you may want to communicate. You're still in an IRC, remember. To talk to another user, you use the say command, as follows:

```
say Hello, are you lost?
```

The other players see this message on their screens

```
<nick> says, "Hello, are you lost?"
```

where `<nick>` is the user nickname that you used to connect to the MUD. You can talk to people only in your room using this command, just as you can talk to people only in your channel on the normal IRC. Be sure to do some exploring to find people to talk to.

11

If you want to send a message to a player who is somewhere in the MUD, you can use the page command, as follows. It keeps you from having to search throughout the entire MUD just to talk to someone.

```
page <user> <message>
```

Here *<user>* is the nickname for the user you're trying to contact. *<message>* is, of course, the message you are trying to send to that person. Pages are visible only to the user you're contacting.

What if you want to speak with only one person? To do so, you use the whisper command, as follows:

```
whisper <user> <message>
```

This command sends your message to the user you specified if he or she is in the same room with you. This command is the same as the whisper option in normal IRC use.

One more basic command you can use in general MUD games is the act command. This command makes your character do something—for example, waving to everyone, as follows:

```
act waves to everyone
```

All the players in the room with you see

```
<nick> waves to everyone
```

where *<nick>* is again your nickname. Using this command can provide a lot of fun when actions speak louder than words.

Combat

In some MUDs, you can fight with other players and computer-driven monsters. Combat MUDs are the most common form of MUD, so you shouldn't have to look hard to find one.

Power is the goal in a combat MUD. Players fight monsters and each other to gain points. The more points you get, the more strength you gain. The more strength, the more power.

As a player, you begin as a simple fighter and progress to the rank of wizard. You move up in rank by completing quests, solving puzzles, killing monsters, and interacting with other users. Each of these tasks gives you more points, enabling you to buy weapons, armor, or knowledge to increase your strength.

A few commands such as wear, wield, and kill are used throughout combat MUDs. After you purchase a piece of armor, you must wear it to use its protection. The wear command is simple; you enter the following command to put on your helmet:

```
wear helmet on head
```

Some MUDs keep track and recognize certain body parts. Others aren't so advanced.

To protect yourself, you need a weapon. With a certain number of points, you can purchase a sword. To arm yourself with this sword, or any weapon, you use the `wield` command, as follows:

```
wield sword on right hand
```

This command places the sword in your right hand, ready for battle.

So you have your sword and armor, and you just stand there. No! Now you're ready to conquer the MUD. Only a few things are standing in your way. Literally. A group of angry trolls is about to attack you. You need to use the `kill` command quickly. Simply type

```
kill troll
```

and the battle begins. You may win and gain points as well as any treasure the trolls may have been carrying. You may also lose, in which case you will lose points and be transported to the central area to regenerate.

This is just one example of the type of action that awaits you in the MUD. There are MUDs for all types of personalities and scenarios: knights and dragons, space alien invasion, robotic adventures, or underwater expeditions. Enjoy the action and have fun playing.

11

Summary

IRC is a multiuser network of servers that span the globe. All one-to-one conversation restrictions of the old talk program are gone. IRC can now support tens of thousands of users on numerous channels. Conversations are now limited to the user, rather than the software. IRC clients make accessing the networks easier for the beginner.

Multiuser dungeons make up the adventure gaming area within the Internet. Role-playing to specific themes, from knights to spacemen, adds to the addictive qualities of MUDs.

Workshop

The following workshop helps solidify the skills that you learned in this lesson.

Q&A

Q What's a bot?

A A *bot* is an automated program that runs on an IRC server. Usually, their names end with "Bot," "Srv," or "Serv," but not always. Bots can also be programmed to give basic responses to a conversation. The "person" you're talking with may not be a person at all.

Q What if someone tells me to type something? Should I take his or her word for it and try typing the command?

A No! Never type anything anyone tells you to, unless you know what the command does. Problems with the security of your account could be caused by certain commands. Some jokers just like to pick on the newbies.

Q Do I have to tell anyone some of my personal information, such as my real name, e-mail address, or phone number?

A No, you can tell people whatever you want them to know. Being anonymous is one of the selling points of IRC. You also can experience the excitement of being someone else while playing a MUD, which makes it so addictive.

Quiz

Take the following quiz to see how much you've learned.

Questions

1. What does IRC stand for?
   - (a) Interlink Response Correction
   - (b) Internet Relay Chat
   - (c) Inhuman Roughneck Combatant

2. What does MUD stand for?
   - (a) Mad Users Domain
   - (b) Multipurpose User Device
   - (c) Multiuser Dungeon

3. The common use of IRC is to
   - (a) Talk with friends
   - (b) Make new friends
   - (c) Talk with strangers
   - (d) All the above

4. What is an avitar?
   - (a) A grand wizard in MUD
   - (b) A persona in 3-D chat
   - (c) A person who flies a plane

Answers

1. (b) Internet Relay Chat
2. (c) Multiuser Dungeon
3. (c) IRC is like a cocktail party on the Internet. The purpose is to provide a real-time conference area for users to discuss whatever happens to be on their minds.
4. (b) An avitar is your image in 3-D chat. This image is how you appear to other users in the 3-D chat world.

Activity

Download an IRC client from one of the FTP sites, and try out a channel or two. Begin by starting a conversation with one of the visitors. If that person doesn't want to talk, don't get discouraged; just try someone else.

You may find that the 3-D chat worlds are a little easier to master if you're a new user. Download Worlds Chat from their Web site and give it a try. Be sure to choose an avitar that fits your style. I like the giant blue bear myself.

11

Hour 12

Internet Phone and Video

In Lesson 5, "Understanding E-Mail," you learned how cheap it is to communicate via the Internet. The cost of sending messages back and forth to relatives, friends, and colleagues is practically nothing when you figure the number of messages you can send in a short amount of time.

Now consider sending voice rather than text across the Internet. Add into that the ability to carry on real-time conversations, and you're talking about using Internet phone software. Internet phones, or Web phones as they are sometimes called, enable you to talk directly to another person halfway around the world simply by using the Internet.

In this lesson, you can find answers to the following questions:

- ☐ What is an Internet phone?
- ☐ Where do I get Internet phone software?
- ☐ What are some uses of an Internet phone?
- ☐ How do I place a call?
- ☐ What's my Internet phone number?

Internet phone use is beginning to grow; new software and increased features will likely be available soon. You should find, however, that the tips in this lesson apply to most Web phone packages.

Theory Behind the Web Phone

Since the beginning of the Internet, data has been transmitted from network to network and from computer to computer. Because the human voice can now be digitized, it only seems natural that tools for transmitting speech along these networks would be developed.

Enter the Web phone market. Now you can bypass the long-distance phone companies altogether. The global telecommunications network has been replaced by the collection of networks known as the Internet. A digital data signal that represents a voice is sent to the next computer rather than an analog signal that connects to the handset of a standard phone.

Making a call to my brother Dave, for example, is no more difficult than checking a Web site for the day's sports highlights. I call up Dave's computer by using my Web phone's phone book, by typing in his IP address, or by selecting his name from a list of current online users. Assuming that Dave is online at the time and that we are using the same Web phone software, he is notified by the standard phone "br-ring" or some other signal. Dave can accept my call with the click of a button, and we can save ourselves the cost of a long-distance phone call. If only the process were that easy every time. Later in this lesson, I'll give you tips to make calling your friends, relatives, and so on rely less on luck (in my case, Dave happened to be online) and a lot more productive.

Now back to the theory: When you speak, your Web phone software digitizes your voice into packets of data. These packets are transmitted through your modem, across the Internet— bouncing from server to server, to your caller's modem, through his or her software, and finally back into an audible signal—or your voice.

The main bottleneck with this scenario is the bandwidth required. For a true telephone-quality connection, you would need to transmit about 8 kilobytes of data per second. Unfortunately, a typical 28.8 Kbps modem can handle only around 3K per second. What the hardware is lacking, you can try to make up with software design.

Web phone vendors have tried to pump more information into every kilobyte of data they transmit. Every Web phone application now uses some type of audio compression software, or *codec*. The codec receives your analog voice signal from the microphone and compresses it into a digital signal. On the opposite end, the codec converts the digital signal back into an analog signal that can be reproduced at the computer's speakers.

NEW TERM   **Codec:** This term is short for compression/decompression. A mathematical algorithm is responsible for encoding an analog signal into digital form. It also decodes a received digital signal into an analog signal.

Connection Tips

In this section, I provide a few hints to make connecting and conversing with an Internet phone easier and more enjoyable.

If your Internet service provider offers static or fixed IP addresses, get one. A static IP address is one that doesn't change every time you dial into your provider. Connecting with another person is easy if you always know his or her IP address. With a standard, dynamically assigned IP address, you lose one form of dialing directly to that person's computer because his IP address changes with each connection to their ISP. Many Web phone vendors maintain servers listing the online users of their software so that connecting to another user is easier, but these servers can go down, leaving you little hope of making a connection.

I highly recommend using at least a 28.8 Kbps modem. Any lower speed does not give a reliable connection. Transmission of a conversation over even a 14.4 Kbps connection leads to garbled speech and lower sound quality.

When you want to place a Web phone call, plan a rendezvous time and place with your caller. Not many people can afford to sit and wait for the Web phone to ring. Nor do they enjoy searching through hundreds of chat rooms for a person to talk to. Logging onto a vendor's server waiting for a person to call can also lead to your receiving miscellaneous calls from strangers wanting to talk to anyone to test their installation.

Use settings that maximize the performance of your software. Choose the correct codec for your connection speed. Identify your correct hardware settings within the Web phone application. Also, adjust the input and output settings on your microphone and speakers to reduce echo and feedback.

Headphones are great when you're using a Web phone application. With some connections, you may experience distortion or transmission delays. Headphones place your ears closer to the source. So, from this vantage point, you can often more easily understand what the other person is saying. Using headphones also means you don't have to worry about possible feedback effects and distortion from microphone and speaker interaction.

You should purchase a full-duplex sound card if you don't have one. This type of sound card enables you to carry on normal conversations with your caller. Full-duplex cards allow both users to talk simultaneously. Half-duplex cards, which are installed in all but the more recent

12

machines, can carry only one speaker at a time (similar to a CB radio). During installation, most Internet phone applications will tell you what type of sound card you have installed in your computer.

Last, but not least, speak clearly and slowly directly into your microphone. Most Web phone software is voice activated, so as long as you're talking, it is transmitting. If you lower your voice and speak softly, you may not register as talking within the application, and nothing you say will be sent to the other person.

A Typical Web Phone Conversation

I've covered the basic principles behind a Web phone, but I haven't talked about how to use one. As an example, I'll explain how to use the most popular Web phone application, Internet Phone by VocalTec, to demonstrate the following:

☐ Locating a remote user

☐ Dialing and establishing a call

☐ Using typical Web phone features

Because not all phones offer the same features, some phones may not offer all the options of Internet Phone. I chose Internet Phone for this demonstration because many magazines have rated it their top choice for Web phones. You can download a seven-day trial version from the VocalTec Web site (`http://www.vocaltech.com`), shown in Figure 12.1.

Figure 12.1.

The VocalTec Web site provides the demo version of its Internet Phone software.

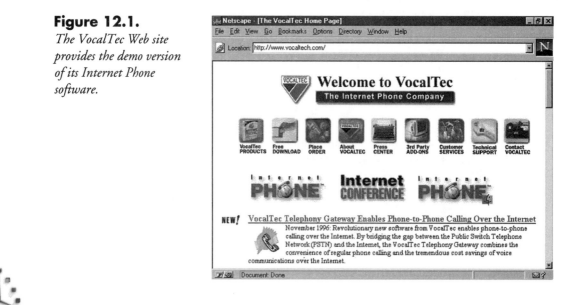

Dialing into Your ISP

None of this phone software would do you much good without a connection to the Internet. To begin the example, you need to connect to your Internet service provider.

See Lesson 4, "Internet Service Provider Options and Pointers," for more information on Internet Service Providers (ISPs) and how to connect your computer to the Internet.

JUST A MINUTE

You don't need to do anything out of the ordinary when you dial in. Just follow the directions that the ISP provided when you opened your account. The Web phone application runs over the same protocol as many other Internet applications. Your ISP should already be capable of using Web phone software, so no changes should be required on that end. A corporate firewall, on the other hand, may not allow use of the particular port that Internet Phone uses. You should contact your system administrator if you run into problems connecting to the Internet Phone directory servers.

Launching the Web Phone Application

When you run the installation program, a copy of the Web phone application and all the files needed for the program to run correctly are installed on your hard drive. Locate the Internet Phone application and double-click it. If you're using Windows 95, you can also find the Internet Phone application listed in your Start menu.

After you establish your Internet connection through your ISP, launching Internet Phone opens two Internet Phone windows. One is the phone control window, and the other is the Global Online Directory (GOLD) window.

Internet Phone automatically tries to connect to one of the GOLD servers on the Internet when you launch the application. For this reason, it's good to have your connection to your ISP already established.

JUST A MINUTE

The software tries to connect you to one of the 20-plus Iphone servers around the world. These GOLD servers are in constant contact with each other and provide a real-time list of the current users. By connecting to one of these servers, your name is simultaneously added to the Online Users list on all the other servers, as you can see in Figure 12.2.

12

Figure 12.2.

The Global Online Directory lists all the current Online Users and Chat rooms.

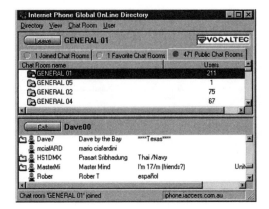

Connecting to one of the GOLD servers may take a few minutes. You can watch on the screen as the software connects to the server. If the server has too many users or does not respond, another server is called until a connection is made.

Controls and Displays

The Internet Phone control window displays an animated assistant and three primary buttons, as shown in Figure 12.3. The animated assistant serves to notify you of incoming calls, displays your current online status, and identifies users during a conversation.

Figure 12.3.

The animated assistant in the Internet Phone control window is waiting for a call.

By clicking the Answer button, you can accept an incoming call, like picking up the receiver on a normal telephone. After a call has been made, the button changes to Hang Up. You can click the Hang Up button to end a conversation. The Hold button mutes your microphone, not allowing the other user to hear you. You use the last button, Redial, to call back the last person dialed automatically.

To the left of the animated assistant are four more icons (starting at the top):

☐ Send voice mail message: This feature enables you to send an audio message to another person via e-mail. The other person needs to also have Internet Phone or VocalTec's Voice mail player on his or her machine.

☐ Text chat window: This feature enables you to begin a text-based chat session with your caller in a process similar to IRC. A text window is opened on both machines, and all keyboard activity is displayed simultaneously on both computers.

☐ Whiteboard window: The whiteboard, as shown in Figure 12.4, is a simple graphics tablet on which both phone callers can draw, write, or type. It is similar to Windows Paint.

☐ File transfer: Within Internet Phone, you also can transmit files directly to the other person. They can include bookmark files, address books, or chapters to an upcoming book.

Figure 12.4.

The whiteboard enables users to draw, diagram, or collaborate using a graphics tablet.

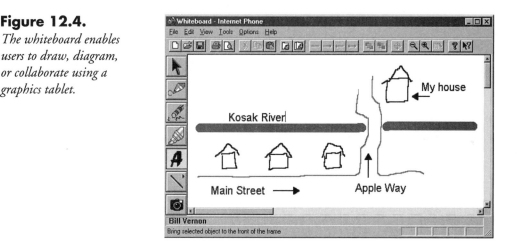

Under the animated assistant are three additional panels. They display real-time user information during your conversation. The panels may not always be visible when the application is launched. Click the appropriate button to toggle any of the panels open or closed. The arrow on the button signifies which panels are opened.

The Call Center gives you direct access to the Online Directory, your Personal Directory (like your phone book), and the Web Directory. It also lists the individuals whom you have called for quick reference back to them. The Session List keeps a running tally of your current connection status as well as any previous calls you have placed. The Statistics panel records a real-time log of incoming and outgoing data signals, the codec used, and the transfer rate. This panel is good to use if you notice your connection is hampered with sudden *dropouts*.

> **NEW TERM** **Dropout:** A dropout is a sudden loss of digital signal that cuts off the person speaking. A dropout is generally caused by incorrect audio settings on a user's microphone and speakers.

Global Online Directory

The Global Online Directory (GOLD) window provides a list of individuals who are currently online. It also maintains the status of chat rooms used by callers. Chat rooms are great places to rendezvous or just find someone to talk to. Private chat rooms are "unlisted" and can be created when you want to talk to family or business associates. Access to these rooms is limited to only those people who know they exist.

Dialing the Recipient

You can place a call to another person in the following different ways:

- [ ] Locate using GOLD: You can look for a person in the Online Users list in the GOLD window. If you want to find someone new to talk to, this list is a great tool.
- [ ] Find by IP address: If you know the other person's IP address, you can enter it into the Call Center panel and then click the Call button. This way, you can connect directly with the other user. This method works only if the other person has a static IP address.
- [ ] Use the Find feature: In some versions of Internet Phone, you can search all the chat rooms at once. Enter the person's nickname and if the person is online, the client returns the user's information and the option to call him or her.
- [ ] Call Back: From the Call Center, you can select the user from the list of past connections. If the person is currently online, a call is placed to him or her.
- [ ] Use Quick Dial: As you can do with speed or memory dialing on a traditional telephone, you can add users who are repeatedly called to the quick dial menu. This way, you can call users, wherever they are, with a single mouse click.

After you initiate the call, the animated assistant dials the number. Just to give you some familiarity, a telephone rings until the other person accepts your call. Your conversation can begin when the connection is complete, so watch for the signal from your assistant.

Receiving a Call

If you are online, another person can place a call to you. If this should happen, you may be notified in the following different ways:

☐ Your animated assistant begins knocking on your screen to get your attention.

☐ A ringing telephone sound is played.

☐ The name of the person calling is displayed in the Call Center panel.

To accept the call, click the Answer button on the Internet Phone control window, as shown in Figure 12.5.

Figure 12.5.

The animated assistant tells you that someone is trying to call.

12

Conversing

Conversing is the best use for the animated assistant. If either you or the person you're calling is using a half-duplex sound card, you are limited to one person talking at a time. The assistant shows who is currently talking, who is listening, whether no one is talking (silence), or if you're both trying to talk at the same time, as you can see in Figure 12.6. If you're using a full-duplex card, you both can speak just as if you were using a standard phone.

JUST A MINUTE

The next step in Internet phones is the addition of video. At the end of this chapter is a list of Internet video phones. If you have a camcorder or one of those eyeball cameras, you can send video to your caller.

Figure 12.6.

The assistant shows the current activity during the conversation.

Ending the Conversation

When you're done talking to the other person and you've said your "good-byes," click the Hang Up button on the Internet Phone control window. The connection is cut. You're immediately ready to start another call by selecting another user.

Other Web Phone Applications

The following is a short list of other Web phone applications. All of them are available on the Internet.

Traditional Internet Phones

☐ Netspeak Corporation's WebPhone (http://www.netspeak.com)

☐ DigiPhone from Third Planet Publishing (http://www.planeteers.com)

☐ TeleVox from Voxware (http://www.voxware.com)

☐ FreeTel (http://www.freetel.com)

12

Internet Video Phones

- ☐ VocalTec's Internet Phone with Video (`http://www.vocaltec.com/iphone4/video.htm`)
- ☐ Intel's Internet Video Phone (`http://www.connectedpc.com/iaweb/cpc/iivphone`)
- ☐ CU-SeeMe (`http://www.goliath.wpine.com/cu-seeme.html`)

Summary

In this lesson, you learned about Web phones. Although they are not quite ready for corporate life, common recreational use has become widespread. You learned the theory behind the Web phone and learned some useful terms, such as codec, half-duplex, and full-duplex. I also gave you some hints for using Internet phones and making better connections.

Next, I walked you through a sample Web phone conversation using the Internet Phone application. You learned how to locate, call, and converse with another person. Finally, I listed other Web phone software packages that are available.

Workshop

The following workshop helps solidify the skills that you learned in this lesson.

Q&A

Q Now that I have Internet Phone, should I cancel my long-distance carrier?

A No, telephony and Web phone technology in general are not advanced enough to replace normal phone use.

Q How much does using a Web phone cost?

A The software can run between $30 and $60 for a registered version. The other cost is your Internet connection.

Q A friend of mine is using a different Web phone than I am. Can we still talk?

A No, as of yet you are only able to call someone who is running the same software as you (no Web phone standards are in place).

12

Quiz

Take the following quiz to see how much you've learned.

Questions

1. What can you type in to call another person?

    (a) Home telephone number

    (b) IP address

    (c) Social Security number

2. With what type of card can only one person talk at a time?

    (a) Half-duplex card

    (b) Full-duplex card

3. What is the minimum speed suggested for Web phone use?

    (a) 9600 baud

    (b) 14.4 Kbps

    (c) 28.8 Kbps

Answers

1. (b) As long as the person has a static IP address, you can call him or her using the IP address.

2. (a) Half-duplex card

3. (c) Connecting with a 28.8 Kbps modem is the slowest recommended speed for consistent voice transmission.

Activity

Download one of the Web phone packages from the Internet. Call a friend who also has Internet access and try out the package. Decide which software you're going to use, what chat room you're going to meet in, and who is going to call whom.

12

PART
IV

The World Wide Web

Hour

Hour 13

Navigating the Web

In Lesson 3, "Introduction to the World Wide Web," you learned a lot about how the Web works. As you read on, you put the Web on the back burner to become familiar with some of the great things the Internet has to offer. But now you're ready to meet the most interactive and dynamic part of the Net head on.

In this lesson, you find the answers to the following questions:

- ☐ How can I deal with so much information on the Web?
- ☐ How do I navigate around the Web?
- ☐ What are all those buttons for on my browser?
- ☐ Can I keep track of where I've been?
- ☐ How do I keep a permanent record of my favorite sites?

Whether you use Netscape Navigator or Internet Explorer, most of the information in this lesson applies. I give examples for both browsers. For more detailed information on these two browsers, refer to Lesson 14, "Netscape Versus Internet Explorer: Finding the Right Browser."

Coping with Information Overload

Experienced Internet users are constantly inundated with complaints about how useless the Internet has become because too much information is available. When one Web site can index over 50 million Web pages, you obviously can find a lot of information.

But think about this fact for a moment. Is this really anything new? Have you ever been to a major city or university library? Could you handle all the information in all the books in even one of these libraries? Probably not.

In a real sense, the Web is no different. A great deal of information is available, yes. But, like in many of the libraries you visit, tools are available to help you find what you need. Also, though it may not look like it at first, the Web does have an organization that enables you to span vast distances of resources in a short period of time.

TIME SAVER

Don't panic. These words made famous by Douglas Adams in *The Hitchhiker's Guide* series are applicable here. Perhaps the biggest key to conquering the Internet and the Web is simply to remain calm. If you like, you can even take a towel!

Before you learn about some of the actual tools you'll use to find your way around, think about how many people are able to go into a large library without getting overwhelmed; then apply those principles to the Web. By doing so, you can have a set of mental tools to keep in mind as you tackle the tangled Web.

- ☐ Familiarity breeds…well, familiarity. No one has ever gone into a library for the first time and been comfortable. You need to walk around some, find out where different types of books are located—get to know the place. Apply this rule to the Web. Surf around some; just look around to get a feel for where things are located and get a feel for what it's like.

- ☐ The right tools are invaluable. Just as you'd never try to keep the locations of six different library books in your head, don't try to do too much on the Web either. Use your browser's History and Bookmark features (which I describe later in this lesson) to help you. The Web is a big place, so don't be afraid to write things down either.

- ☐ Go ahead and ask questions. Take advantage of what you've learned about newsgroups and e-mail to get information about the Web. Friends, professionals, and others who are accessible electronically make up a great team of Internet "reference librarians."

13

☐ A card catalog is the best tool to help you find information in the library. Internet search engines, covered in Lesson 16, "Searching the Web for Virtually Anything," are a must-have on the Internet. You will find yourself searching the Web a lot to locate only that information you're interested in.

Exploring Navigation Basics

You must be familiar with several basics to start exploring the Web. You must understand how individual pages on the Web can be viewed and explored, you need to know how hyperlinks work, and you need to be familiar with browser toolbar buttons. Once you're familiar with these important parts of the Web, you're well on your way to becoming an experienced Web user.

Navigating Web Pages

If navigating an individual Web page seems simple and obvious to you, you might want to skip to the next section. You might be surprised, however, at the number of beginners who fail to realize how to get around on a Web page.

The key is in realizing that any particular Web page can be as long or as short as the Webmaster programs it to be. Many people, when they get on the Web for the first time, think that what appears on their screen is all there is. The page in Figure 13.1, for example, contains a lot of text, links and "action," but you should notice one thing right away. Note that both the horizontal and vertical scroll bars are active, which tells you that this page is wider and longer than will fit in the screen.

Figure 13.1.

You can probably tell that there's more than meets the eye on this Web page.

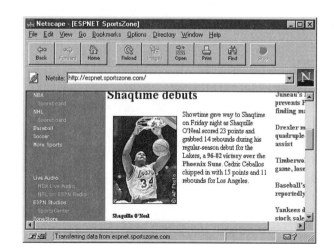

TIME SAVER

Maximizing your browser window to take up your entire monitor is always a good idea. This way, you can ensure that you view the most possible information. The only time this may not be true is if you have a large (17-inch or bigger) monitor, in which case adjusting your browser to take up a half screen should be fine.

Unless the specific piece of information you want is at the very top of a page, you should make a habit of scrolling down a Web page when you first encounter it. By doing so, you know how much and what type of information is on the page you're looking at.

Following That Link

The simplest and most useful tool on the Web is the *hyperlink*. This underlined and colored word can take you to a page next door or halfway around the world. The hyperlink is the key to the nonlinear nature of the Web.

The hyperlink also is the reason that the Web is so easy to use. With a quick glance, you know immediately where you can go from any page. The page shown in Figure 13.2 (http://www.shareware.com), for example, has text links to New Arrivals, Search, Bag the beta, and more. Because these words look different from other words on the page, you know you can click them to go to another page.

Figure 13.2.

Text hyperlinks are easy to see and follow on the Web.

Hyperlinks —

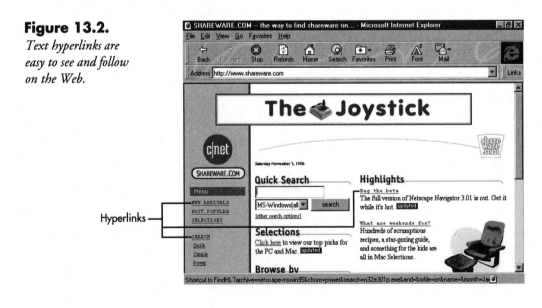

13

Not all hyperlinks are so obvious, however. Often, Webmasters create graphics that are themselves hyperlinks. Obvious graphical hyperlinks have colored borders around them so that you know they are hyperlinks.

Webmasters are more commonly putting graphical hyperlinks on their pages now to create a more realistic feel to them. If you look again at the page in Figure 13.2, you will see a chair in the bottom-right corner. Even though it doesn't have a border around it, the chair is a link, too.

TIME SAVER

When you're trying to find links on a page with a lot of graphics, pay special attention to your cursor. Whenever it passes over a link on a page, it turns from a cursor into a hand. When your cursor becomes a hand, you know you're looking at a hyperlink.

You also should know about one last type of graphical hyperlink: the image map. An *image map* is a special type of graphic that takes you to different pages depending on where on the graphic you click. If you see a graphic with a row of books, for example, you might go to a different page depending on which book your cursor is over when you click.

Using Toolbar Buttons

You need to do more than simply click links to go from one place to another. You need another set of tools to help you. Most major browsers offer a number of toolbar buttons to help you navigate the Web. The exact names and functions of these various buttons vary from browser to browser, but the most-used buttons are usually always the same. Table 13.1 gives you a breakdown of the most common buttons.

Table 13.1. Common toolbar buttons.

Button	Function	Browser
Back	Takes you back to the most previous page visited.	Explorer and Navigator
Forward	After using the Back button, takes you forward one page	Explorer and Navigator

13

continues

Table 13.1. continued

Button	Function	Browser
Home	Takes you to the user-defined home page	Explorer and Navigator
Stop	Stops current page from loading into your browser	Explorer and Navigator
Print	Prints current page	Explorer and Navigator
Reload/Refresh	Requests the current page be loaded into the browser	Explorer and Navigator
Find	Lets you quickly search for a phrase on the current page	Navigator
Font	Allows you to change the size of the displayedfont	Explorer

These buttons, along with hyperlinks, will allow you to do a large majority of your Web browsing. Both browsers, however, offer an additional set of buttons that let you accomplish even more. Table 13.2 displays a few of these buttons.

Table 13.2. Additional browser buttons.

Button	Function	Browser
What's New/Today's Links	Takes you to a list of new Web sites	Explorer and Navigator
Software/Product Updates	Enables you to view a page about the latest software related to a particular browser	Explorer and Navigator
Net Search/Search/People	A number of buttons that enable you to search for a variety of things	Explorer and Navigator

13

Button	Function	Browser
Destinations/ Microsoft/ Services	Buttons that take you to a variety of resources at Netscape or Microsoft	Explorer and Navigator

Figure 13.3 shows the toolbars of both Netscape Navigator and Microsoft's Internet Explorer. Both browsers enable you to adjust which buttons you actually display on your screen. For more details on these two browsers, go to Lesson 14.

Figure 13.3.
Netscape Navigator and Microsoft's Internet Explorer offer a wide variety of options to help you navigate and explore the Web.

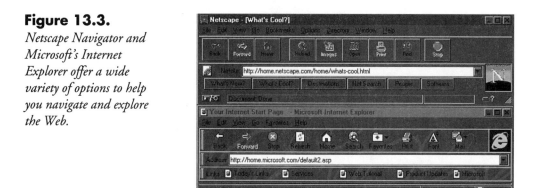

History Does Repeat Itself

If you were to walk around a large library without any clues as to where you were going, you would probably get lost before long. Fortunately, many libraries have those colored lines on the floor to tell you where you're going and where you've been.

This same type of tool comes in the form of the Go menu in both Internet Explorer and Netscape Navigator. As you visit each page during a particular session on the Web, your browser makes a note of where you've been in what is sometimes called a *history file*.

You can access the history file through the Go menu to go back instantly to any of the pages you've visited. Figure 13.4 shows a sports addict's history file after a bit of cruising.

Figure 13.4.

The history file tells you everywhere you've been during a particular session on the Web.

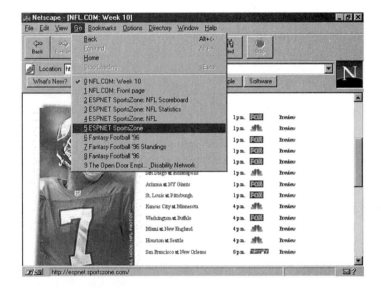

You need to know one more thing about how your browser keeps track of where you've been. Obviously, the information about each page you've been to has to be stored somewhere on your computer. This storage area is called *cache*, which can be either a portion of your computer's RAM or hard drive where data is temporarily stored for fast retrieval. Obviously, the more room available for cache, the more links your browser can remember.

If you find that your history file never gets very long, you can try to improve your situation by doing the following:

☐ Close as many open applications (besides your browser) as you can. The memory that closing these applications frees up can often allow your browser to keep a longer history file.

☐ Turn off the helpers. If you don't find yourself using Java or some of the other built-in capabilities of your browser, disabling them may free up more memory when you start your browser.

☐ Adjust your computer's virtual memory. Increasing your virtual memory can improve performance for your browser.

CAUTION

In the Windows 95 Virtual Memory control panel, you get this warning: These settings can adversely affect system performance and should be adjusted by advanced users and system administrators only. Be careful when adjusting these settings in Windows 95 or any other operating system, and make note of the original settings so that you can restore them in case something goes wrong.

13

Making a Permanent Record of Your Travels

I can think of one serious downside to the history file. The second you quit your browser, your history is erased from the Go menu. As a result, you start with an empty Go menu every time you start your browser.

JUST A MINUTE

Internet Explorer does keep the history file active between Web sessions. To view your history from past sessions, however, you must choose Go I Open History Folder. Explorer also enables you to adjust how far back you keep your history. Choose View I Options I Navigation and then adjust the History setting to choose your taste.

Even if you didn't have to start over each time, you would probably want a way to go instantly to an often-visited or favorite site without having to find it every time. Most major browsers have this "bookmarking" capability. Though different browsers call it by different names (as you'll learn in the next lesson), I refer to these markers by the generic term "bookmarks" for now.

Adding Bookmarks

Adding a bookmark in either Netscape or Explorer is easy. Simply go to a site for which you want a permanent record and choose Bookmarks|Add Bookmarks in Netscape or choose Favorites|Add To Favorites in Internet Explorer. That's it.

From now on, by simply clicking the Bookmarks or Favorites menu, you see all the sites you can access with a click. When you first start to surf the Internet with a browser, this process will be sufficient. As you become more experienced, however, and need to keep track of more sites, you'll need to be able to do a little more. Both browsers make modifying your bookmarks "drag-and-drop easy."

13

Editing Bookmarks in Netscape

Soon you'll discover you've created a long list of bookmarks that are so disorganized that you almost wish you didn't have them at all. In Netscape, making your bookmarks more organized is easy.

After you make a few bookmarks yourself, choose Bookmarks|Go to Bookmarks. A window like the one shown in Figure 13.5 then appears. Changing the order of your bookmarks from this window is as simple as clicking a bookmark and dragging it up or down. When you release your mouse button, the bookmark appears in its new place.

Figure 13.5.

The Bookmark editing window in Netscape is easy to use.

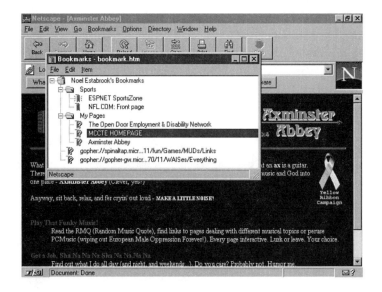

You may want to complete other tasks with your bookmarks, however, such as putting related bookmarks in the same folder or deleting bookmarks. The following is a rundown of the most commonly used bookmark editing options. (Figure 13.6 shows the bookmark editing window after some of these changes have been made).

☐ Choosing File|Import imports bookmarks from another browser for inclusion in your Netscape bookmark list.

☐ Choosing Item|Insert Bookmark enables you to enter a bookmark manually by name and URL.

☐ Choosing Item|Insert Folder enables you to create a folder in your bookmark list. After you've created it, you can drag and drop related bookmarks into the folder for easy organization.

☐ Choosing Edit|Delete removes a bookmark from your list.

Figure 13.6.

All these bookmarks were edited within this window.

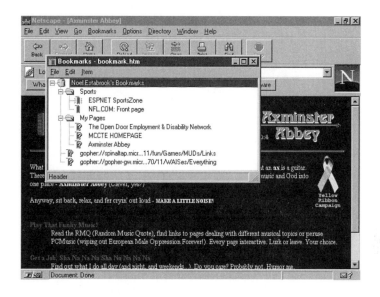

Editing Favorites in Explorer

Editing favorites (bookmarks) in Internet Explorer is also easy. Choosing Favorites|Organize Favorites takes you to a window that looks almost identical to any other Windows 95 window, as you can see in Figure 13.7.

Figure 13.7.

Organizing favorites is similar to organizing any other information in Windows 95.

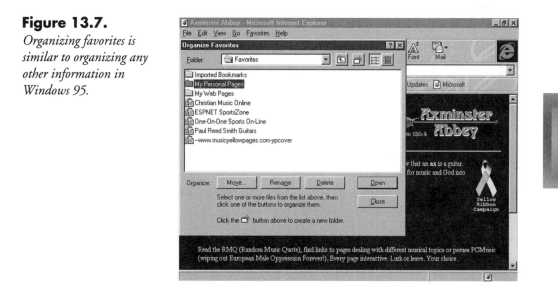

Explorer is slightly more limited in how you can organize and edit bookmarks. You can't simply move their order, for example, by dragging and dropping. You can only move them from one folder to another. The basic functions are still available, however:

☐ Folder Button: Clicking the Folder button at the top of the window enables you to create a new folder into which you can move related bookmarks.

☐ Delete Button: This button removes a selected favorite from your list.

☐ Move Button: Clicking this button brings up a dialog box that enables you to move your bookmark to any location.

No matter what browser you use, creating and organizing bookmarks is simple with just a little practice. You will find that you can organize literally hundreds of bookmarks to be available at your fingertips.

Summary

This lesson explained how the Web is similar to any large library and how you need to apply some of the same rules when dealing with the amount of information that's available. You also learned about many of the tools available to help you organize the Internet.

You know that you can easily access toolbar buttons to help you navigate and get specialized information. You also learned that Web browsers keep an easily accessible history of where you've been. Finally, you learned how to keep and organize a bookmark list of your favorite places on the Internet.

Workshop

The following workshop helps solidify the skills that you learned in this lesson.

Q&A

Q I've seen the term "cookies" around and don't know how they work. What are they?

A A cookie is a file that a server puts on your machine when you access it. The next time you visit the server (or other cookie-capable servers), this file can be read and additional information can be deposited into it. Some people consider this use an invasion of privacy and don't accept cookies. To have control over whether you choose to accept cookies, choose View|Options|Advanced and then select the Warn Before Accepting "Cookies" option in Explorer, or choose Options|Network Preferences|Protocols and then select the Accepting a Cookie option.

Q **I am color blind and have a very difficult time reading many of the Web pages that are out there. What can I do?**

A Netscape Navigator gives you the option of always displaying every Web page only as you want to see it. In Navigator, choose Options|General Preferences|Colors. Choose a set of fonts and background colors that are easy for you to read and then select the Always Use My Colors, Overriding Document option.

Quiz

Take the following quiz to see how much you've learned.

Questions

1. The problem of "information overload" really doesn't present any problems that haven't existed before.

    (a) True

    (b) False

2. Which of the following toolbar buttons is found in Netscape but not Explorer?

    (a) Back

    (b) Open

    (c) Home

3. Which of the following isn't a hyperlink on a Web page?

    (a) Text

    (b) Graphic

    (c) The browser window scroll bar

Answers

1. (a) True
2. (b) The Open button is found only in Netscape
3. (c) The browser window scroll bar

Activity

Your biggest task, both now and in the future, will be to have a large and easily accessible list of bookmarks. Well, you might as well start now. Spend an hour or so cruising the Net, making at least 10 bookmarks as you go. After you're done, edit the bookmarks into at least two different categories. If you don't want to keep them all, feel free to delete some of them after you've organized them.

Hour **14**

Netscape Versus Internet Explorer: Finding the Right Browser

Now that you know a little bit about the Web, you need to know how to get there. In this lesson, you explore two of the most widely known browsers used to view the Web: Netscape Navigator and Microsoft's Internet Explorer. What's the difference? Which is best for you? This lesson is designed to help you find the best browser for you.

In this lesson, you find the answers to the following questions:

☐ What are some of the basic things I need to know?

☐ What are some current Netscape features?

☐ What are some current Internet Explorer features?

☐ Can you give me some examples of how they're different?

☐ What version should I use?

Browser Basics

Web browsers are basically the same. Each one displays text and graphics, hyperlinks to other pages or places, and each displays this information in an easy-to-read format, much like a word processor.

As you learned in Lesson 13, "Navigating the Web," all Web page browsers have common areas. Buttons and toolbars are the most common features that you will use when exploring the Web. Luckily, each browser uses these features, so knowing the basics of one will assist you in knowing them all.

Figures 14.1 and 14.2 show the differences between the Netscape Navigator and Internet Explorer interfaces. Both figures display the full range of features available for both browsers. You can, however, customize them both to change their look and feel.

Figure 14.1.

Microsoft Internet Explorer's toolbar.

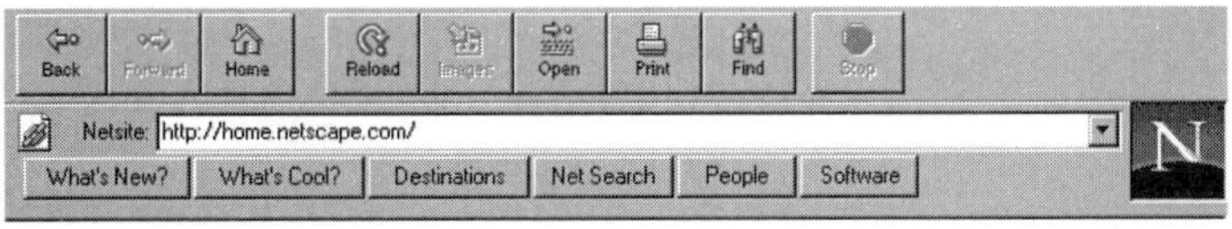

Figure 14.2.

Netscape Navigator's toolbar.

COFFEE BREAK

A Brief History of Time

Netscape and Microsoft were not always the *de facto* standards of the Internet. The Web took off only about four years ago, and at that time only one browser—named Mosaic and available for free—was in use. Mosaic was written by Marc Andreessen, who went into business for himself making a new browser called Netscape.

Just two years ago, 10 to 15 different browsers were on the market, all free, all vying for supremacy. Netscape's innovations, customer service, and timely upgrades helped it reign supreme.

Microsoft got into the game late but brought its resolve (and huge cash reserves) to the marketplace to impose its standards. The story isn't over as these two companies are locked in a battle to have the best browser or, more likely, to achieve the largest market share.

14

Where to Go and How to Get There

In the preceding lesson, you learned that you can make permanent records of sites you've visited so that you can return to them later. Both of the browsers reviewed in this lesson have extensive bookmarking features. Although both of them contain this feature, they both handle bookmarks slightly differently. I cover this aspect of both features in greater detail later in the lesson.

Safe and Secure

One feature that browsers use to attract corporate customers is their ability to safely send credit card numbers and financial information transmitted over the Internet. These browsers guarantee this capability by encrypting—scrambling the contents—of Web pages.

Encrypting is a big boon to businesses who want a safe way to get your money for their products in the most convenient way possible. Of course, this capability sets up a system by which companies with Internet content, Web pages and the like, can charge *micropayment* fees for your use and purchase of their products over the Internet. Both Netscape Navigator and Internet Explorer offer secure environments for these transactions to take place.

NEW TERM **Micropayments:** Micropayments are a method by which companies can keep an "electronic charge account" for you. Micropayments offer an affordable way to charge anywhere from one cent to one-hundredth of a cent as payment for services or products offered over the Internet.

When Browsers Need Help

Web browsers can't "do it all" when it comes to viewing movies, listening to radio broadcasts, decompressing downloaded files, and providing interactive content. To assist in these activities, they employ plug-ins and helper applications (see Lesson 15, "Helping Your Browser with Plug-Ins," for more details).

JUST A MINUTE

In the early days of Web browsers, helper applications were needed for just about everything, but both Netscape and Internet Explorer are adding these features as plug-ins, which are internal browser applications that handle many features that used to be "farmed out" to external helper applications.

14

Collaboration Across the Office or Across Country

Both Netscape and Internet Explorer include tools that enable you to collaborate with others across the Internet. They also offer text-based chat modules such as Internet Relay Chat (IRC) for group discussions. Also included with both browsers are Internet phone capabilities, which enable you to place telephone calls over the Internet.

JUST A MINUTE

> The thought of using the Internet for long-distance calls is attractive, especially now that connection fees are much lower than long-distance fees. The downside is that both participants must be using the same browser and be online at the same time. Netscape claims answering machine capabilities, and Internet Explorer won't be far behind.

Mail and News Tools

Both Netscape and Internet Explorer have e-mail and Usenet news clients; Figure 14.3 shows an example. Although you can use these tools, you may find that you want to use more full-featured clients if you spend a lot of time using e-mail or newsgroups. For more information on clients you can use for e-mail and news, refer to Lessons 6, "Person-to-Person Communication with E-Mail," and 10, "Getting the Scoop: Using Newsgroups," as well as Appendixes B and C for Windows and the Macintosh.

Figure 14.3.

Netscape offers a basic e-mail client, as does Internet Explorer.

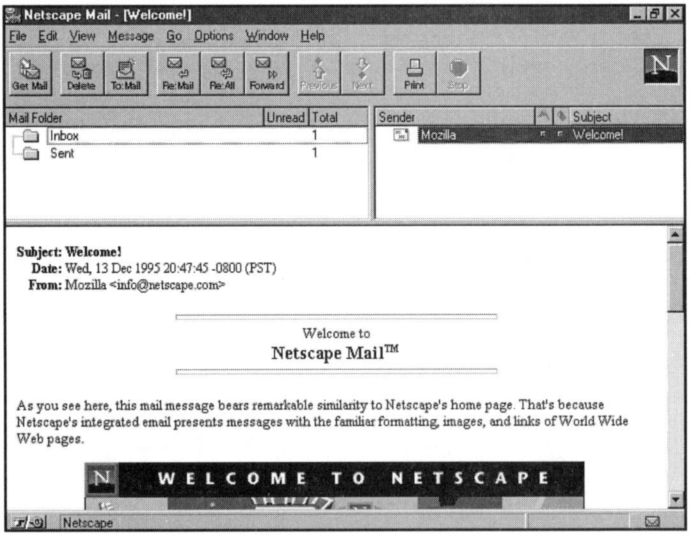

Netscape Mail - [Welcome!]

File   Edit   View   Message   Go   Options   Window   Help

Get Mail | Delete | To:Mail | Re:Mail | Re:All | Forward | Previous | Next | Print | Stop

Mail Folder	Unread	Total	Sender	Subject
Inbox		1	Mozilla	Welcome!
Sent		1		

Subject: Welcome!
  Date: Wed, 13 Dec 1995 20:47:45 -0800 (PST)
  From: Mozilla <info@netscape.com>

Welcome to
Netscape Mail™

As you see here, this mail message bears remarkable similarity to Netscape's home page. That's because Netscape's integrated email presents messages with the familiar formatting, images, and links of World Wide Web pages.

WELCOME TO NETSCAPE

Netscape

Current Netscape Features

Netscape is the current browser of choice by a two-to-one margin in relation to all the other Web browsers available. This use is due to many factors, not the least of which is the fact that Netscape was the first truly full-featured Web browser available to the public.

Theoretically, the Web is based on open standards, but because many Webmasters want their sites to look good on the popular browsers, they often use Netscape's special programming extensions to make their sites more attractive. As a result, other companies have had to clone Netscape's capabilities so that they can compete.

Netscape, unlike Internet Explorer, is free only to students, libraries, and nonprofit organizations. Those people who do use it under the "free" license are not offered any technical support. Although you can use Netscape on a trial basis, you must eventually purchase it.

TIME SAVER

Depending on who your Internet service provider is, you don't always have to pay for Netscape. Your Internet service provider may give you Netscape as part of its service package. Bell South, Sprint, America Online, CompuServe, and AT&T all provide Netscape free of charge. You can even call them for technical support.

Netscape Calls Them Bookmarks

I've already told you about ways that browsers keep track of places you've been. With Netscape Navigator, you use bookmarks, as shown in Figure 14.4, to revisit Web sites. Using Navigator, you can access bookmarks by clicking the Bookmark menu and then clicking where you want to go.

Netscape stores these bookmarks in a file that you can then use in other ways. You can customize it to have separate folders for specific topics, and you can export the list for other Internet-savvy programs to use. Navigator bookmarks are also easy to edit, change, and delete.

14

Figure 14.4.

In addition to using the Bookmarks menu, Netscape also enables you to open an editable window of your book-marks.

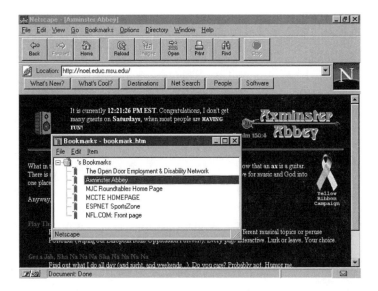

More Netscape Features

Netscape has many more features that make it a powerful and useful browser. Here are a few more:

☐ In-Box Direct is a feature that expands the capability to receive interactive Web pages—including pictures, video, audio, and more—that can be received and viewed in an e-mail message.

☐ Netscape automatically adds the `http://www.` and `.com` in an address so that you have to type in only a single word to access that site (but make sure it's the right word). If you type `cnn` in the Location: field, for example, Netscape automatically takes you to `http://www.netscape.com`.

☐ A fully configurable interface and feature set is one of Netscape's strongest points. You can decide for yourself how you want to use it and what features you want to use. You can also customize the look of the Netscape screen to make a comfortable browsing environment.

14

JUST A MINUTE

Currently, Netscape finds only addresses that begin with www and end in com. For addresses that begin and end differently, you still need to type them in manually.

The Future

The race for the best browser seems to be a race of features and usability. Even Netscape admits it can be outdone. Microsoft's ActiveX technology, which is discussed in the next section, for example, is currently scheduled for a future version of Netscape.

Also up and coming is the ability to perform audio conferences with multiple participants. Voicemail, too, is on Netscape's agenda, along with chat functions that are usually associated with the IRC. Of course, another common trend for both browsers is a continued increase in interactive capability.

Current Internet Explorer Features

Microsoft's Internet Explorer was a late arrival to the browser world. As a result, Microsoft cloned Netscape rather than fighting the established standard. And clone Netscape it did because most pages made for Netscape look virtually identical in Internet Explorer. Even though Internet Explorer is playing catch-up with Netscape, Microsoft will be a force in the browser market.

Internet Explorer tries its best to make you feel comfortable if you're converting from Netscape. You can change Explorer's interface to match Netscape's almost button for button if you want.

Microsoft Calls Them Favorites

What Netscape calls bookmarks, Internet Explorer calls *favorites*. Explorer's favorites work much like Netscape's bookmarks in that you can access them through the Favorites menu as well as opening a window that enables you to edit, organize, and delete your favorites, as shown in Figure 14.5.

14

Figure 14.5.

Internet Explorer uses
favorites, which are easy
to customize and edit to
suit your needs.

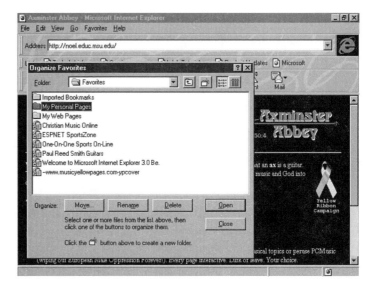

More Internet Explorer Features

Like Netscape, Internet Explorer has many other features that make it convenient and easy to use. Here is a list of some of them:

☐ The most notable aspect of Internet Explorer is its price—free. You can download it right off the Microsoft home page free of charge. Remember, though, that there is something to be said about software that is free: You get what you pay for. Internet Explorer comes with no customer support.

☐ Completely unaddressed by Netscape is Internet Explorer's capability to increase or decrease the size of the text in the viewer with the click of a button. This feature is great if you're trying to read the fine print of some page or you want larger letters to reduce eye strain.

☐ Internet Explorer is much smaller and takes up less memory than does Netscape Navigator. This feature can be a big advantage to users who do not have 16MB of RAM on their computers.

☐ ActiveX is Microsoft's answer to Netscape's plug-ins. ActiveX components act like plug-ins, but Microsoft claims they are more dynamic because you can download

14

them along with the page that uses them. ActiveX differs from plug-ins by being able to represent an application interface, like a spreadsheet or database, right in the browser window.

The Future

Compared to Netscape, Internet Explorer may soon seem like a whole new product because it will be tightly integrated into the Windows 95 operating system (beginning with version 4.0) to a point that you can't tell where one starts and the other ends. Of course, this will be a problem for Macintosh users.

This transformation will begin when you are able to view files and folders on your system's hard disk as hypertext. The new HyperText option will make every window look like a Web page. The names of files and folders will be in hypertext; you simply click the underlined name to open that item.

Finally, another coming feature called WebCheck will monitor Web pages in your Favorites folder or on your desktop and automatically notify you of changes to those pages.

Same Site, Different Browsers: Some Examples

So, is a browser a browser or is one superior to the other? The answer depends on where you point that browser. Most content on the Internet is relatively neutral in regard to which browser views it. Of the browser-specific content out there, however, most of it is still directed toward Netscape, even though a significant amount is geared toward Internet Explorer's capabilities. The best way to determine which browser is best is by looking at two sites that push the browsers to their limits.

Netscape's Winning Features

As an example of Netscape's winning features, the object shown in Figure 14.6 is a three-dimensional image that can be rotated and viewed from all sides. Imagine walking through a supermarket on the Internet and being able to pick up items and look at them from all angles!

14

Figure 14.6.

*This site is Netscape-
centric.*

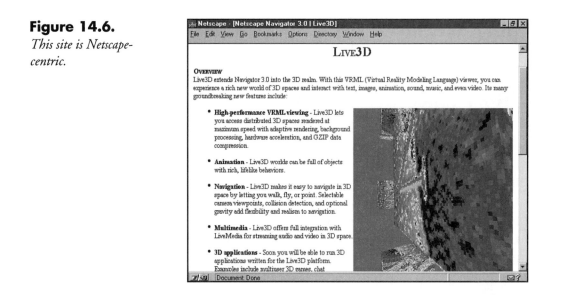

Internet Explorer does a fine job of showing regular text, but notice that the object in Figure
14.7 is in a separate window, not in the page like Netscape. You lose the effect of the Web
page if the objects aren't located within it.

Figure 14.7.

*This example shows the
same site as Figure 14.6
but using Internet
Explorer. Big difference.*

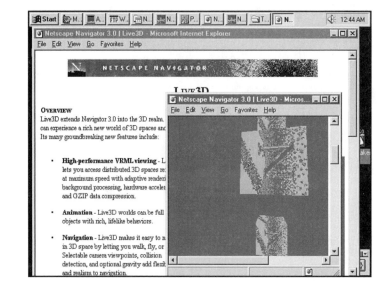

14

Internet Explorer's Winning Features

To be fair, Internet Explorer displays some sites much better than Netscape. Look at Figures 14.8 and 14.9 for an example. The site shown in Figure 14.8 uses ActiveX to achieve what I described earlier as an application interface. That is, it looks like an actual spreadsheet. You can move the scroll bars, and the new calculations are made instantly, changing the graph on the fly.

Figure 14.8.

This site is Internet Explorer-centric. Notice all the areas where you can enter data; using this site is just like using a calculator!

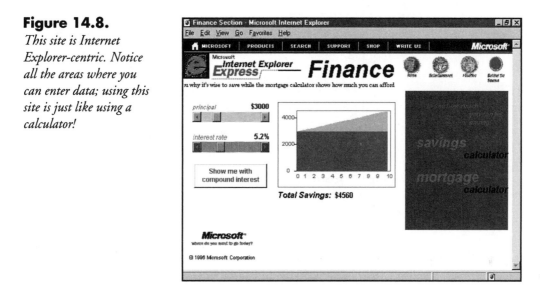

The current iteration of Netscape doesn't do ActiveX at all, so in Figure 14.9 you can see the blank space and what looks like random characters in the shaded box. Netscape has said that future versions of its software will include ActiveX support. Currently, you can buy a plug-in from Ncompass called Script Active that does allow Netscape to view ActiveX elements. (Go to http://www.ncompasslabs.com/products/scriptactive.htm for a free evaluation copy.)

14

Figure 14.9.

This figure shows the same site as in Figure 14.8, but through Netscape's eyes. Not so interactive, is it?

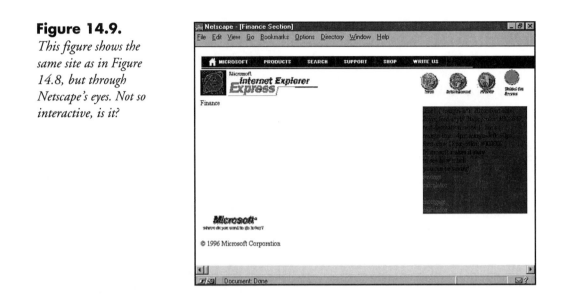

The examples shown in this section are sites designed for specific browsers. Keep in mind, though, that their similarities far outweigh their differences. Ordinary daily use of either browser should produce satisfactory results.

Get 'Em While They're Hot: What Version to Use

The problem with the breakneck speed at which software companies must bring out upgrades is that software still has many bugs. When you're deciding when and how far to upgrade your browser, you should be cautious.

CAUTION

In the software industry, you may hear of a universal warning about version numbers that end in a .0 or contain an a or b (which stands for alpha and beta versions, respectively). These versions sometimes have incompatibilities, bugs, and performance issues that have not been addressed. Waiting until the .01 or .1 versions appear before upgrading is often wise.

14

Getting the newest version isn't always in your best interest because the product may not have been fully tested. One of the qualities that makes an older version of software attractive is its user-tested stability. When you're dealing with Internet browsers—and software in general—like wine, there is something to be said about vintage and maturity. When you're ready to upgrade, the best way to find out about new versions is to check the Netscape or Microsoft home page regularly.

Less Filling, Tastes Great

Older versions of browser software may not have all the bells and whistles that newer versions have, but they are usually smaller and use less memory. Netscape Navigator 3.0, for example, requires almost twice as much memory to run as 2.0 does. You should keep this factor in mind.

Do you really need to view the movies on the MTV site? If your computer is an older model, viewing movies may not even be an option, so don't bother with features you can't use. The newer browsers are primarily directed at the latest version of system software and memory requirements that run your computer.

JUST A MINUTE

> The future of browsers is already upon us. Version 4 of both browsers will probably be available when you read this book, and planning for versions 5 and 6 is already under way. Do these people ever sleep?

Summary

In this lesson, I took you through a quick tour of Netscape Navigator and Microsoft Internet Explorer. You learned the basics of browsers, as well as their similarities and differences. Despite their many differences, you discovered that the two don't contrast greatly. Each browser has an integrated e-mail and newsgroup client and the capabilities to show movies, play sounds, and even make calls around the block or around the world. The biggest single difference is probably the price. The browser you choose depends on how many features you want and how much memory your computer has.

14

Workshop

The following workshop helps solidify the skills that you learned in this lesson.

Q&A

Q I'm interested in speed. Which one is faster: Netscape Navigator or Internet Explorer?

A Both, depending on whom you ask. Netscape and Microsoft have "documented" evidence that their browser is much faster than the other. Really, telling which is fastest is not easy when you take into account the type of machine you have, the RAM and hard disk size, and the speed at which you connect to the Internet. Get out that stopwatch and try them both.

Q If both browsers are so similar, which one should I use?

A The answer depends on what you want to use the browser for. Are you using it to access a specific Netscape-centric Web site? Or did your computer come bundled with all the Microsoft applications you could ever want, including Internet Explorer? Really, the best thing to do is try them both and see which one fits into your routine. Ask your friends and coworkers which one they use and why. Ultimately, your choice is a matter of personal taste.

Quiz

Take the following quiz to see how much you've learned.

Questions

1. Which feature is not available in both browsers?
   (a) ActiveX technology
   (b) The ability to keep a permanent record of visited sites
   (c) A customizable interface
2. Which browser has an integrated e-mail and newsgroup reader?
   (a) Netscape
   (b) Internet Explorer
   (c) Both

14

3. What functions are not included with Netscape and Internet Explorer today? The ability to

   (a) Telephone a friend in Bombay

   (b) Work with others simultaneously across the Internet

   (c) Use voice mail

Answers

1. (a) Currently, only Internet Explorer offers this feature.

2. (c) Both

3. (c) This feature will be included in the next version of both programs.

Activity

If you have downloaded either Netscape Navigator or Internet Explorer version 3.0 or later, have a little fun by going to the Virtual City repository located at `http://www.vir.com/~farid/ctrepos.htm`. Cruise through some of the countries and cities listed to get an idea of what the virtual world is like as seen through the eyes of a Web browser. To look for even more 3-D worlds, go to `http://webspace.cgi.com/intro.html`.

14

Hour 15

Helping Your Browser with Plug-Ins

Most browsers are designed to display text and graphics with generally no problems. What about the new technology, however, and third-party software manufacturers that want their wares to be visible and usable on the World Wide Web? Here, the world of plug-ins begins.

In this lesson, you find the answers to some of the more basic questions about plug-ins, such as the following:

- ☐ Where do I find plug-ins?
- ☐ How do I install plug-ins?
- ☐ Do plug-ins work with my browser?
- ☐ Which plug-ins are "necessities"?

CAUTION

Before delving too far into the hows and wheres of plug-ins, I want to add my personal caution to downloading in general. When you download a program—any program—you are taking the chance of unleashing a potentially harmful virus or malice application. Please be careful when downloading files. Download only from reputable sources that can be trusted. Netscape, Microsoft, and other such vendors are safe havens for obtaining software via the Internet. If at all possible, only download the original files from the original vendor's site. With that little note, let's learn more about plug-ins.

What Are Plug-Ins and How Do They Work?

Start with a quick review. Your Web browser can display only three file types: text, GIF, and JPEG. The text category includes plain text files and HTML (Hypertext Markup Language) documents. GIF (Graphics Interchange Format) and JPEG (Joint Photographic Experts Group) are graphical formats for images and backgrounds. So, before plug-ins, almost everything you could view in a browser was in one of these three formats.

JUST A MINUTE

By default, a traditional browser can display only three file types: text, GIF images, and JPEG images. Through the use of plug-ins, you can increase that number immensely.

It follows that the basic function of a plug-in is to enable you to view a file type other than text, GIF, or JPEG. Instead of redesigning, reengineering, and redistributing browsers for each new file type, software developers have developed plug-ins for use with the most popular browsers. This way, applications or files developed with their applications can be used on the Internet.

Okay, so plug-ins are a good idea, but what are they? Well, a plug-in is typically a small program or file that is loaded into your Web browser when it is launched. Most plug-in–capable browsers have a plug-ins folder in their application directory. The browser looks to this folder when it is being launched to find any plug-ins that it can load for use. The minimum version for plug-in support for Netscape Navigator is 2.0; for Microsoft's Internet Explorer, it is 3.0.

15

15

These plug-ins may not be apparent to you until you encounter an *enhanced Web page.* In this case, the plug-in works with the browser to display the embedded audio, video, or whatever the developer has added to the site.

NEW TERM **Enhanced Web page:** An enhanced Web page includes a file type that is viewable within a browser that is loaded with the proper plug-in.

Before the advent of plug-ins, you had to rely on the applications loaded on your hard drive to view certain material. If you wanted to download and view a Word document, you had to have Microsoft Word on your machine. Table 15.1 shows some basic helper applications and what file type they are used to view.

Table 15.1. Examples of helper applications.

Application	Use
Microsoft Word	Viewing Word documents
Microsoft Excel	Viewing Excel spreadsheets
Microsoft Powerpoint	Viewing Powerpoint presentations
MS Paint	Viewing bitmap images
WinZip	Decompressing downloaded files

The use of plug-ins has released the need to have certain applications on your machine. The Microsoft Word plug-in now allows your browser to display the Word document. Other plug-ins expand this further by allowing the user to edit, save, and upload a file right in the browser itself. You can see how much time and money this work can save. By not requiring the application to launch and load each working document, the user works directly in the web browser. By not loading each computer with the barrage of applications, the company saves money and valuable hard drive space.

Installation Basics

Typically, your browser creates a plug-in directory when it is installed on your machine. If you're using Netscape, for example, you can find the directory on your hard drive in the Netscape folder. Here's where the directory is located, based on the type of operating system you are using:

Win95/NT `C:/Program Files/Netscape/Navigator/Program/plugins/`

Win31 `C:/Netscape/plugins`

Mac In the Netscape folder `labeled Plug-ins`

Most plug-ins will be installed into this directory. The whole process is normally very simple. You can generally install a plug-in in one of three ways:

☐ You download the zipped (compressed) file. After expanding it, you move the files to the correct directories.

☐ You download the plug-in file itself and place it in your browser's plug-in directory.

☐ You download a self-installing executable and run the file. Running the executable automatically places the files in your plug-in directory.

Most sites include good directions for installing their plug-ins. Be sure to read these instructions for possible incompatibilities or special system requirements.

Are Plug-Ins Practical?

Should you rush out and install every plug-in that's available on the Web? No. Doing so would be a terrible waste of time and disk space. A good rule of thumb is that you install a plug-in when you encounter a Web site that is advertising its pages as enhanced for use with a specific plug-in or you have a general need for the added functionality a plug-in offers. You can use a plug-in, for example, to listen to ABC news reports from your laptop, as in Figure 15.1.

Figure 15.1.

Listening to ABC news via the RealAudio plug-in.

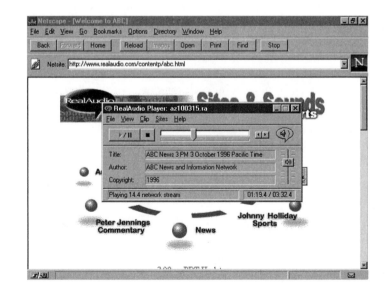

15

At Netscape's Web site (http://home.netscape.com/comprod/products/navigator/version_2.0/plugins/) at the time of this writing, 102 plug-ins were available for downloading from their Inline Plug-ins site for use with their Navigator browser. Add these plug-ins to the scores of sites using ActiveX technology for use with Microsoft's Internet Explorer, and you've got yourself a whole lot of possible downloads.

A plug-in also can make your browser into a viewer. As a viewer, it cannot make any changes to the file; it can only display the file for you. This capability leads to a very economical situation for some groups. Instead of loading Microsoft Office onto everyone's machine, for example, now you can install the plug-ins only for people who don't use the applications for more than reading the online files.

Netscape's and Microsoft's approaches to the plug-in world are to configure their respective browsers to react to different file types. Each of these browsers can alert you when you begin to download a Web page that requires a particular plug-in that you don't have installed on your machine. The alert, like the one shown in Figure 15.2, presents you with the option of going to a site to download and install the needed plug-in.

Figure 15.2.

A browser's alert that you need a plug-in to view this site.

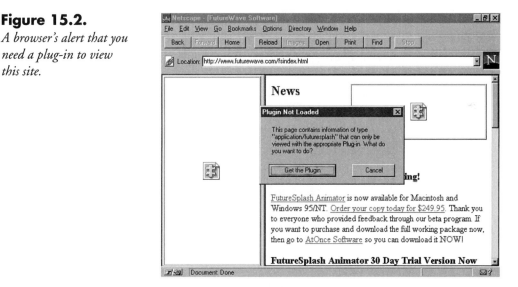

In Microsoft's case, the site displays a security certificate verifying that this site is authorized to distribute the plug-in. This certificate also serves as protection to your system because installing a file from the Internet always leaves the opportunity for a malicious program to infect your hard drive. If you decide to accept the certificate, the plug-in is automatically downloaded and placed in the appropriate location on your hard drive. The process doesn't get much easier than that.

RealAudio, Real-Time

As I stated earlier, one reason to install a plug-in is to be able to listen to news reports from your laptop. The RealAudio plug-in (http://www.realaudio.com) from Progressive Networks delivers "Audio on Demand." It delivers streaming, CD-quality audio to your computer via the Internet.

NEW TERM **Streaming:** Streaming audio means that the clip begins playing as soon as the file download begins. You therefore don't have to wait for the entire file to download before you can hear it.

Download and Install

The RealAudio Player is offered in a couple different forms. The basic player plug-in is available for free downloading. Another version of this plug-in, Player Plus, offers increased sound capabilities and more user features. Here, I describe the installation of the free plug-in, but the procedure should be the same for both of them.

To Do: Download and Install the RealAudio Player

1. From the RealAudio Web site (www.realaudio.com), choose Download RealAudio 3.0 or go directly to the download site (www.realaudio.com/hpproducts/player/download.html).

2. To install the free plug-in, click the Download Now link on the right side of the screen, as shown in Figure 15.3.

Figure 15.3.

Choose the free RealAudio Player or purchase the RealAudio Player Plus.

15

3. Select the plug-in version, your operating system, and fill in your name and e-mail address. Select the checkbox if you would like to receive updates on RealAudio software. Click the button at the bottom of the form to submit the information.

4. You're presented with the download sites for the plug-in. Choose the location nearest you for better results, saving the file to a location on your hard drive.

5. Run the installation program that you just downloaded. The installer (named ra32_3 or similar) restarts your browser and sends you to the RealAudio Web site. At this point, you're ready to visit sites using RealAudio technology.

CAUTION

If you're working within a company firewall, the port that RealAudio uses may not be available. You should check with your system administrator to see if this port is open. Because RealAudio uses a nonstandard port on the Web server, some companies may view it as a security risk.

ABC News via RealAudio

One of the best sites displaying the RealAudio technology is the ABC News Reports site (www.realaudio.com/comtentp/abc.html). Updated hourly, the same news used by the television and radio stations is broadcast from the web site.

Users can hear Peter Jennings as he delivers his daily commentary on global and national matters, listen to Johnny Holliday deliver his sports report, or hear the general news that is updated hourly. The archives of all three newscasts contain news feeds back to the beginning of the year.

Catch the Shockwave

Shockwave by Macromedia (www.macromedia.com) captures the power of Macromedia's suite of tools—Director, FreeHand, and Authorware—and delivers it over the Internet. Director, a professional presentation application, is used by graphic artists and visual production companies. FreeHand is a powerful graphic artist's tool kit, and Authorware is the world's leading authoring tool for interactive information.

Macromedia recently released a new collection of plug-ins: Shockwave Deluxe. The Deluxe version contains the plug-ins for Director, Authorware, FreeHand, and SoundEdit 16. SoundEdit 16 is a powerful digital audio application used to develop soundtracks for various platforms—from movies to CD-ROM games to Internet Web sites.

Most of the big names in multimedia have developed Web sites using Shockwave technology. These "Shocked" sites include Disney, Sony, MCI, Paramount, and hundreds more. Let's take a few minutes and run through the procedure for bringing your machine up-to-speed with Shockwave.

To Do: Install the Shockwave Plug-In

1. Click the Get Shockwave button on the Macromedia Web site (www.macromedia.com), as shown in Figure 15.4, or go directly to the Shockwave download area (www.macromedia.com/shockwave/download/).

Figure 15.4.

On Macromedia's Web site, click the Get Shockwave button to install the plug-in.

Get Shockwave Button

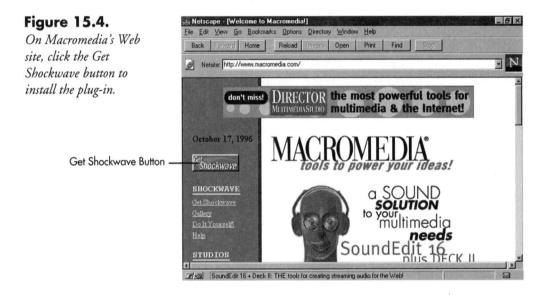

JUST A MINUTE

The Shockwave installation program comes in two flavors: Shockwave and Shockwave Deluxe. The original Shockwave package includes the plug-ins for Director and SoundEdit16. The new Shockwave Deluxe package contains plug-ins for Director, SoundEdit16, Authorware, and FreeHand.

2. Fill in your personal information if you want to receive e-mail regarding information on Shockwave. This information is optional and will not limit you from using the software.

3. Select your operating system and language. Select the flavor of the package you want: Shockwave or Shockwave Deluxe. Click the final Get Shockwave button.

15

4. The location of the installation program appears as a link labeled Download NOW!. Clicking this link begins the download process. A window may appear asking you where to save the file; choose a location on your hard drive.

5. Locate the install program (`n32z0007.exe` or similar) on your hard drive and run it. You are prompted to select the browser and location to install plug-in files. When the installation completes, restart your browser.

Now you're ready to view some example of using Shockwave on the Internet. Let's try out your new plug-ins on Macromedia's SSotD. That's Shocked Site of the Day for the uninitiated.

Shocked Site of the Day

I thought the Macromedia site was cool, but some people actually use it to do more than make buttons flash. Entire arcade style games use Shockwave. Why not take a quick trip?

Now that you have your browser armed to handle the Shockwave files, look at some examples. The best place to start is the Macromedia Web site. On it, you can find examples of Macromedia's own work, as well as links to all sorts of sites using Shockwave technology.

In the Shockwave Gallery is a collection of sites that range from educational to mass media. Companies from CNN to Apple are in the spotlight as major Web sites featuring the Shockwave plug-in. Also check out the Shocked Site of the Day. These sites include full arcade-style games using Shockwave technology to deliver outstanding sound and graphics.

Overview of Other Plug-Ins

As I mentioned earlier, Netscape records more than 102 plug-ins available for use with its browser. I can't list all of them, but I can give you a slight tasting of some of the features that await. Remember, check out the Netscape Plug-in page for the complete list (`http://home.netscape.com/comprod/products/navigator/version_2.0/plugins/`).

Bubbleviewer

If you get tired of looking at the same flat graphics on a Web site, check out the Bubbleviewer plug-in by Omnivision (`www.omnivision.com`). With the Bubbleviewer plug-in, your browser can display 360-degree, spherical photographs called PhotoBubbles. You're placed at the center of a 360-degree experience. You can zoom in and out, and you can look left, right, up, and down in 360-degrees of freedom.

Saab and Toyota are just a few of the Web sites using PhotoBubbles. Also, be sure to visit the Philadelphia Museum of Art. Go to the Omnivision Web site for a complete list of sites featuring PhotoBubble technology.

Live3D

The Live3D plug-in (`http://home.netscape.com/comprod/products/navigator/live3d/index.html`) is part of the standard installation of Netscape Navigator 3.0 for Windows 95 and Windows NT. Because it is preloaded, you can instantly visit sites using Virtual Reality Modeling Language (VRML) technology. You can walk through gardens, for example, or test drive a new car.

FutureSplash

You can design Web sites with small, fast, vector-based animations and multimedia screens with the FutureSplash Animator by FutureWave Software (`www.futurewave.com`). The FutureSplash Animator could be considered the common man's Macromedia Director. It isn't nearly as powerful, but it gives great results in a short amount of time. At the time of this writing, a trial copy of the FutureSplash Animator was available at the FutureWave Web site.

The hit TV show *The Simpsons* now has an official page on the Fox Network site (`www.foxworld.com/simpsons/simpsons.htm`). The developers of this site used the FutureSplash Animator to design interactive buttons and screens of animation of Bart, Lisa, and Homer. Take a look at this site after you install the FutureSplash plug-in.

KeyView

The mother of all plug-ins has to be KeyView (`http://www.ftp.com/mkt_info/keyv2.html`) by FTP Software. It slices. It dices. This little wonder delivers more than 200 file formats to your browser's window. KeyView is cross-platform capable, displaying both Macintosh and Windows files. You can use KeyView as a Netscape plug-in or by itself to perform everyday operations such as print, convert, copy, and compress from one file format to another.

15

Summary

In this lesson, you learned the basics of adding functionality to your Internet browser by using plug-ins. With plug-ins, you can use your browser to view files that you cannot view normally. Launching a helper application is no longer necessary. Some plug-ins can work as viewers, relieving the requirement to have the full application present on the machine. Some browsers have been developed to prompt you to install a needed plug-in.

Some of the best multimedia Web sites are making full use of the capabilities of plug-ins. These enhanced sites provide audio, video, and VRML worlds that you can view and enjoy right within the browser window.

Workshop

The following workshop helps solidify the skills that you learned in this lesson.

Q&A

Q How can I make enhanced Web pages?

A Most of the third-party software companies provide their plug-ins for free use. They do so because you have to purchase their applications to create the files to use on your Web site. To use RealAudio on your site, for example, you have to purchase the RealAudio Encoder software.

Q Do I have to pay for these plug-ins?

A Well, the answer to this question depends on the plug-in. Some are free because they only display proprietary files made with an application you have to purchase. Others are shareware that you can try before you buy them.

Q Can I remove plug-ins?

A Yes. Look for the plug-in in the Plug-ins folder in your browser's directory. Delete or move the file, and your browser will not load the plug-in. Some plug-ins are even listed in the Add/Remove Software section in Windows 95.

Q Do I need a different plug-in for every file type?

A Yes and no. Some plug-ins, such as KeyView, display many different file types. Some applications, however, develop files that you can view only with custom plug-ins. In this case, you need to install the appropriate plug-ins to view these files.

Quiz

Take the following quiz to see how much you've learned.

Questions

1. Plug-ins launch the external application on your machine.
    (a) True
    (b) False

2. In what form do plug-ins download?
    (a) Zipped (compressed)
    (b) Executable
    (c) Single file
    (d) All the above

3. How do you know you need a plug-in to view a site?
    (a) The browser warns you with an alert message.
    (b) The browser crashes.
    (c) You can't see the site at all.

Answers

1. (b) False. Plug-ins use the browser to access the files. The full application does not have to be installed on your computer.

2. (d) A plug-in can be in any form—zipped, as an executable installation program, or a single file.

3. (a) Your browser notifies you that the site you are about to visit requires a plug-in. You are given the option of downloading the plug-in.

Activities

Go to the RealAudio site and install the RealAudio plug-in. Listen to the nightly news report from the ABC RealAudio page or hear a program from National Public Radio. See if any of your local stations support RealAudio on their Web sites.

Download the Shockwave plug-in for your machine and visit the Macromedia Shocked Site of the Week. Play one of the Shocked games with a member of your family or a friend.

15

Hour 16

Searching the Web for Virtually Anything

You now know enough to realize that you cannot possibly locate everything you want and need by simply surfing the Web. You need some sophisticated tools to help you sift through the billions of Web pages and other available resources.

Fortunately, many of these tools are available for free, and they're right at your fingertips. In this lesson, I show you how to search for virtually anything using the best tools available.

When you're done with this lesson, you'll know the answers to these questions:

- ☐ What are the basic search concepts I need to know?
- ☐ How do I conduct searches using Yahoo! and Excite?
- ☐ What are other search engines I can use?
- ☐ What do I use if I want to search newsgroups?

No matter what browser you're using, all these sites are available to you.

Searching Basics

When you're using a search engine on the Web, several concepts and techniques are almost universal and don't vary a great deal from site to site. Before you look at some specific sites to search, perhaps you might find it helpful to know some of these basic elements.

Searching Options

No matter what search engine you use, you always follow the same basic steps: point your browser to the search site, find the field to enter your search term, and then click the search button. You may find some variation, of course, but you usually follow the same basic pattern. Figure 16.1 shows what a typical search site looks like.

Figure 16.1.

The Infoseek search site offers a typical search interface.

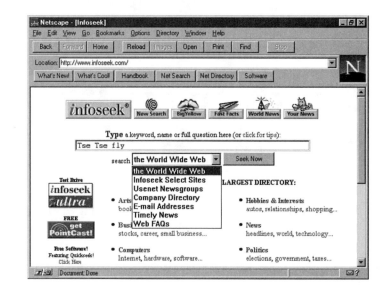

Most search engines now offer you a number of choices on how to conduct your search. The most common, as you can see in Figure 16.1, is a choice of where to search. Using Infoseek, located at http://www.infoseek.com, you can search the World Wide Web, Usenet newsgroups, FAQs, e-mail addresses, and more.

Most search engines now give you a choice of many different sources to search. In this lesson, I focus mainly on searching the Web, but feel free to try out some of the other options as well.

Keep in mind that this type of search is best when you're looking for a specific word, phrase, or other element.

The other option usually available to you is the choice of browsing through a directory by category. At Infoseek, you can browse directories on topics such as Art, Business, Sports, and Travel. Browsing categories can be effective when you're just looking for general information in a specific area but aren't looking for a specific result.

Framing Your Search

The search terms you use really determine your success. The words and *operators* you use to help you in your search can greatly improve or reduce the effectiveness of your searches.

NEW TERM   **Operators:** Operators are usually anything that modifies a term or equation. In the equation 2 + 2 = 4, the plus sign is an operator. When searching on the Web, you can often use special symbols or words to build a search "equation" that is often more effective than searching for a single word or phrase.

As with other elements within search engines, a fair amount of variability exists from one search site to another. Most search engines can make use of Boolean operators, which are designed to put conditions on a search. These operators, as well as a few other common operators and techniques, are listed here:

- ☐ AND or +: This Boolean operator requires that both terms be present to produce a hit. A search on cars AND mustangs (or cars +mustangs), for example, would likely rule out all hits on Mustang horses and produce only those results on Ford Mustang cars.

- ☐ OR: This Boolean operator accepts hits from either term. A search on mustangs OR cars, for example, would produce hits in which either term is present.

- ☐ AND NOT or -: This Boolean operator enables you to exclude a term specifically. As an example, mustangs AND NOT cars (or mustangs -cars) would require that only documents containing the word mustangs and not accompanied by cars would be produced as hits. In a sense, the AND NOT operator is the opposite of the AND operator.

JUST A MINUTE

Most search engines require that all Boolean operators be in all capital letters so that they can be distinguished from the search terms themselves.

☐ Case: Many search engines are also case sensitive. Here's some advice: If you're searching for a proper name, such as `Queen Victoria`, go ahead and capitalize the proper names; doing so may make for a better search.

☐ Real Language: Many search engines now can interpret real language searches. Searching for `learning how to speak Spanish`, for example, can often produce good results. The Excite search engine, which I talk about later in this lesson, allows such searches.

TIME SAVER

> Almost every search site has a `Help` or `Search Tips` link on its search page. In addition to general search advice, links take you to a page that outlines some specific techniques that work particularly well for the site. I highly recommend that you take the time to look at these links when going to a search site for the first time.

You also can define many other settings such as your real name and other personal information and how many articles to download at a time. As a rule, sticking with the settings that come preconfigured with your client is fairly safe.

Displaying Search Results

The last (and easiest) part of any search is displaying the results. In general, most search engines display the results similarly. The search results, also called *hits*, are generally displayed as a URL or Web page title followed by a description of the page or a snippet of actual text from the page.

Many search engines also put a percentage or other number next to each hit to indicate how strongly it matches your search term. At these search sites, the results are usually listed in order from strongest to weakest hits. In addition, most search engines display only between 10 and 25 hits per page but give you the option of viewing more pages of hits if you want. Figure 16.2 shows a typical search results page with all these elements.

Figure 16.2.

This page of search results is representative of what you will find throughout the Web.

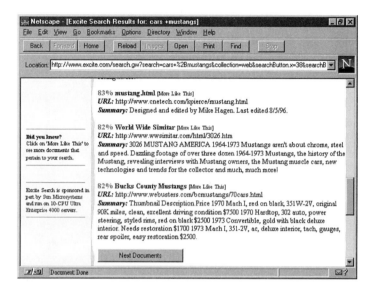

Using Yahoo! to Find Information

Yahoo!, the original Web search engine, is still going strong today. Started by David Filo and Jerry Yang when they were graduate students at Stanford University, Yahoo! contains hundreds of thousands of pages in its database. Like many other sites, it enables you to both search by term and browse by category. Yahoo! offers many unique options to people searching for information on the Web.

Searching for a Term

Although many people use Yahoo! to browse by category, it is an effective search engine by itself. Try a search now.

To Do: Searching for Terms

1. Go to the Yahoo! search site at `http://www.yahoo.com` and click the `options` link. You also can go directly to this page by pointing your browser to `http://www.yahoo.com/search.html`.

2. Type `Star Trek` in the keys field.

3. Choose to find only new listings added during the last month.

4. As your operators, select the All keys and Complete words options. This way, you can make sure that both words appear in documents found. Choosing these options also ensures that words such as "startled" aren't returned as hits.

5. Tell Yahoo! to display 10 listings per page. Your screen should look like Figure 16.3.

6. Click the Search button.

7. After a few seconds, the results will be displayed 10 at a time for you to look through.

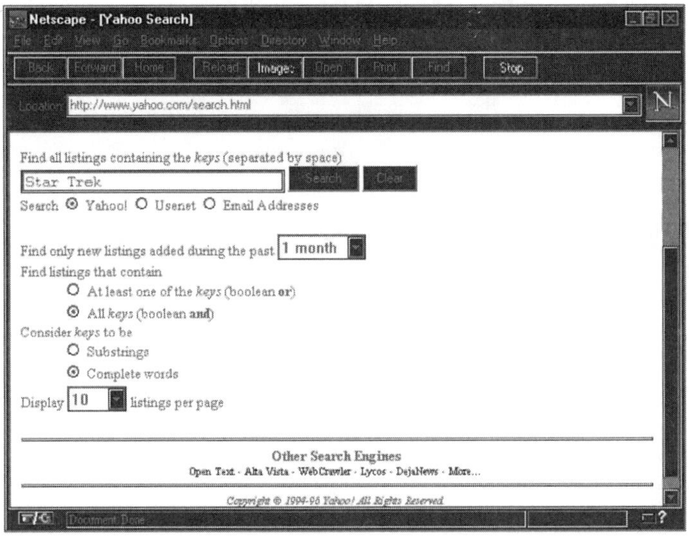

Figure 16.3.

You can search for Star Trek information using Yahoo!.

At the time this book was written, Yahoo! found 88 matches for Star Trek sites added in the last month. That's quite a few. Just for fun, you might repeat the search and ask that Yahoo! return all sites entered in the last three years just to see how much more information is available.

TIME SAVER

Yahoo! offers one very nice feature you should know about. If you scroll down to the bottom of a Yahoo! search results page, you see an Other Search Engines option, followed by links to several other search engines. If you click one of these links, Yahoo! automatically submits your latest term to the search site you clicked. Using this feature is an excellent way to search several sites at once.

Searching by Category

Yahoo! is probably even better known for its browsable categories than its capability to search by terms. Yahoo! is divided into 14 categories, which are then divided into subcategories. Obviously, if you're going to perform a search by category, you need to know which category your search belongs to. To compare a standard search with a category search, look for Star Trek again.

To Do: Searching by Category

1. Start at the Yahoo! search site by returning to http://www.yahoo.com and scroll down to Yahoo!'s listing of categories.

2. Because Star Trek is likely to be found under Entertainment, click that link. You then see a listing of each entertainment-related category Yahoo! has in its database.

3. At this point, you have two choices: Movies and Films or Television. Look for information on the television series by clicking Television. (Notice that you can conduct a standard search at any point during this process.)

4. Scroll down until you see the Shows link and then click it.

5. Because Star Trek was a science fiction show, click the Science Fiction/Fantasy/ Horror link.

6. If you scroll down, you see a Star Trek link. Click it to see all the listings under Star Trek, as shown in Figure 16.4.

Figure 16.4.

The Yahoo! Star Trek category has lots of links.

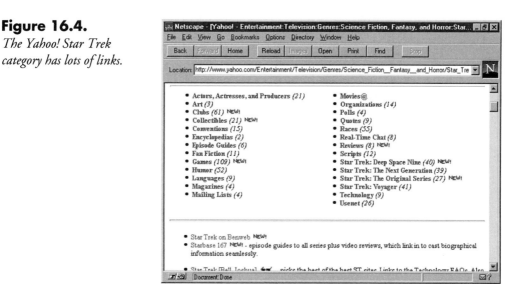

You may think that a category search may be more time-consuming to get somewhere than a standard search would be, but it really isn't. After you find Star Trek, you have a listing of only the pages you want to see. Remember that with a standard search, you have to view hits a few at a time and wade through dozens of sites before possibly finding the one you want.

Another major advantage in using Yahoo!'s category search database is that while you're searching for your subject, you can surf at the same time. While looking for Star Trek, for example, you might notice that you can view some Dr. Who Web pages.

TIME SAVER

When you're searching for a complicated category, such as computer training manuals, which category would you start with? Generally, try using the biggest category first. In this instance, you can probably find more information on computers than on training (Education) or manuals (Reference). So, try searching under the Computer category first.

Getting Excited

One of the best search sites available is Excite. Most of Excite's usefulness comes from its size and accuracy. Excite uses *Intelligent Concept Extraction* (ICE) to search over 50 million fully indexed Web pages. The ICE method allows for highly accurate searches based on real language searches, as well as more standard search types.

Excite claims to be the fastest, largest, most feature-rich, and accurate search engine on the Internet. My experience has been that this claim could very well be true. Excite searches are typically fast and almost always bring up hits that I can use.

One of Excite's best characteristics is its ease of use. Simply enter your search phrase, click Search, and you're off. If you point your browser to Excite at http://www.excite.com, for example, and conduct a standard search for Star AND Trek, Excite offers over 92,000 pages from which you can choose, as you can see in Figure 16.5.

In addition to the standard search, Excite also enables you to search for information by city through its City.Net service (http://city.net/), browse by category browsing through its ExciteSeeing Tours (http://tours.excite.com), and perform reference searches for maps, shareware, dictionaries, and more. It is truly a must-see search site.

Figure 16.5.

Excite produces several hits quickly from its large, searchable database.

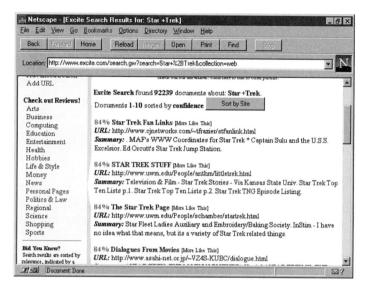

Examining the Best of the Rest

Dozens of search engines are available for you to choose from. Several of them offer unique advantages. DejaNews, a search engine for Usenet, is covered briefly here. Some other search engines, such as the Four11 directory of e-mail addresses, are covered in other lessons.

TIME SAVER

Even though all search engines try to be comprehensive, you can almost always find sites with one index that you wouldn't find with another. So if you search one index and don't find quite what you're looking for, try another and then another.

Though some people view the multiple "competing" indexes of the Internet as a waste of resources, experienced searchers are grateful for the multiple coverage. As the Web continues to grow exponentially, it seems ever more unlikely that any one procedure or program would ever be able to index it all successfully. But by the time you search three or four indexes on the same topic—and follow a few links to related sites—you'll have a very thorough picture of what's available.

DejaNews

DejaNews is the "official" Usenet search site. In my opinion, using DejaNews is without a doubt the best way to find information on Usenet. DejaNews offers a Quick Search when you're looking for articles on a particular topic. You can also conduct a Power Search, which helps you further refine your search to make it more effective. With DejaNews, you can even enter a topic you're interested in, and it provides you with a list of related newsgroups you might want to go to.

Continuing with the Star Trek theme, do a search for Spock on DejaNews.

To Do: Searching on DejaNews

1. Point your browser to DejaNews at `http://www.dejanews.com`.
2. Type `Spock` in the Quick Search field.
3. Click the Search button. You then see results similar to those pictured in Figure 16.6.

Figure 16.6.

That pointy-eared Vulcan is still alive and well on Usenet.

Inktomi's HotBot

Another search site that bears looking at is Inktomi's HotBot site (`http://www.hotbot.com`). Like Excite, HotBot has a very impressive index to search.

16

HotBot also has a unique search interface. A click to their Expert search page reveals a truly powerful and flexible search engine, as you can see in Figure 16.7. With Hot Bot, you can restrict your search by time, location, and domain. You can even search for a particular type of media.

Figure 16.7.

HotBot gives you many options to search.

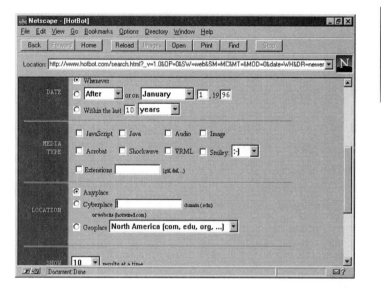

Search Site Grab Bag

Covering all the search engines available on the Internet would be impossible. As of this writing, over 250 search sites are already available. Table 16.1 lists some of the better search engines not covered in this lesson.

Table 16.1. Other search sites.

Site	Address
Infoseek	http://www.infoseek.com/
Alta Vista	http://www.altavista.digital.com/
Magellan	http://www.mckinley.com/
Lycos	http://www.lycos.com/
Open Text	http://www.opentext.com/
WebCrawler	http://www.webcrawler.com/

Also take a look at Table 16.2 for a listing of some other unique search sites.

Table 16.2. Unique search sites.

Search Site	Purpose	URL
shareware.com	Searches for shareware	`http://www.shareware.com/`
Four11	Searches e-mail addresses	`http://www.four11.com/`
MetaCrawler	Searches by geographic region	`http://metacrawler.cs.washington.edu/`

Summary

In this lesson, you learned a great deal about how to search on the Web. In addition to seeing examples of excellent search sites such as Yahoo!, Excite, DejaNews, and HotBot, you also learned how to search.

You learned how to use Boolean and other operators to help you in your search. You also discovered how to interpret search results, how to conduct a standard search, and how to browse a category directory. If you want to learn how to search even more resources, take a look at Lesson 20, "Finding People, Places and Things on the Net."

Workshop

The following workshop helps solidify the skills that you learned in this lesson.

Q&A

Q I am always being told that thousands of documents match my search query. How many of them do I really have to look at to find what I want?

A Certainly not thousands. If you have defined your search effectively, you can usually find what you're looking for in the first 20 to 30 hits. Rarely does a useful hit show up after the 50th hit or so.

16

Q **You're right, a lot of search sites are available. Can you recommend two or three that I should stick with?**

A This question is one that will get 10 different answers from 10 different people. I can tell you that I use Excite and Infoseek most. I usually can find what I'm looking for with Excite. It is fast, I don't have to wait a long time for results, and the hits are relevant. My advice to you is to try one of four or five different sites for a few days and then pick one or two that you're most comfortable with. Keep them all in mind, though, for those times when you might have to really dig deep to find what you're looking for.

16

Quiz

Take the following quiz to see how much you've learned.

Questions

1. A search for steak +knives would bring up which hit?

    (a) The Ancient Combat Knives Web Site

    (b) The On-Line Butcher Shop

    (c) Whackem N Hackem Steak Knives In Cyberspace

2. Web-based search sites are effective for searching much more than just the World Wide Web.

    (a) True

    (b) False

3. If you're searching for information on Harley Davidson motorcycles, which search would probably be the most effective?

    (a) Harley Davidson Motorcycles

    (b) motorcycles

    (c) Harley Davidson

Answers

1. (c) Whackem N Hackem Steak Knives In Cyberspace
2. (a) True. You can search newsgroups, look for people, and do much more.
3. (a) Harley Davidson Motorcycles

Activity

Because you will probably want to find the best search site you can, here's a way to do it. Pick something you want to look for. For best results, don't pick a one-word category like cars, but choose something more specific such as surfboard sales. From all the search sites in this lesson, choose five and conduct an identical search on each one. Make note of how many hits each site produces, how relevant these hits are, and how comfortable you are using each site.

PART
V

Finding Information on the Net

Hour

Hour 17

Getting Files with FTP

At this point, you've hit all the "big ones" —World Wide Web, e-mail, Usenet. Now you know what all the fuss has been about. But wait, you can still discover some lesser-known yet powerful tools. Next in line is File Transfer Protocol, or FTP. Using FTP is one of the most popular methods of obtaining software and documents on the Internet.

By the end of this lesson, you'll be able to answer the following questions about FTP:

- ☐ What is FTP and how does it work?
- ☐ How do I access FTP sites?
- ☐ How do I get around FTP sites to get what I want?
- ☐ What is the best way to get the files I want?
- ☐ How do I actually download files?

Using the two most popular Web browsers, Netscape and Internet Explorer (discussed in Lesson 14, "Netscape Versus Internet Explorer: Finding the Right Browser"), you can FTP files right from a browser window. For added functionality, however, you can obtain clients designed specifically for FTP (see Appendix B, "Shareware Products for Windows").

FTP in a Nutshell

File Transfer Protocol. The phrase may sound intimidating when you first hear it; however, it's really not. As you learned in Lesson 1, "The Internet: What's It Really Like?" a protocol is nothing more than a set of rules. Thus, FTP is nothing more than a set of rules for transferring files. Easy, eh?

But perhaps you want to know more about what FTP is like. Hang on—the following section is for you.

What Is FTP?

Imagine, if you will, a super-library—one with aisles of books, videos, CDs, power tools, and everything else imaginable. Furthermore, imagine that every time you check out a book or other resource, another one pops on the shelf to take its place. Now imagine no due dates, no library cards. Just browse and get what you want.

But don't stop there. Imagine further that you can contribute to the library yourself, providing materials that you have to offer for others, as well. FTP is pretty much like that. Among the many machines on the Internet are some that are dedicated to being electronic "libraries." Each library allows you to upload or download files of text, graphics, and software tools that you can read, view, and use on your home computer.

JUST A MINUTE

Unlike a library, some of the files available via FTP do cost a little. Files for which you pay some small fee are usually called *shareware* programs (as opposed to free software, called *freeware*). The authors of these programs "share" them for a small fee so that they can afford to write even more. Still other software authors put out limited use *demo* software to entice you to buy the complete product. Believe it or not, some of the best software in the world started out as freeware and shareware.

FTP is a fast, efficient, and reliable way to transfer information. It was one of the first Internet services developed to enable users to transfer files from one place to another. This service is designed to enable you to connect your *local* machine to a *remote* computer on the Internet, browse through the files and programs that are available on the computer, and then retrieve those files to your computer.

17

NEW TERM **Local/Remote:** You will see the terms "local" and "remote" a lot in reference to FTP. A local machine is your computer—after all, you can't get any more local than your desktop. A remote machine is simply a server to which you connect via means of a modem or network connection.

Where Is FTP?

The servers that keep all these files for you are commonly called *FTP sites.* Each site is its own self-contained electronic library containing information, files, and applications on every topic imaginable. You don't really take files from FTP sites, though; you transfer them from the FTP site to your own computer.

An unfathomable amount of information is available on FTP sites—trillions and trillions of bytes worth. Some basic types of information are briefly mentioned here; for more information on what these files are called, refer to the section titled "Names: The File Frontier."

17

☐ Text files: Text files of infinite variety are available via FTP. Get a copy of the lyrics to your favorite Bob Dylan song, grab a copy of *Alice in Wonderland,* or peruse the latest wisdom on good manners on the Internet.

☐ Multimedia files: Pictures, 3-D renderings, stereograms (you know, those things you have to stare at for 45 seconds before you can see them?), even movie clips are available with FTP, too.

☐ Applications: From e-mail clients to programs that help you balance your checkbook, they're all there. Software of every type, flavor, and color is available with FTP.

Of course, hundreds of variations of these three basic categories do exist, but I hope that this list gives you an idea of the types of resources to which FTP gives you instant access.

Anonymous FTP

Unfortunately, as great as much of the information is, it's not always available to everybody. Many FTP sites are set up for a specific purpose or for a particular group of users. This limited purpose succeeds in somewhat restricting the access to some of the resources that are available via FTP.

The good news is that lots and lots of sites are available to everybody. These sites are called *anonymous* FTP sites. They are called "anonymous" because they don't require you to identify yourself in order to gain access to the site. Rather, you're invited in as a "guest" to browse and retrieve files as you want.

JUST A MINUTE

Just because an FTP site is an anonymous site does not necessarily mean that it has unlimited access. A site may limit the number of anonymous users during business hours, restrict anonymous users to particular areas, require that you enter your e-mail address as a password, or not allow for the download of certain files from the site, as you can see in Figure 17.1. So keep in mind that free instant access may not let you take all the candy in the candy store when you want to take it.

Figure 17.1.

Many FTP sites restrict use to certain times of the day and to a particular number of users.

```
Netscape - [FTP Error]
File  Edit  View  Go  Bookmarks  Options  Directory  Window  Help

 Back   Forward   Home      Reload   Images   Open    Print    Find      Stop

Location: ftp://mac.archive.umich.edu

 What's New!   What's Cool!   Handbook    Net Search   Net Directory   Software

Could not login to FTP server

        All allowed connections are being used at this time.

Due to overwhelming usage during business hours, restrictions to ftp acces
are now being enforced.  PLEASE be considerate and ftp during non-"busines
hours" as much as possible.  Also, please keep connection times short.

Weekends:                                              60 connections
Weekdays from 11pm 'til 4am (EST):                     60 connections
Weekdays from 6pm 'til 11pm, and 4am 'til 6am (EST):   30 connections
Weekdays from 6am 'til 6pm (EST) ("business hours"):   10 connections

The best way to access the archive files is via AFS.  If you have
AFS installed, "cd" or make a link to /afs/umich.edu/group/itd/archive.

Gophering to "gopher.archive.umich.edu" is the next best alternative,
as is our WWW interface ("http://www.umich.edu/~archive" or
"http://www.archive.umich.edu").

Document Done
```

The wide range of files on anonymous FTP sites means that something really is available for everyone. From novices to experienced programmers, you can find something for you.

17

JUST A MINUTE

Not all FTP is anonymous. Many times you may have access to an FTP server that requires a valid user name and password. Logging on to these is simple: Just use your system user ID as your login (provided by your system administrator) and your password. After you've logged on, using FTP this way is identical to using FTP anonymously.

FTP Structure and Syntax

Before you can download anything from an FTP site, you must first get onto a site and then know how it is structured. When doing so, you need to know three basic pieces of information: the site name, the directory path of the file you want, and the actual name of the file.

17

TIME SAVER

Often, you may not know the specific location of the file you're looking for. Usually, you can conduct a search on the Internet. You can find an excellent place to search for software on the Internet at http://www.shareware.com/. For more specifics on searching for files on FTP, refer to Lesson 20, " Finding People, Places, and Things on the Net."

You already learned about domain names in many previous lessons. FTP site names generally (but not always) begin with ftp. As you also know, the protocol portion of an FTP URL is ftp://.

Whether you're using a Web browser or an actual FTP client, you shouldn't have any problem getting on. Just remember, if your client asks for a user ID or login ID and password to get onto a site, just use anonymous as your user ID and *your@email.address* as your password, as shown in Figure 17.2.

Figure 17.2.

With most FTP clients, like WS_FTP, you can enter all relevant information before getting on a site.

Session Profile	
Profile Name: WSArchie	Ok
Delete... Save New	Cancel
Host Name: ftp.demon.co.uk	Advanced...
Host Type: Automatic detect	Help
User ID: anonymous	☑ Anonymous Login
Password: noele@pilot.msu.edu	☐ Save Password
Account:	☐ Auto Save Config
Initial Directories	
Remote Host: /pub/ibmpc/winsock/apps/ws	
Local PC:	
Comment:	

Like a Tree

The second element you need to know is the *directory path* of the file you want. Directory paths are much like the branches of a tree with each subdirectory "branching" off from a previous one. If you were to climb a tree, for example, you would start at the trunk, climb on a branch, then move out on a limb, and so on.

FTP sites are the same. The "trunk" of the FTP site is called, not coincidentally, the *root directory*. From this directory, you choose the branch directories (called subdirectories) from the root directory. Figure 17.3 shows a simple directory tree on a hypothetical FTP site.

Figure 17.3.

An FTP site's directory path even looks sort of like a tree.

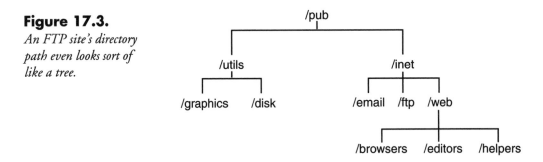

First, notice that directories on FTP sites all begin with a slash (/). Each slash represents one level, or branch, on the FTP site. If the file you want is in /pub/inet/web/browsers, for example, you take the /inet branch from the /pub trunk, go to the /web limb, and then jump to the /browsers twig (okay, maybe I'm stretching the analogy a bit). Presumably, the file you want is in that last subdirectory.

17

Navigating these paths is easy once you're used to it. If you're using a Web browser, selecting directories and using the Forward and Back buttons enables you to navigate nicely.

If you're using an FTP client, such as WS_FTP, you can still click directory names to move down. To move back up, however, you need to remember to double-click the double-dot (..) at the top of each directory window. The double-dot is another throwback to times before GUI interfaces and is standard syntax for "go up a directory."

Names: The File Frontier

Probably the most confusing part of FTP is the really strange names that files seem to have. If you don't know what you're doing, they can seem almost indecipherable. You can keep in mind a couple points when dealing with filenames, though.

First, know that most files you find on FTP sites are compressed to save space. A compressed file has its original code "compacted" into a smaller file. This means that you have to "decompress" files that you download before you can use them.

Second, quite a few compression utilities are available, which also means that you need to know many different filename extensions. Table 17.1 gives a breakdown of the most common file extensions on FTP sites today.

Table 17.1. File extensions explained.

Extension	Platform	Compressed	Decompress with
.txt	PC or Mac	No	N/A (text file)
.ps	PC or Mac	No	PostScript printer file
.exe	PC	Yes/No	Executable or self-extracting
.zip	PC	Yes	WinZip
.sit	Mac	Yes	StuffIt Expander
.sea	Mac	Yes	Self-extracting
.hqx	Mac	Yes	Binhex StuffIt Expander (this encoding is usually added to a compressed file).
.bin	Mac	No	A program like Macbinary II will convert this file.

Of course, you will see other extensions. Extensions such as .gz, .tar, and .Z are UNIX files that you most likely cannot use. You might be able to use other compressions that are outdated or rare, such as .lzh or .arc; it never hurts to try. When all is said and done, you end up with something like the window shown in Figure 17.4.

Figure 17.4.

Both remote and local files and directories are all visible from one FTP client.

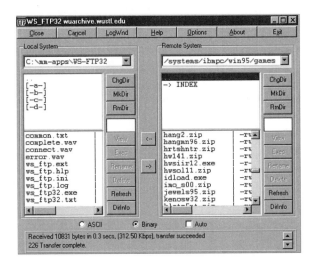

TIME SAVER

Many Web browsers and FTP applications "post-process" files. That is, if you have an decompression program installed on your machine, the client automatically decompresses the file for you after it's downloaded. Check your client's documentation to see if your software has this capability.

Downloading Files

I've given you all the pieces. Now you're ready to put them together and download that first file to your hard drive. Starting out with something easy, like a decompressed text file, is probably a good idea.

TIME SAVER

Most Web browsers simply display a text file in a browser window instead of downloading it. If you want to save the file to your hard drive, right-click the filename and then choose the option that enables you to save the file.

17

To Do: Downloading Files

1. Point your client to `mirrors.aol.com` (FTP client) or `ftp://mirrors.aol.com`.

2. Take the directory path `/pub/music/lyrics/d/dire.straits/`.

3. Choose one of the albums listed, and download it to your computer's hard drive.

4. Open a word processing program.

5. Open the file you just saved to your hard drive and view it.

Next, download something useful. You may have already glanced at Appendix B and noticed that WinZip is listed as a great utility for decompressing files. Well, why don't you go ahead and download the latest demo version right now?

To Do: Downloading the Demo

1. Point your FTP client (or Web browser) to `ftp.winzip.com`.

2. Take the directory path `/winzip/winzip/`.

3. Choose one of two files to download at this point. If you have Windows 95, choose `winzip95.exe`. If you have Windows 3.1, choose `wz16vXX.exe` (where *XX* represents the most current version).

4. Download the appropriate file to your hard drive.

5. Choose File|Run (in Windows 3.1) or Start|Run (Windows 95) to run the file you just downloaded.

6. Choose the WinZip Setup option, and follow the directions to set up WinZip.

TIME SAVER

> If you are using a Mac, you might want to go ahead and download StuffIt Expander. Simply go to `http://www.aladdinsys.com/consumer/expander2.html` and follow the instructions provided on the page.

Browser Versus Client

Probably the biggest choice you face when using FTP is the software you'll use. You have two basic choices: a Web browser or a client designed specifically for FTP. Each solution has its own drawbacks, but you should carefully consider a few factors.

Usability

The first issue is that of usability. For ease of use, a browser wins hands down. Using either Netscape or Internet Explorer, the process of finding and downloading files is as easy as browsing the Web—everything remains point-and-click. You can use a Web site, such as http://www.shareware.com/, to find the files and then click your way to the file you want to download. Figure 17.5 shows such an example.

Figure 17.5.

Browsers offer you Web ease for finding and downloading files.

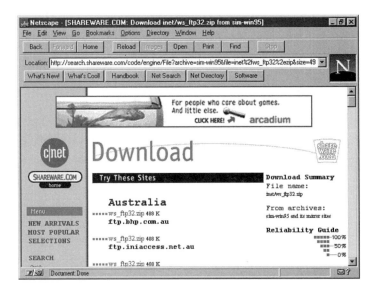

I'm not saying that FTP clients are hard to use—they really aren't. However, figuring out exactly how to use these clients definitely takes longer. Also, your using FTP clients doesn't mean that you can't still use a browser to find files—you can. In fact, many FTP pros regularly use the strengths of both browsers and FTP clients to get files quickly and efficiently.

Flexibility

The second real issue to consider when choosing a browser versus a client is flexibility. How many different tasks a browser or client can perform is also of utmost importance. On this measure, the FTP client wins without question.

For the most part, using a browser, you can find, download, and upload files, and that's about it. A client, however, offers an entire world of functionality. Many clients, such as WS_FTP for Windows and Fetch for Macintosh, actually act as miniature file managers as well as FTP clients. You can usually change download directories and filenames, delete files, and download multiple files all from one piece of software, as you can see in Figure 17.6. Often, you can also view and even launch files right from within the FTP client.

Figure 17.6.

Do you want to save some time by downloading several files at once? Don't use a Web browser!

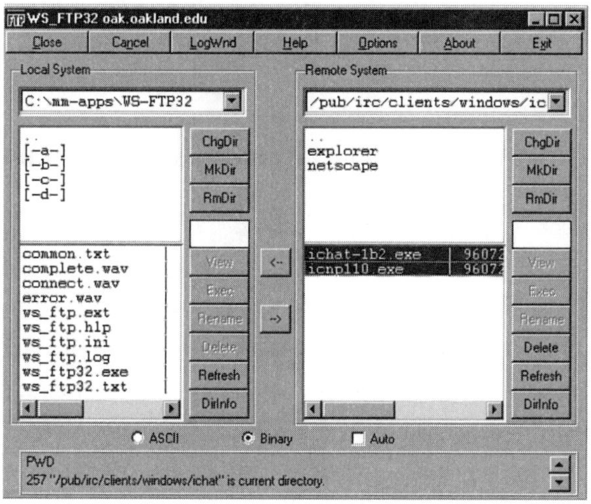

You will probably find yourself using both a browser and a client to use FTP. For many everyday FTP tasks, a browser works fine. For the times you need a more powerful tool, you may want to take advantage of what an FTP client has to offer.

Summary

In this lesson, you learned about what FTP is and how it works. Now you know that two different types of FTP sites exist, one of which (anonymous FTP sites) you can access to get all types of files, documents, and software.

You also learned how FTP sites are organized so that you know how to find, explore, and get what you want. Finally, you learned how to download files using FTP, as well as some of the pros and cons surrounding what type of FTP software to use.

Workshop

The following workshop helps solidify the skills that you learned in this lesson.

Q&A

Q I know that all this great stuff available via FTP really isn't free. Is that true?

A Sort of. Many files, particularly software, are generally offered as shareware. Shareware is software that is distributed freely. If you find that you use shareware on a regular basis, however, you are usually asked to send in a small fee ($10 to $25). This way, shareware developers can continue writing useful, inexpensive software for you to use.

Q Do I have a limit on how many files I can download?

A Not really. The only restriction you usually have is time. Using a modem connection, downloading very large files can take up to an hour or more. How you pay for your Internet service and how much time you have to spend online are most likely the determining factors in how much you actually download.

Q Is a file extension really platform specific?

A Yes and no. Consider an example. Suppose that you have a very large text document that you want to compress. If you're using a PC, you can use WinZip to compress the file and call it `text.zip`. Another person can download this same file to a Macintosh, unzip it using StuffIt Deluxe, and view it without a problem. Generally, software and applications with compressed file extensions are platform specific.

Quiz

Take the following quiz to see how much you've learned.

Questions

1. Of the following choices, which one describes a directory path?

   (a) `ftp.site.com`

   (b) `/pub/graphics/util`

   (c) `docviewer.zip`

2. Which of these files would be fastest to download?

   (a) `goodfile.tar.gz`

   (b) `goodfile.zip`

   (c) `goodfile.txt`

3. An anonymous FTP site doesn't require any information from you in order for you to use it.

   (a) True

   (b) False

Answers

1. (b) `/pub/graphics/util`

2. (c) Files with no compression are always fastest.

3. (b) False. You must provide a user ID of anonymous and a password of your e-mail address to log on.

Activity

Now you can really apply what you've learned and still have some fun. In this lesson, you downloaded WinZip. Now go out and download a compressed file. First, go to `http://www.shareware.com` and search for games. Find a compressed game that looks interesting, download it, and then decompress it. Yes, you can play some before moving on to the next lesson.

17

Hour 18

Gopher Even More

Many people consider Gopher to be the precursor to the World Wide Web. In many ways, it was. In today's Web-crazed world, however, Gopher has been almost forgotten. Don't be fooled. A lot of good information is still out there on Gopher, and in this lesson, I intend to help you find it.

In this lesson, you find the answers to the following questions:

- ☐ What is Gopher and how does it work?
- ☐ How do I find Gophers?
- ☐ What do Gopher sites look like?
- ☐ What type of information can I find on Gopher?
- ☐ What are some examples of Gopher information?
- ☐ How is Gopher different from the WWW?

Although you can find Gopher clients, such as WSGopher for Windows and TurboGopher for Macintosh, they are rarely used anymore. Browsers such as Netscape and Internet Explorer can access and use the information on Gopher well.

Is Gopher Just Another Rodent?

Besides being a cute little animal and the mascot for the University of Minnesota, a Gopher is another type of site on the Net that is full of information. In fact, it's no accident that this type of Internet site bears the name of this northern university's mascot.

Gopher was originally developed at the University of Minnesota in the 1980s to solve a particular campus computing problem. A typical large university, U of M contained many departments with many files that different people needed to share and access. They still needed to make this information easy to access and controllable by each department, however.

Enter Gopher. A system was developed whereby many types of information could be displayed and accessed in a simple, menu-based structure, as shown in Figure 18.1. In fact, the University of Minnesota defines a Gopher as "software following a simple protocol for tunneling through a TCP/IP internet."

Figure 18.1.

The Mother of all Gophers is located at the University of Minnesota's site (gopher://
gopher.micro.umn.edu).

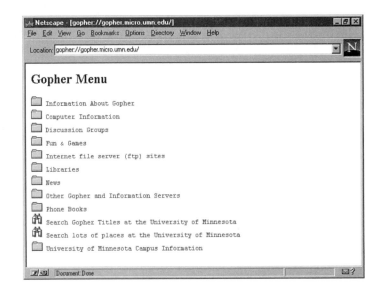

For the first time ever, users could access useful information by selecting menu items that were actually in English (if you can imagine that). Soon others saw the usefulness of this helpful system.

Where Should You Start?

A great place to start using Gopher is actually at the University of Minnesota's Gopher site. Also at Minnesota's Gopher is a directory with links to practically every Gopher server in the world. You can locate it at the following URL:

```
gopher://gopher.tc.umn.edu:70/11/Other%20Gopher%20and%20Information%20Servers
```

TIME SAVER

If typing in a URL like the preceding one gives you goose bumps, you can go about it in an easier way. From U of M's Top Level Gopher at gopher://gopher.micro.umn.edu, simply click the Other Gopher And Information Servers link and make a bookmark for the resulting page shown in Figure 18.2. This way, you can save a lot of typing.

Figure 18.2.

Your link to the entire world of Gopher starts at the University of Minnesota.

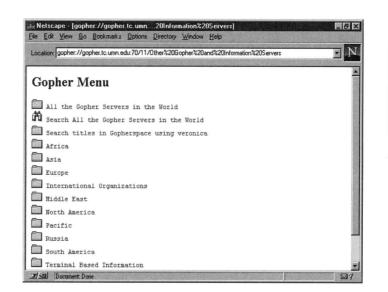

18

As you can see, this Gopher gives you the opportunity to go to an alphabetical listing of every Gopher server in the world. In addition, you can look at Gopher servers by region or even conduct a search for and of different Gopher servers worldwide.

What's Gopher Really Like?

You already know that Gopher sites consist of menus that contain information, but what are some of the specifics involved in navigating *Gopherspace?* The first thing you need to do is learn how to recognize when you're using Gopher.

NEW TERM **Gopherspace:** Gopherspace is simply the term used to describe the portion of the Internet that contains Gopher sites. It is one of cyberspace's subdivisions, if you will.

If you're navigating the Internet using a Web browser, you may not always realize when you've left the Web and entered Gopherspace. You can look for a couple of telltale signs.

First, if you have your browser display the location, you can see that a Gopher site's location begins with gopher://. Second, notice the line-by-line menu structure for which Gopher is known. Gopher sites can often look similar to FTP sites in a browser, but just remember that FTP menu items rarely consist of English words and headings.

Burrowing in Gopher

Navigating Gopherspace using a Web browser is easy. In fact, it's really no different from navigating the Web. Every menu item in Gopher appears as a hyperlink in your browser. Simply click a menu item to proceed to the next one.

Much like links on the Web, Gopher links can take you to many different types of resources. Depending on what browser you use, these different links are preceded by an icon or a word to indicate what types of resources the link points to. Table 18.1 gives a breakdown of common Gopher links.

Table 18.1. Common Gopher links.

Link Type	Link Name Extension or Symbol
Gopher Menu	English phrase or heading; folder symbol
Text file	English phrase or heading or .txt
Image file	Usually .jpg or .gif; maybe .bmp
Search	English phrase; binoculars symbol
Movie file	Usually .mov, .mpg, or .avi
Sound file	Usually .wav or .au.
Telnet session	English phrase; computer terminal symbol

18

As a rule, links to Gopher menus simply take you to other Gopher pages; links to image, movie, sound, or text files are treated as such links would be treated on the Web, as are searches and Telnet sessions. (Look at Lesson 19, "Telnet to the Internet," for more details on Telnet.) Keep in mind, though, that a Search link in Gopherspace generally searches only Gopher sites and other databases, not the Web.

What's on the Menu?

Just as navigating in Gopher is similar to finding your way around the Web, the file and directory structure of Gopher is similar to that found on FTP sites. (See Lesson 17, "Getting Files with FTP," for details.) Briefly, every Gopher site has a *Top Level menu* such as the one shown in Figure 18.1. Each one of these menus then acts as its own "top level" menu for the menus below it.

One major difference, however, does exist between Gopher and FTP directory structure. Whereas FTP directories can lead only to other subdirectories and files, Gopher directories can lead to subdirectories and files, as well as search engines, databases, Telnet sessions, Web sites, FTP sites, and other Gopher sites. For a simple example of Gopher menu structure, look at Figure 18.3.

18

Figure 18.3.

The tree-like structure of a Gopher menu can lead you almost anywhere.

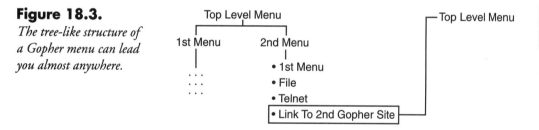

Just like with FTP, most of your navigation in Gopher consists of clicking hyperlinks and using the Back and Forward navigation buttons frequently.

What Can You Find on Gopher?

I mentioned at the beginning of this lesson that a lot of useful information really is available via Gopher. If you burrow around Gopher, you will begin to find some of the menus and files that make Gopher a good source of information to this day.

As you will learn in Lesson 20, "Finding People, Places, and Things on the Net," you can search Gopherspace using Veronica to find even more information on Gopherspace. In addition, in the following sections I show you a couple of the resources to which Gopher can give you easy access.

Using Gopher to Telnet

As you will learn in Lesson 19, by using Telnet, you can connect directly to other computers on the Internet.

One thing you won't learn in that lesson, however, is one particularly easy way to find some of the most useful Telnet sites on the Net, as you learn next. Gopher is an excellent resource for locating public access Telnet sites on the Internet. Foremost among these sites are libraries. Many large libraries have their card catalogs and holdings available for searching on the Internet. These libraries, with the help of Gopher and Telnet, can offer you a wealth of information.

To Do: Telnetting

1. From the University of Minnesota's home Gopher at `gopher://gopher.micro.umn.edu`, click the `Libraries` link.

2. Click `Library Card Catalogs via Telnet`.

3. Click the `Library Catalogs from Other Institutions` link.

4. Follow the `Americas/United States/Michigan/` link.

5. With your Web browser configured with a TN3270 Telnet client (see Lesson 19), go to the `Michigan State University` library.

TIME SAVER

Notice that most libraries have both a Telnet session link and a file link for each library. Reading a library's accompanying text file to get any specific login directions before using the site itself is always a good idea.

Figure 18.4 shows how your Web browser automatically brings up the appropriate application to get you into just about any library you want. Before going on, you may want to browse around the MSU MAGIC online library for a while. On your way to finding this library, notice that you passed hundreds more. MSU MAGIC online library is a great place to start if you need to do library research of any kind.

18

Figure 18.4.

When it comes to Telnet, you need two applications to get connected.

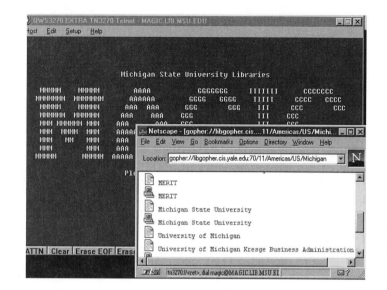

Gopher Jewels

As you now know, Gopherspace consists of millions of interconnected menus and files. What you may not know is that another attempt has been made to make Gopher sites accessible by topic in an effort to reduce the necessity for complex searches and following dead-end links.

This topical organization of Gopherspace is accomplished by Gopher Jewels, a system maintained at the University of Southern California. Getting to Gopher Jewels is easy. From `gopher://cwis.usc.edu`, click `Other Gophers` and `Information Resources` and then click `Gopher-Jewels`. You then see a screen like the one pictured in Figure 18.5.

Spend a little time exploring these topical menus. Notice that each submenu enables you to jump to a previous menu or search Gopher Jewels. This capability gives you one more way to use Gopher powerfully and efficiently.

18

Figure 18.5.

Gopher Jewels offers topical access to Gopherspace.

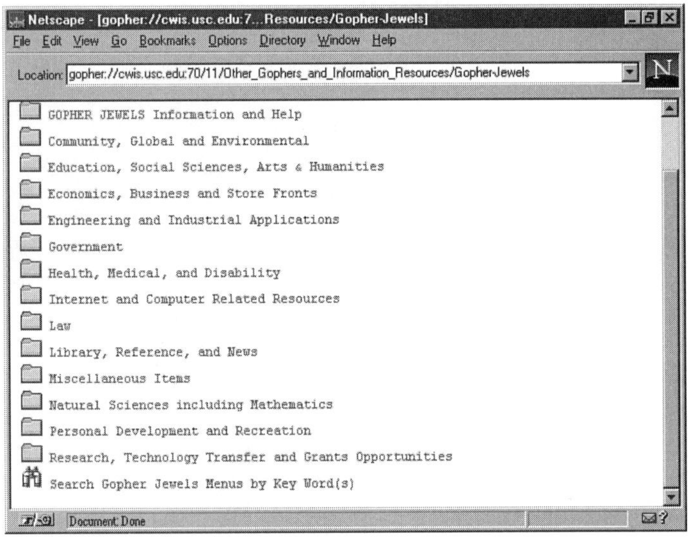

Gopher Examples, Please?

You now have several different ways to explore much of the useful information that is on Gopher. Before you're done, though, perhaps you would like to see a few examples of Gopher in action.

How's the Weather?

Gopher provides a lot of information on the latest in weather, including satellite pictures of recent weather in different areas, as well as complete forecasts. Probably the best place to find current weather forecasts is the Gopher site at Michigan State University.

To Do: Checking the Weather

1. Go to MSU's home Gopher at gopher://gopher.msu.edu.
2. Click News & Weather and then click the Weather links.

   From here, you can go in one of many directions:

3. For the latest satellite weather images, click University of Illinois Weather Central and then Satellite Images. You can then view a wide range of images, as shown in Figure 18.6.
4. If you want a current forecast, with your browser configured with a Telnet client (see Lesson 19), click the University of Michigan Weather Underground. You can also get forecasts from Australia if you're interested in the weather "down under."

18

Figure 18.6.

Viewing satellite weather is easy when you're using Gopher.

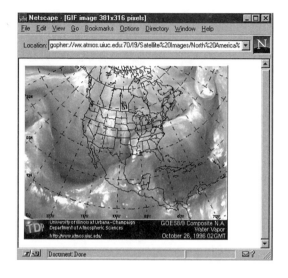

"Money for Nothin' and the Books Are Free"

One of the most popular literary trips on the Internet, and available through Gopher, is Project Gutenberg. This project has put hundreds of non-copyrighted books on the Internet in electronic form. Quite a few sites give you access to the Gutenberg *E-texts;* next, you take a look at one.

NEW TERM **E-text:** This term stands for "electronic text." E-text is becoming a popular way to put textbooks, non-copyrighted books, and other literature on the Internet.

To Do: Viewing E-Texts

1. Go to gopher://gopher.etext.org/.
2. Click Gutenberg.
3. Click newuser.txt or index.html to find out more about Project Gutenberg.
4. If you remain on the main Gutenberg menu, you can click any one of the years listed to find the books published for that year. Click etext93, for example, to find those books published in 1993.
5. Click one of the INDEX.GUT links to find out what all the funny-looking links actually contain.
6. Click the book you want to see. You could click rgain10.txt, for example, to take a look at *Paradise Regained* by John Milton, as shown in Figure 18.7.

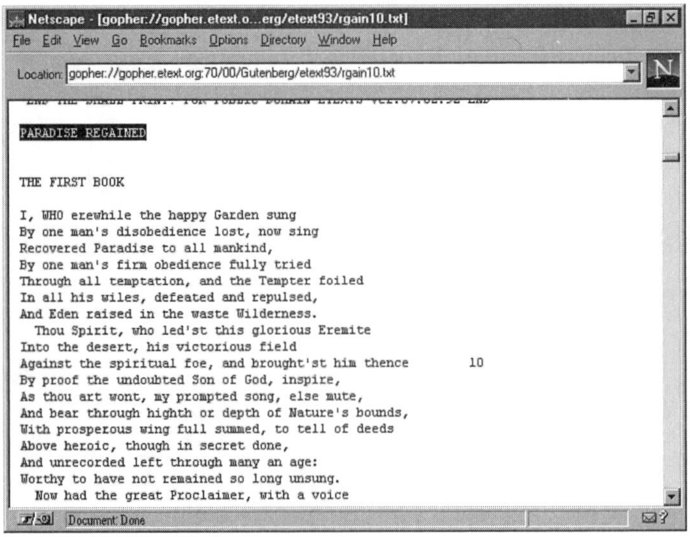

Figure 18.7.

After you scroll through a couple pages of disclaimers, the book appears.

Obviously, much of the information available on Gopher might also be available on the World Wide Web or other sources. For simplicity of interface and amount of information offered, however, Gopher is a useful tool that Internet veterans still make use of today.

Summary

In this lesson, you learned about Gopher, which was created at the University of Minnesota and grew into a menu-driven worldwide source of information.

Next, you learned about how Gopherspace is organized, what types of files you could expect to find, and what are some of the resources available through Gopher. Finally, you looked at some useful Gopher sites in action.

Workshop

The following workshop helps solidify the skills that you learned in this lesson.

Q&A

Q I can see that Gopher might be useful, but it sure would be nice if there were a way to search for information on Gopher. Is there?

18

A There sure is. But I'm going to keep you in suspense a little longer. If you can't wait, however, you can go to Lesson 20 to find out how to search for more interesting information on Gopher.

Q Does Gopher offer any information that really isn't available anywhere else?

A Yes. The amount of information that's available on Gopher that may not be available anywhere else, however, is getting smaller all the time. The biggest advantage to Gopher is that many resources (such as libraries, Telnet sites, and other information) are easier to access from Gopher because much of the "clutter" of the World Wide Web isn't there.

Quiz

Take the following quiz to see how much you've learned.

Questions

1. What's the URL of the first Gopher site?

    (a) `gopher://gopher.micro.umn.edu`

    (b) `gopher://gopher.msu.edu`

    (c) `gopher://gopher.etext.org`

2. Which of these files would you likely not find in Gopherspace?

    (a) Text files

    (b) Images

    (c) Sound files

    (d) None of the above

3. Gopher sites are practically obsolete.

    (a) True

    (b) False

Answers

1. (a) Remember that the University of Minnesota started it all.

2. (d) You can find just about anything on Gopher.

3. (b) False. Some might say that Gopher is obsolete, but it still has way too much good information for it to be obsolete. Of course, for anything new, the Web is the direction everyone is going.

Activity

Just to see what really is available in Gopherspace, pick any generally broad topic that you're interested in. Next, go to Gopher Jewels and see what information you can find on that topic.

18

Hour 19

Telnet to the Internet

Back in the old days, the only way to communicate with a computer was to "log on" as a user on the system and type away line by line. Compared to today's Web and other graphical interfaces, direct computer logons seem like they belong in the Smithsonian. But wait…

In this lesson, you find the answers to the following questions:

☐ What is Telnet and how does it work?

☐ How can I get Telnet to work with my Web browser?

☐ Are different types of Telnet available?

☐ What do I need to log on to a computer via Telnet?

☐ What are some examples of Telnet sites and information?

Understanding Telnet

For you to understand what Telnet is, my explaining what it isn't might be easiest. When you use a Web browser, e-mail or newsgroup client, or just about any other application on the Internet, you never actually "see" what is on the computer you're connecting to. Instead, your client contacts the server, gets the information it needs, displays it on your screen, and then disconnects from the server.

Telnet is in fact just the opposite. Telnet requires that you actually be connected to the server computer at all times to maintain communication. In this environment, all interactions are conducted in a *command-line environment* where your communication and the server's responses appear in a text format, as shown in Figure 19.1.

NEW TERM **Command-line environment:** In this environment, you type text on a line, the server responds with text, you type in another command, and so on. These interfaces often require special commands and keystroke combinations to perform special functions.

Figure 19.1.

A Telnet session is about as Plain Jane as you can get.

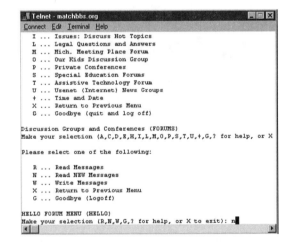

Though Telnet sessions may not be much to look at, a wealth of information is available using Telnet. Many libraries, local bulletin board systems, and more are all available via Telnet connections. Once you know your way around Telnet, you may make it one of your standard Internet tools.

Telnetting from the Web

Because you must keep contact with the server at all times to maintain a Telnet connection, the standard Internet clients don't work. Instead, you must have a client that performs the necessary Telnet functions for you.

In addition, you may often run into Telnet sites while exploring Gopher or the World Wide Web. So, having your Web browser configured to call a Telnet client automatically whenever you click a Telnet link is also helpful.

The Flavors of Telnet

Before you can tell your Web browser which Telnet client to use, you need to have one first. Before you proceed, however, be aware that you will run into two types of Telnet: VT100 and TN3270.

You need to know two things about these different terminal protocols. First, each of these terminal types requires its own client. Second, be aware that VT100 is by far the most common terminal type in use, but TN3270 is a common terminal type for libraries to which you can telnet. Usually, a TN3270 client will connect to VT100 sites.

Before you set your browser to handle Telnet clients, you need to know where to get them:

☐ VT100 clients: If you use Windows 95, you're in luck because a built-in VT100 Telnet client is located in `c:\windows\telnet.exe`. If you're using Windows 3.1, you need to get this client via FTP. A very good one is Yawtel (Yet Another Windows TELnet client), available through `ftp://ftp.winsite.com/pub/pc/win3/winsock/`. As of this writing, Yawtel was at version .9 (`yawtel09.zip`), but a later version may be available by the time you read this lesson. For Mac users, you can use NCSA's Telnet available at `ftp://ftp.ncsa.edu/Mac/Telnet/Telnet2.7/2.7b4/`. You can also use a new product called NiftyTelnet available at `http://andrew2.andrew.cmu.edu/dist/niftytelnet.html`.

☐ TN3270 clients: Whatever version of Windows you use, QWS3270 is a stable TN3270 client. You can download it from `ftp://ftp.ccs.queensu.ca/pub/msdos/tcpip/qws3270.zip`. For the Mac, you can use TN3270 available at `ftp://mirror.apple.com/mirrors/Info-Mac.Archive/comm/inet/tn3270-25b2.hqx`.

After you install these clients on your hard drive, you're ready to tell your browser how to use them.

Helping Your Browser with Telnet

Configuring your browser to use these Telnet clients is a relatively easy process. You only need to find out where your browser is configured to use helper applications and then plug in the correct filename. The following steps show you how to configure Netscape Navigator 3.0 to use Telnet clients.

To Do: Configuring Netscape to Use Telnet

1. In Netscape, choose Options|General Preferences.

2. Click the Apps tab.

3. Click in the Telnet Application field. Then type in `c:\windows\telnet.exe` if you're using Windows 95 or the correct path and filename for any other Telnet client you're using.

4. Click in the TN3270 Application field and enter the correct path and filename for your TN3270 client. Your window should look something like the one shown in Figure 19.2.

5. Click OK, and you're ready to go.

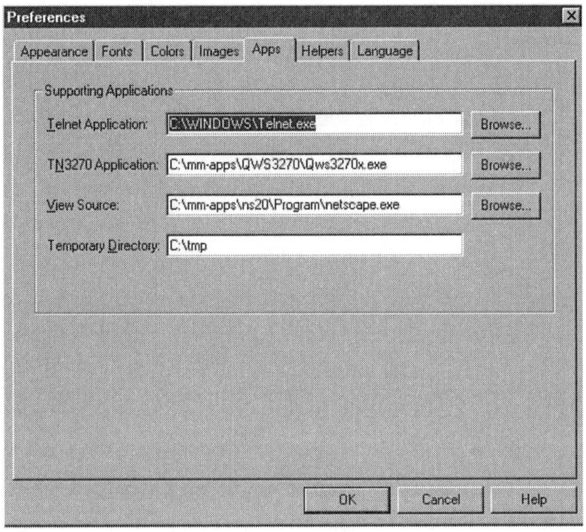

Figure 19.2.

Netscape is easy to configure, so you can Telnet around the world effortlessly.

Internet Explorer is both easier and harder to configure than Netscape. For standard Telnet sessions, Explorer comes preconfigured. You have to do a little work, however, before it can handle TN3270 sessions.

To Do: Configuring Explorer to Use Telnet

1. In Explorer, choose View|Options.

2. Click the Programs tab, and then click the File Types button.

3. Scroll down in the resulting window until you see the URL:TN3270 Protocol item and double-click it.

4. Click the Edit button. Then either browse to find your TN3270 client, or enter it directly, as shown in Figure 19.3.

5. Click the OK and Close buttons until you return to the Internet Explorer window. You're now ready to go.

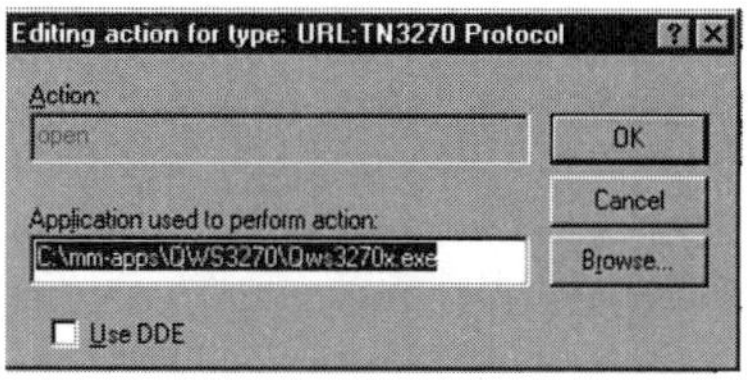

Figure 19.3.

The process takes awhile, but you can tell Explorer how to use TN3270.

Editing action for type: URL:TN3270 Protocol

Action:
open

Application used to perform action:
C:\mm-apps\DWS3270\Dws3270x.exe

☐ Use DDE

OK
Cancel
Browse...

TIME SAVER

If you enter a Telnet URL directly in the Location field of Internet Explorer, leave out the standard //. If you want to Telnet to here.there.com, for example, you simply type telnet:here.there.com.

No matter what browser you use, you should be able to Telnet to any machine in the world in a matter of minutes.

19

Telnet Essentials

Unlike other types of sites you'll encounter on the Web, you don't gain automatic entrance to Telnettable Internet sites. You're likely to encounter several general types of Telnet sessions on the Internet:

☐ Freenets: These organizations offer limited bulletin board system-like access onto the Internet, although some Freenets offer no Internet access at all.

☐ BBSs: Bulletin board systems contain information specific to the organizations that sponsor them. They are often similar to Freenets, except that they rarely offer any type of Internet access.

☐ Libraries: Probably the most common type of Telnet site, library systems usually enable you to search an electronic card catalog for individual library resources.

☐ MUDs and MOOs: MUDs (Multiuser Dungeons) and MOOs (MUDs-Object-Oriented) are sites that you can log on to with the specific purpose of playing a game, sharing information, or talking with other "mudders." Originally, these sites were created for playing dungeon-type games, but now many MUDs and MOOs are designed for sharing academic information and other more useful purposes.

These different types of sites require different information when you log on and use different commands once you're on. I cannot give exhaustive coverage of all you'll need to know here, but I can offer some general information.

Getting On

Libraries are really the only sites that often do not require any type of login or password information for you to get on. As for Freenets, BBSs, MUDs, and MOOs, the information they require is generally straightforward.

As a rule, you are required to enter a user ID, or login ID, and possibly a password. Most often, if you're visiting one of these sites for the first time, you can use a login ID of new, guest, or visitor.

Often, these IDs don't require a password. When a password is required, the login prompt tells you the information you need to give. Figure 19.4 shows a typical Telnet login screen.

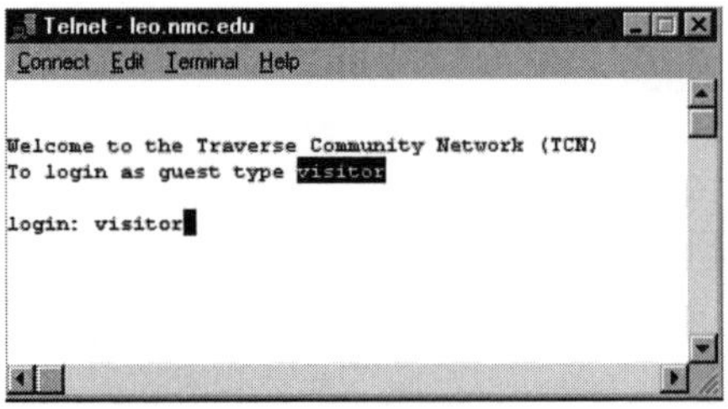

Figure 19.4.

Most Telnet sites tell you what information they need before you log on.

```
 Telnet - leo.nmc.edu                          _ □ ×
Connect  Edit  Terminal  Help

Welcome to the Traverse Community Network (TCN)
To login as guest type visitor

login: visitor█
```

As a visitor or new user, you are often asked to give your name and other personal information to become a registered user. Usually, you need to become a member of the site to gain access to many of the offered features.

19

TIME SAVER

Always look for a text link next to a Telnet session link. These links often give you information such as the login ID and password that you'll need to log on to the site. Most browsers also display a small dialog box informing you of any login ID you'll need to use before your Telnet client connects to the site.

Again, many libraries don't require any login at all. Of those that do, library (or an abbreviated form of the library's name) is usually requested. The Alma College Library in Michigan, for example, asks you to log on as aclib.

You will probably run into dozens of other login IDs, but you will generally be told what they are before you have to log on.

What to Do After You Get There

After you are on one of these sites, the choices of what you can do are almost endless. However, don't worry. As with login and password information, most Telnet sites offer help menus and self-explanatory directories that prompt you every step of the way.

If you're logged into a BBS, chances are you're using a Galacticom bulletin board. Galacticom is probably the most popular BBS, but they all work pretty much the same. Figure 19.5 shows a typical Galacticom BBS menu. Keep in mind, though, that even non-Galacticom boards look similar.

Figure 19.5.

A typical BBS looks much like the one shown here. Notice the self-explanatory menu items.

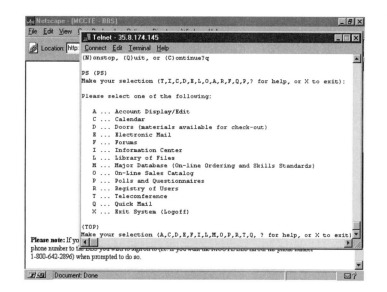

Many libraries are also similar to use. You can generally search them by a number of different criteria such as Subject and Author. Figure 19.6 shows a typical Telnettable library.

Figure 19.6.

Electronic libraries also give you explicit directions on how to use them.

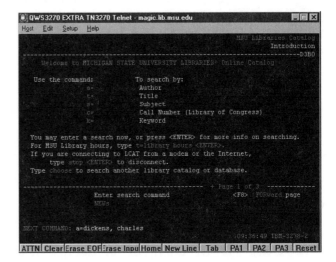

MUDs and MOOs are a little trickier and require more practice to use. For more details on how MUDs operate, refer to the "Getting MUDdy" section later in this lesson.

Telnet Examples

Now you're ready to see some of these sites in action. The following sections give you some idea of what is available in the world of Telnet. Telnet may not be flashy, but it sure has some substance.

Using FedWorld

FedWorld, which contains a lot of information, is probably one of the biggest Telnettable BBSs around. The following section tells how to get to it.

To Do: Starting to Use FedWorld

1. Go to `telnet://fedworld.gov` and login as NEW.

2. You will be asked several questions about yourself, which you should answer. FedWorld will then leave you a piece of e-mail on your account with an attached user's manual.

19

3. After reading your mail, you come to the main menu.

4. From the main menu, select Option 1 to proceed to FedWorld.

5. Choose J to get a listing of Federal job openings.

6. From the next menu, choose Z to select jobs by state.

7. Select the option for whichever state you're interested in.

8. Feel free to browse around and search for a job. You may have to experiment a bit. As you can see in Figure 19.7, getting a Federal job may take awhile.

Figure 19.7.

If you're a qualified weapons assessor, this job's for you!

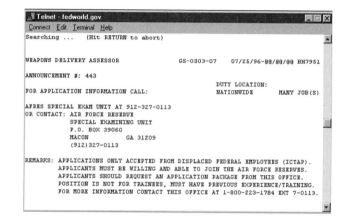

Getting MUDdy

Now take a look at the interactive world of MUDs and MOOs. These Telnettable sites offer all sorts of possibilities. For this example, you're going to look at Elendor, a MUD dedicated to "a literary and role-playing study of Tolkien's Middle Earth."

Point your browser to telnet://elendor.sbs.nau.edu. If you want to log on as a guest, type connect Nomad nomad. This way, you can wander to your heart's content. You can also create a character when you log on.

When you log on to one of these worlds, you should first look for login instructions, which often tell you where to go for help. In Elendor, for example, you are told to type WHO to find out who else is logged on.

TIME SAVER

In the world of MUDs, case matters. If you're trying to find out who is on, don't type who; type WHO.

Besides WHO, several other commands are common. QUIT enables you to leave the world you're in, and help gives you descriptions of different types of commands.

To Do: Getting Help with MUDs

1. Type help commands to get a listing of the commands available in the MUD. When you do, you'll see that one of the commands is pose.

2. If you're curious as to what this command actually does, type help pose to see a description like the one in Figure 19.8.

3. Look at the help for different commands. Focus mainly on the action commands because they are used most often.

Figure 19.8.

Now you know what the pose *command does in a MUD.*

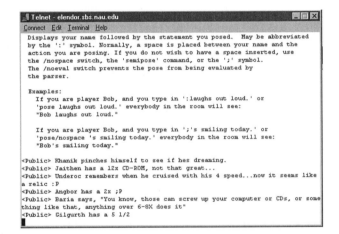

In Figure 19.8, notice that several lines start with <Public>, followed by sentences. These lines represent the discussions that often occur in these worlds.

TIME SAVER

> Probably the best way to find your way around is to ask somebody for help. In Elendor, you can use the page command. The command page Aragon=Can you help me?, for example, notifies the character logged on as Aragon that you would like some help. Generally, people in these worlds are more than happy to help if you are polite and sincere.

Using the rest of the commands is generally a matter of trial and error. Walk around, look at objects, go to rooms that have others in them, and just spend some time "mudding around." You may find yourself hooked.

19

Summary

You learned a lot of information about Telnet in this lesson. You learned that you can Telnet to different resources, such as BBSs, MUDs, and libraries. You also know that you can configure your browser to two types of Telnet—VT100 and TN3270—for automatic access.

You also learned how to log on to Telnet sessions and what to do after you get there. Finally, you looked at some examples of popular types of Telnet sessions.

Workshop

The following workshop helps solidify the skills that you learned in this lesson.

Q&A

Q I'm not real crazy about the Telnet client that comes with Windows 95. Are any others available?

A Quite a few are available—some better than others. For the definitive listing of Telnet clients to try, point your browser to `http://www.shadow.net/tucows/term95.html`.

Q I use both Netscape Navigator and Internet Explorer, and I'm having problems getting Telnet to work all the time. What should I do?

A First, make sure that they're both configured to handle Telnet correctly. Next, remember that Netscape Telnet URLs start with `telnet://` or `tn3270://`, and Explorer's start with `telnet:` or `tn3270:`. If worse comes to worst, put your cursor over the Telnet link and make note of the domain name. Then you can manually open your Telnet client and connect to the site yourself.

19

Quiz

Take the following quiz to see how much you've learned.

Questions

1. Which of the following is not a Telnet type?
    (a) VT100
    (b) Term63
    (c) TN3270

2. Web browsers cannot conduct Telnet sessions by themselves.

   (a) True

   (b) False

3. Which of the following are popular implementations of Telnet?

   (a) MUDs

   (b) Libraries

   (c) BBSs

   (d) All the above

Answers

1. (b) Term63

2. (a) True. Browsers need Telnet clients to help them out.

3. (d) All the above

Activity

The next time you have an hour or so to while away, explore some of the virtual worlds of Telnet. As your starting point, go to gopher://spinaltap.micro.umn.edu:70/11/fun/Games/ MUDs/Links/all. You also can use any of the search engines covered in Lesson 16, "Searching the Web for Virtually Anything," to search for MUDs or MOOs.

Hour **20**

Finding People, Places, and Things on the Net

In Lesson 16, "Searching the Web for Virtually Anything," you learned how to search various parts of the Internet for information and resources. As you now know after reading the preceding three lessons, however, a lot more than just the Web is available. That probably means that you can search for a lot more, too. Right? Right.

In this lesson, you get the answers to the following questions:

- ☐ How can I locate people on the Internet?
- ☐ Can I search Gopher like I can search the Web?
- ☐ How do I search for files on FTP sites?
- ☐ Can I find files on the Web?

TIME SAVER

> You can access all these services from a Web browser. After you use some of the search engines in this lesson, you might want to combine them with your favorite Web search sites in a Bookmark folder for easy access.

Finding That Special Someone

If I had written this section two years ago, it would have contained very little information. Today, however, more ways are available to find someone that you might be comfortable with. Many search engines can help you locate people on the Internet today.

JUST A MINUTE

> Some of these search engines rely on people registering themselves with the service. Be aware that results will likely vary a great deal from engine to engine.

As you look at a few examples, you're going to look for the same person—me. This way, you get an opportunity to see not only how each search engine works, but also how effective and up-to-date it might be. I'm almost afraid to know what's out there, but let's get started anyway.

Finding People with InfoSpace

One of the more comprehensive people finders available is InfoSpace, which is located at `http://www.infospace.com/`. You can use their AccuMail service to find me.

To Do: Using AccuMail in InfoSpace

1. From the InfoSpace home page, click the AccuMail link.
2. At the next page (`http://www.accumail.com`), click in the Last Name field and type `Estabrook`.
3. Click in the First Name field and type `Noel`.
4. Scroll down and click the Look It Up button.
5. Look at the results, as shown in Figure 20.1. As of this writing, five of my e-mail addresses are listed. Four of them are correct; one is old and no longer valid (`nestabro@nova.gmi.edu`).

20

Figure 20.1.

How can one person have all these e-mail addresses? It ain't easy.

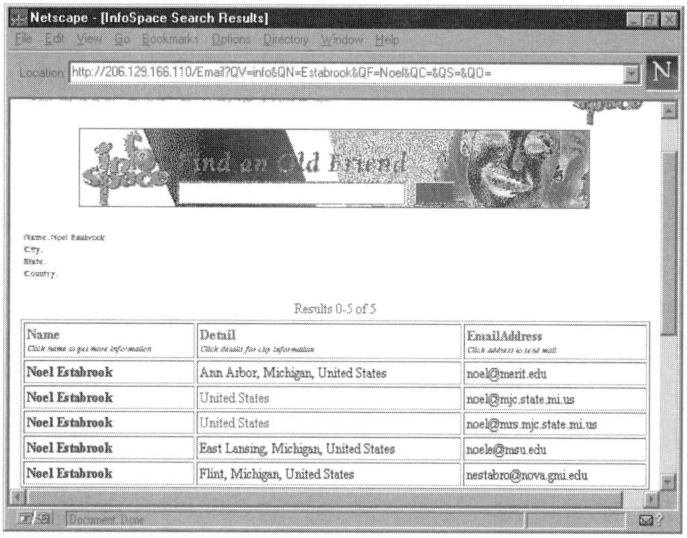

AccuMail enables you to restrict your search by country, state, and city. You can take advantage of these options if you're looking for Joe Smith.

JUST A MINUTE

Finding People with Four11

Another people finder on the Internet is the Four11 Directory, which is located at http://www.four11.com. It was really the first Web-based people locator on the Internet.

With the Four11 Directory, you can restrict your search by area much like you can in the Info-Space directory. It also includes a SmartName feature, which locates names like *Bob* and *Bobby* when you do a search for *Robert*. If you know the domain of the person you're looking for, you can enter it as well.

To Do: Using Four11 to Search for People

1. From the Four11 home page, click in the First Name field and type Noel.
2. Click in the Last Name field and type Estabrook.
3. Click the Search button. The results page brings up a listing of real names followed by a domain.

4. Click the name to go to that person's listing. When you search for Noel Estabrook, for example, one of the results is `Noel W. Estabrook @msu.edu`. For this exercise, click `Noel W. Estabrook`.

The resulting page pictured in Figure 20.2 shows some of the e-mail addresses Four11 has for me. In this case, all three of them are accurate.

Figure 20.2.

Four11 makes finding people easy.

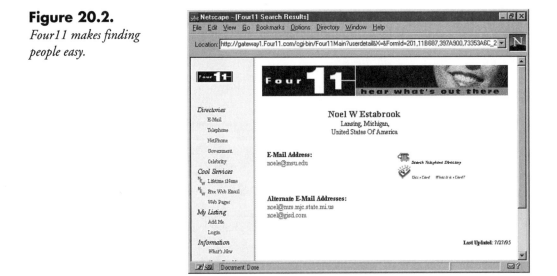

The Best of the Rest

Of course, other search engines are available. Most of them are Web-based and easy to use. A few of them are available via Gopher and Telnet and are harder to use, but they can still be useful. A few of them are briefly highlighted in the following sections.

WhoWhere

The WhoWhere people finder is located at `http://www.whowhere.com`. This service doesn't have many search options, but it's a fast and simple people locator. On a search for Noel Estabrook, it found eight e-mail addresses, five of which were correct.

JUST A MINUTE

> I mentioned that not all the located e-mail addresses are correct. So how do you know which ones are? Well, you really don't. Fortunately, most of the people you look for won't have a dozen e-mail addresses to choose from!

20

Knowbot

Knowbot is an old but sometimes useful Telnettable search engine; it's located at `telnet:/` `/info.cnri.reston.va.us:/185`. After you enter your e-mail address to get into the search engine, simply type `query` and the name of the person you're looking for at the command prompt. Knowbot then searches several databases to find the address. Unfortunately, it did not show any listings for Noel Estabrook.

Gopher and Telnet Phone Books

Many institutions have their own phone books. If you know where the person you're looking for works, these phone books are good places to go for accurate e-mail addresses. You can access these phone books from just about any starting point.

If you start from `gopher://gopher.msu.edu`, you should click, in order, `Phone Books & Other Directories`, `Phone Books — Other Institutions (Notre Dame)`, and then `All the directory servers in the world`. You see a list of hundreds of institutions worldwide. If you scroll down to `Michigan State University Faculty/Staff` and search for Noel Estabrook, you can find one accurate e-mail address.

One other place to go to is Netfind at `http://www.lib.rpi.edu/Computing/Email/netfind.html`. You will find pointers to a number of Telnettable "white page" databases of e-mail addresses.

Using Veronica to Search Gopher

After learning about Gopher in Lesson 18, "Gopher Even More," you might be wondering how to search Gopherspace quickly for information. Enter Veronica, which is short for the Very Easy Rodent-Oriented Net-wide Index to Computerized Archives (whew!). Several Veronica indexes are available.

Getting Started with Veronica

Most Gopher sites have a link to Veronica search engines somewhere in their menus. An excellent place to start, however, is the Veronica home menu, which is located at `gopher:` `//veronica.scs.urn.edu:70/11/veronica`. Using this short menu of choices, you can find just about all there is to find in Gopherspace.

TIME SAVER

> Before you proceed, you may want to read the information in the `Fre-quently Asked Question (FAQ)` about `veronica` link. Knowing what you're doing before you start can save you a lot of time in the long run.

Composing Your Search

In many cases, simply clicking one of the Veronica search engine links and typing in a search term gets you what you want. You can, however, do a few things to make your job easier:

☐ From the Veronica home menu, click the How to Compose Veronica Queries link, and read the information to become familiar with how Veronica handles searches.

☐ Make use of Boolean operators such as AND. Searching for two or more terms can help narrow your search results significantly.

☐ If you're searching for a common term and want to see only a limited number of result items, use the -m tag on your searches. A search for internet -m100, for example, tells Veronica to display only the first 100 hits it finds for the term "internet."

☐ Know your source. If you know the type of file you're looking for, you can use the -t tag after your search term so that Veronica looks only for items that match the file type you want. If you're looking only for text files with the term "internet," for example, you search for internet -t0. Table 20.1 lists the most common file types to search for in Gopherspace.

Table 20.1. Gopher file types.

Tag Code	File Type
0	Text file
1	Directory
4	Mac HQX file
5	PC binary
8	Telnet session
9	Binary file
s	Sound
g	GIF image
I	Image (other than GIF)
h	HTML (Hypertext Markup Language)

Doing Your Search

Now you're ready to search for something. From the Veronica home page, you need to decide what you want to search for. You generally have two choices: searching by Gopher menus or directories or searching all of Gopherspace.

20

If you're looking for general, well-known terms, you can search Gopher menus. For more difficult searches, you probably should search all of Gopherspace. The first type of search is faster, but the second is more comprehensive. Try one to see what happens.

To Do: Searching with Gopher

1. From the Veronica home menu, click the `Simplified Veronica: Find Gopher MENUS only` link.

2. Click the search field, and type `internet -m100 -t0`. Then press Enter. This search looks for the first 100 hits of text files with the term "internet."

3. View the results; Figure 20.3 shows an example. Then click a few of the links to see what you've found.

Figure 20.3.

It's a good thing you narrowed down your search; otherwise, you would be looking at almost 70,000 hits!

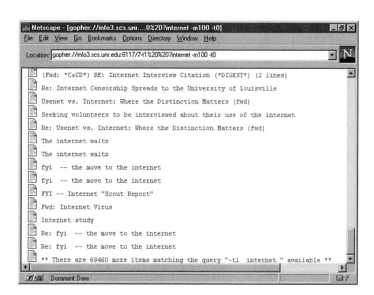

Feel free to experiment with searches to see what you can find. See what the search `internet AND FAQ -m50 -t0` brings up. After you conduct a few searches, you'll have a good idea what's available in Gopherspace.

Searching for FTP Files

If you're looking for files on the Internet, you can go a couple of ways, both of which are covered in the following sections. You can use a search engine called Archie, or you can go to the shareware.com Web site mentioned in Lesson 16, "Searching the Web for Virtually Anything." Both options offer ways of finding almost any file available on FTP sites.

20

ArchiePlex

Using Archie is probably the most popular way to search FTP sites for information. As with almost everything else on the Internet, you can access Archie in more than one way. The easiest way to access Archie, however, is through ArchiePlex gateways on the World Wide Web. You can find a list of every ArchiePlex server at `http://pubweb.nexor.co.uk/public/archie/servers.html`.

TIME SAVER

> The document listing ArchiePlex servers is very popular, and the computer that delivers it is often very busy. To avoid having to download it every time you want to do an Archie search, you can load it once and then save it on your own computer. Choose File I Save As in your browser, and then save the file to your hard drive. After you create a bookmark for this file, you have easy access to ArchiePlex servers.

The NASA ArchiePlex search form page, located at `http://www.lerc.nasa.gov/archieplex/doc/form.html`, is shown in Figure 20.4. To conduct a search, simply enter a search term in the Search for field. You should pay attention to a number of options that make your search more effective.

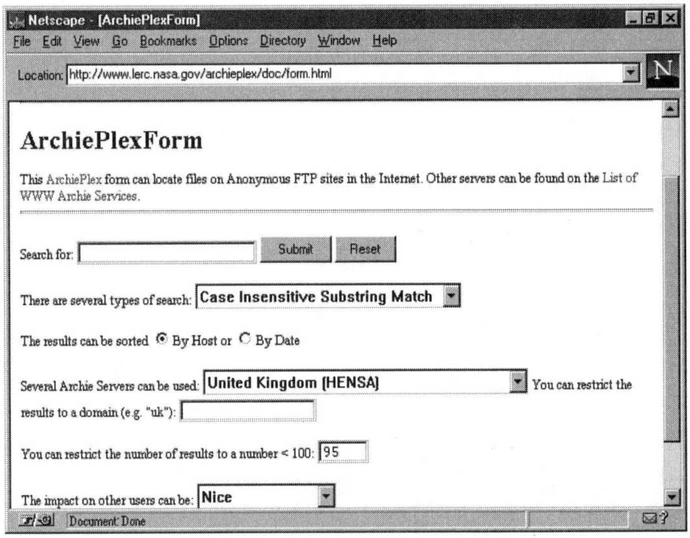

Figure 20.4.

The ArchiePlex search form gives you lots of options to choose from.

Netscape - [ArchiePlexForm]

File Edit View Go Bookmarks Options Directory Window Help

Location: http://www.lerc.nasa.gov/archieplex/doc/form.html

ArchiePlexForm

This ArchiePlex form can locate files on Anonymous FTP sites in the Internet. Other servers can be found on the List of WWW Archie Services.

Search for: [   ]   Submit   Reset

There are several types of search: Case Insensitive Substring Match ▾

The results can be sorted ● By Host or ○ By Date

Several Archie Servers can be used: United Kingdom [HENSA] ▾ You can restrict the results to a domain (e.g. "uk"): [   ]

You can restrict the number of results to a number < 100: 95

The impact on other users can be: Nice ▾

Document: Done

For the types of search, you'll almost always want to choose Case Insensitive Substring Match. You should use Exact Match and Case Sensitive Substring Match when you know exactly what you're looking for.

You can use Regular Expression Match when you know only a partial filename or category of files. If you're looking for an Asteroids game, for example, but aren't sure exactly what to look for, you might search for asteroid* as a Regular Expression Match. Such a search would then result in all hits that contain files with the word "asteroid" somewhere in the name.

The rest of the options are relatively self-explanatory. They enable you to search certain locations, search for files by date or host, and determine how many hits you want displayed and how much of an impact you want to have on other users (always try to be nice!).

To Do: Searching with ArchiePlex

1. From the ArchiePlex search form, type asteroids. For this example, use the Case Insensitive Substring Match option.

2. Don't restrict your search to a particular domain, but enter 50 to restrict the results.

3. Click the Submit button. You then see a list of results similar to the one shown in Figure 20.5.

Figure 20.5.

You may not find these results too useful, but you can always go back and fine-tune your search.

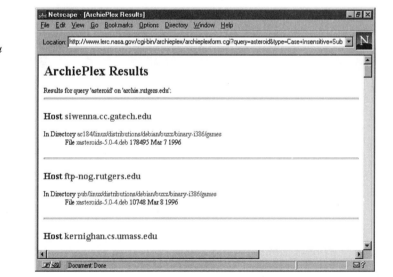

TIME SAVER

In theory, all Archie servers are created equal. But Archie and ArchiePlex, like many programs on the Net, aren't perfect. A search of one Archie server, for example, may bring up nothing, whereas a search on a different server could bring up 100 hits. The moral of the story? If you don't get any matches, try a different form/server combination.

As you can see from Figure 20.5, the results pop up as a nicely formatted Web page that you can then save on your computer if you want. ArchiePlex searches can be slow and complex, so you might want to take a look at the next option.

shareware.com

Probably the best place to search for freeware and software programs on the Internet is shareware.com. From the shareware.com home page located at http://www.shareware.com, you can conduct a Quick Search, which quickly brings up a lot of software for you to download to your machine.

Remember the results you got for a search for the term "asteroid" in ArchiePlex? Now try that same search again at shareware.com. Simply type asteroid in the Quick Search field, select MS-Windows (all) from the pop-up menu, and then click Search. As you can see from Figure 20.6, the results are much better.

Figure 20.6.

From these descriptions, you may have actually found some usable Asteroids games.

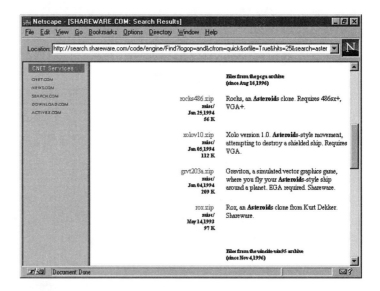

20

JUST A MINUTE

In its database, shareware.com contains both filenames and file descriptions. This means that if a file's name isn't what you might expect it to be, you can still probably find it if your search term is located in the file's description.

Whatever you're looking for, you're sure to find it somewhere on the Net. You now know how to search just about anything on the Internet to find what you're looking for, whether it's FTP, Gopher, the Web, or something else. Of course, you'll probably find other things to search in your travels, but if you master what you've learned in this lesson, plus what was covered in Lesson 16, you should be well on your way to becoming a capable "Net detective."

Summary

This lesson showed you how to find many people, places, and things on the Internet. Using such sites as Four11 and WhoWhere, you discovered new ways to find people. You also learned how to locate Gopher information by using Veronica.

Finally, you learned how to find files using ArchiePlex and shareware.com. With the completion of this lesson, you should now have the tools to find just about anything you want on the Internet.

Workshop

The following workshop helps solidify the skills that you learned in this lesson.

Q&A

Q You spent a lot of time explaining how to find e-mail addresses. But I'm looking for something more mundane, like addresses and phone numbers. What can I do?

A Fortunately, most of the search engines look for this type of information as well. From `http://www.whowhere.com`, for example, you can click the Phone Number & Addresses option (`http://www.whowhere.com/wwphone/phone.html`) to search for someone's name and address. This page even has an option in which you can enter a phone number and find out the person it belongs to!

Q In looking for files on FTP sites, it seems rather obvious that I would want to use shareware.com. Can you tell me why I might want to use Archie?

20

A Yes, Archie is very comprehensive and is an excellent source if you want to look for something very specific or hard-to-find. You are probably right; for simple searches for a category of software or a particularly common file or document, shareware.com is probably your best bet. But if you strike out there, don't forget to give Archie a visit.

Q **On many of the Gopher sites, I've seen another search engine called Jughead. Is it different from Veronica?**

A Yes, it is. Jughead (which stands for Jonzy's Universal Hierarchy Excavation And Display) is a search engine for a single Gopher site. At gopher.somewhere.com, you might find a Veronica engine, for example, that searches all of Gopherspace. A Jughead engine at the same place finds only files located on Somewhere's Gopher site.

Quiz

Take the following quiz to see how much you've learned.

Questions

1. Which one of these tools probably wouldn't work for finding someone's e-mail address?

    (a) Jughead

    (b) Four11

    (c) InfoSpace

2. Which tag would you use to limit the number of hits on a Veronica search?

    (a) -t

    (b) -m

    (c) -n

3. When searching for files on shareware.com, make sure you type in the exact phrase you're looking for.

    (a) True

    (b) False

20

Answers

1. (a) Jughead searches Gopher sites.

2. (b) `-m`

3. (b) False. Remember that shareware.com keeps file descriptions in its database as well so that you can find files more easily.

Activity

Do you have a favorite video game? Space Invaders? Galaga? Centipede? Pac Man? Chances are, a shareware version of the game might be available for your own computer. Use ArchiePlex to try to find "your" game. Then try shareware.com. See if you can find a game that's close to the one you picked. Be forewarned: Most shareware versions of popular arcade games have names that are different from the original. A version of the arcade classic Star Castle, for example, is called Cyclone. Be flexible. Take a chance on a game that might be close to what you're looking for; it might be close enough. If arcade games aren't your thing, feel free to look for something else you're interested in—a recipe or checkbook-balancing program, perhaps.

20

PART VI

Getting the Most Out of the Internet

Hour

Hour 21

The Internet for Home: Entertainment, Travel, and More

Whew! Take a deep breath, because you deserve it. You've learned a lot of information in the last 20 lessons, and now it is time to take a lot of what you have learned and apply it in some fun and useful ways. In particular, this lesson will show you some ways in which you might use the Internet in your home.

In this lesson, you'll learn the answers to the following questions:

- ☐ Can I find information on the movies and other entertainment?
- ☐ Are there services that can help me when I travel?
- ☐ Are there Internet sites outside the United States?
- ☐ Is the Web the only place I can go to get this type of information?

Most of the sites you see in this and the next three lessons were found with experience and a lot of search engines. Always remember to go to a Web search engine or search the newsgroups when you venture into uncharted territory.

Instead of boring you with the same old list after list of supposedly "hot" sites, this chapter takes you through a series of hypothetical situations and shows you how to complete certain tasks. Part of the reason for this is to give you some more practice at what you've already learned. The other reason is that, quite frankly, "What's Hot" lists tend to become outdated really fast.

At the Movies

By the time you read this lesson, the movie *Ransom* is sure to be a huge success (it might even be out on video). As of this writing, however, it's still a week from being released. Do you suppose there is anything out there on the Net about it? You can easily find out.

JUST A MINUTE

It might be interesting for you to follow along with some of this, but with a different movie in mind. Perhaps there's a blockbuster just coming out that you want to find out about. Most of what you'll see here is only available for a limited time!

Thumbs Up?

One of the first things you might want to do is to look up a review of the movie. This is one case in which Yahoo! categories come in very handy. If you point your browser to `http://www.yahoo.com/Entertainment/Movies_and_Films/Reviews/`, you will see a list of dozens of movie reviews and other movie-related Web sites. One of the better sites for movie reviews is *The Washington Post* at `http://www.washingtonpost.com/wp-srv/searches/movies.htm` (see Figure 21.1).

Figure 21.1.

The Washington Post *movie review page— search away!*

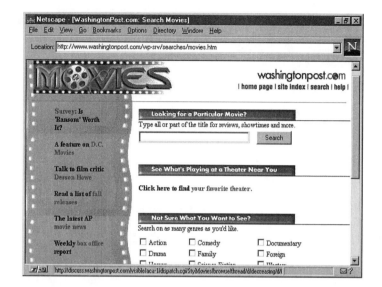

To Do: Look for a Movie Review

1. In the search area that asks you if you are Looking for a Particular Movie?, type Ransom (or a movie of your choice).

2. On the results page, you will see a link for every movie that matched your search term. Find your movie.

3. Click the link that takes you to the movie. In this case, there is a full review of the movie *Ransom* at *The Washington Post* (see Figure 21.2).

Don't be limited just by what you've looked at in this section. There are several movie categories at Yahoo!, and surely you will find several sites that you like. By the way, if you are interested in a "What's Hot" type list, check out Table 21.1, which lists the Web sites for all of the major movie studios. These sites often have video clips of their movies and more.

21

Figure 21.2.

The Post *reviewers are split. Want a second opinion? Go to the* Entertainment Weekly *review.*

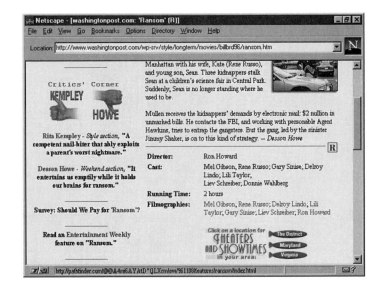

Table 21.1. Movie studio Web sites.

Studio	URL
MCA/Universal	`http://www.mca.com`
Metro Goldwyn Mayer	`http://www.mgmua.com`
Paramount Pictures	`http://www.paramount.com`
Sony Pictures	`http://www.spe.sony.com/Pictures/SonyMovies/index.html`
20th Century Fox	`http://www.tcfhe.com`
Walt Disney Studios	`http://www.disney.com/DisneyPictures/`
Warner Brothers	`http://www.movies.warnerbros.com/`

Movies in the News

Don't forget that there's more to the Internet than just what's on the Web. Usenet newsgroups are always a great place to go for any type of information. In fact, there is an entire hierarchy of newsgroups for movies. All twelve of these groups are under `rec.arts.movies`.

If your news server carries this hierarchy, you might want to check them out. In addition, there is an alt.movies hierarchy. Figure 21.3 shows a movie review by someone like you and me.

Figure 21.3.

rec.arts.movies.reviews *is sure to contain lots of reviews on the movies you want to see.*

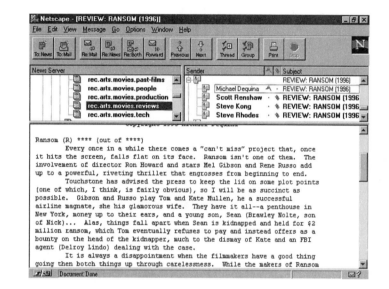

Do You Know the Way to San Jose?

Well, if you don't know the way to San Jose, the Internet certainly does. Among the more innovative Web sites out there is one called MapQuest. If you know your departure point and where you want to go, MapQuest can show you the way. Suppose you live in Lansing, Michigan and you want to go to San Jose, California...

To Do: Create a Map to San Jose

1. Point your browser at http://www.mapquest.com.
2. Click the TripQuest link from the menu at the bottom of the page.
3. At the TripQuest page, type the city and state of your destination and starting point.
4. Click the Calculate Directions button.
5. You now can read, print, or mail the directions, as well as click map blow-ups of your point of origin and destination (see Figure 21.4).

21

Figure 21.4.

There is no faster way to find out how to get there.

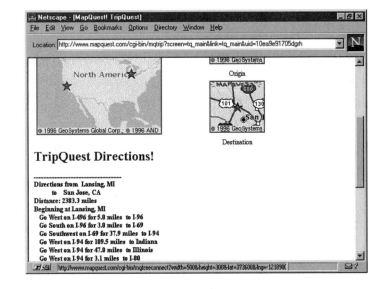

JUST A MINUTE

> I personally have used TripQuest for several trips and found the directions to be very accurate. However, you'll probably want to have an atlas handy when you hit the road just to be safe.

OK, Now What?

After you know how to get there, it might be nice if you could find something to do while you visit. For this, you can use Excite's city.net service:

To Do: Find Something to Do

1. Point your browser to http://www.city.net.
2. Scroll down to the Map A Location section and type San Jose in the city field.
3. Click the pop-up State menu and select California.
4. Click the Map It button.
5. You now can look at an interactive map of San Jose or choose from several activity categories.

Suppose you want to take in a San Jose Sharks hockey game while you are there. If you click the Sports & Rec link, you will go to a page that points you directly to the San Jose Sharks home page at http://www.nando.net/SportServer/hockey/nhl/sjs.htm. Simply scroll down the page to find the 1996-97 Schedule and click it. Actually, I couldn't have gotten luckier—my hometown Detroit Red Wings are playing at San Jose the Thursday I'm going to be there!

COFFEE BREAK

I'd like you to sit back for a moment and think about what you have just finished doing. Do you realize how amazing the Internet really is? Let me bring the point home.

Just to see what would be involved in planning such a trip without the Internet, I tried it myself. I got out my handy atlas to try and map my proposed trip to San Jose. Elapsed time: 40 minutes. Proposed Route: It'll get me there, but it's hardly concise.

I then spent another half hour on the phone trying to find San Jose's travel bureau. When I finally found it, I waited another 10 days for a small packet of information to arrive, which I then spent another hour sifting through to find something in which I was interested.

My total time spent on this project without the Internet? Over two hours of real time plus 10 days of waiting. It's easy to see that even an Internet beginner could do better than that! Remember, the Internet can be very valuable in terms of both time and money.

The Cosmopolitan Internet

There is no doubt that the United States dominates the Internet. Americans by far produce the most traffic and the most information on the Internet. However, other countries are on the Net and are getting more and more prevalent with every passing month.

Instead of picking a specific spot, it might be more helpful to show you some international resources that are of a general nature, because you are sure to be interested in different parts of the world yourself.

Let the World Come to You

One of the best places to start to find ongoing general information about various locations is the listserv, as you learned in Lesson 8, "Communicating with the World: Using Mailing Lists." There are several listservs to which you might be interested in subscribing in order to learn about the world.

One of the best listservs for the globetrotters (or those just interested on global happenings) is the Travel-L listserv. Subscribing is easy.

21

To Do: Subscribe to the Travel-L listserv

1. Compose a new e-mail message to LISTSERV@VM3090.EGE.EDU.TR.

2. Leave the Subject: field blank and type SUBSCRIBE TRAVEL-L in the body of your message.

3. Remember to turn off your signature if you are using one.

4. Send the message. You should begin receiving mail soon.

CAUTION

> Be warned that Travel-L is a very high-traffic listserv. If you are the kind of person who will check your mail only every week or so, you probably should not subscribe to this list.

Basically, this is a list on which people relate their travel experiences about various places they've been. You can find out where the good food is, where to find good jazz, or any of a hundred different pieces of information on places all over the world.

TIME SAVER

> If you don't feel like subscribing to this listserv, you can read the posts from the listserv as a newsgroup. All of the Travel-L posts are sent to the bit.listserv.travel-l newsgroup for anyone to read.

The following are other travel-related listservs of note:

☐ TRAVABLE@SJUVM.STJOHNS.EDU—TravAble Travel for the Disabled

☐ TRAVELUK-L@LISTSERV.AOL.COM—UK Travel e-mail List Server

Worldwide News

If you prefer to find out about the world in other ways, then perhaps you'd like to access some of the many great travel and culture newsgroups that are available via Usenet. There probably are well over 100 newsgroups that deal with these topics.

Many people are interested in various cultures throughout the world. If you use your newsgroup client and employ the methods you learned in Lesson 16, "Searching the Web for Virtually Anything," to search for newsgroups on culture, you will find that there are dozens of newsgroups on countries from Afghanistan to Zimbabwe (see Figure 21.5).

Figure 21.5.

Who says that there is no culture on the Internet?

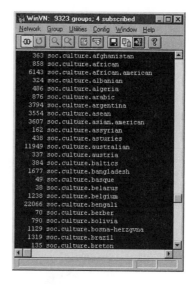

In addition, there are many newsgroups geared specifically toward the traveler. In particular, you might want to check out the `rec.travel.*` hierarchy of newsgroups. You are sure to find information supplied by those who have seen the world first-hand.

TIME SAVER

There is a newsgroup-related FTP site that also has a wealth of information for the globally curious. Point your browser to `ftp://ftp.solutions.net/rec-travel`, where you will find archived travel information by region, country, and topic. In the `rec-travel` directory, click the `cruise` link to find out about cruises.

The Best the World Has to Offer

Of course, the Web won't be left out of the travel game. After all, it *is* the *World* Wide Web! You can find Web sites written in different languages, about other countries and cultures, or any other far-reaching topic you can think of.

21

To Do: Find a Place to Visit

1. Point your browser to your favorite search engine.

2. Think of a country you'd like to find out more about and conduct a search for that country. For a better search, type your country plus the word `travel`.

3. Spend a few moments looking at the results. The first hit under an Excite search for `Australia +travel` was "The Down Under Traveller" Web site (see Figure 21.6).

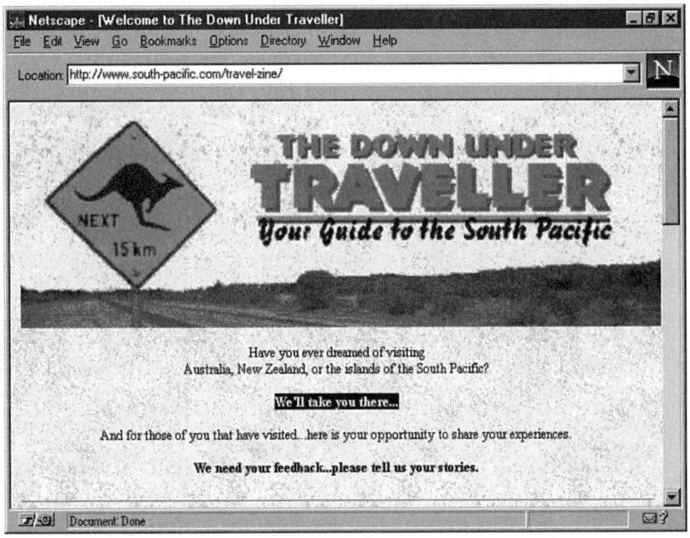

Figure 21.6.

`http://www.south-pacific.com/travel-zine/` *has a lot to offer for those going Down Under.*

For many Web and world surfers, the Virtual Tourist II is one of the favorite Web sites out there. When you point your browser to `http://www.vtourist.com/vt/`, you are presented with a map of the world. You need only click the part of the map in which you are interested until you find what you want.

For example, if you were to use the Virtual Tourist II to come up with information about Australia, you would click your way to the map shown in Figure 21.7.

Figure 21.7.

Clicking any area of this map would take you to city.net menus of information to help you find out more.

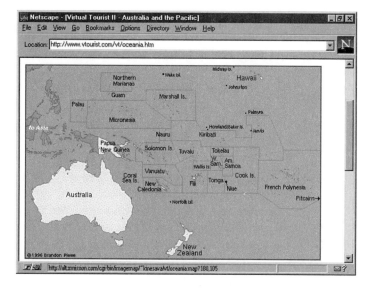

Again, for the traveler looking to see the world through the eyes of the Web, the importance of using search engines is almost inestimable. They generally are always a good place to start. However, keep in mind the many other resources available on the Internet for finding your special "corner of the world."

Summary

This lesson showed you some practical ways to use the Web at home for entertainment, travel, and more. You learned how to find out about hit movies before they ever appear onscreen. You also discovered new and exciting ways to plan your trips.

Finally, you learned that there is a reason for the term "world" in World Wide Web, as you discovered an Internet tour guide in the Virtual Tourist II. You were also able to realize the potential of listservs, newsgroups, and FTP in helping you trot the globe.

21

Workshop

The following workshop helps solidify the skills that you learned in this lesson.

Q&A

Q **Something that I've wondered about while reading this book and wonder even more about now is how current the information really is. Can the information I find be relied on?**

A As a rule, yes. If you run into small Web sites that have names you don't recognize, the resources might not be totally accurate or up-to-date. If you stick with major sites, such as city.net and *The Washington Post*, you are likely to get very accurate information. However, if ever you aren't sure, by all means, check out several resources to make sure the information you're getting is accurate.

Q **I speak fluent German and was wondering if I can actually search for German-speaking sites on the Web.**

A You sure can. My German isn't great, and about the only German word I know is *bier* (German for beer). However, I searched Excite for *bier* and found many German-speaking sites. In fact, the first hit was Bier aus Deutschland at `http://www.bier.de/`. Yes, you can find just about anything on the Internet.

Quiz

Take the following quiz to see how much you've learned.

Questions

1. Which of these options would be best if you wanted information on travel without having to go get it?

   (a) The `bit.listserv.travel-l` newsgroup

   (b) Searching the Web for `travel`

   (c) Subscribing to the Travel-L listserv

2. Using TripQuest eliminates the need for atlases or other resources when traveling.

   (a) True

   (b) False

3. Where is the best place to go for entertainment or travel information if you're not exactly sure where to start?

   (a) Usenet newsgroups

   (b) Any Web search engine

   (c) Listservs

Answers

1. (a)

2. (b) False. The smart traveler always uses several sources of information to be sure.

3. (b) You will rarely go wrong by starting out with an Internet search engine.

Activity

Plan out a trip of your own. It can either be imagined or real, domestic or foreign. See if you can plan a trip, including the route, mode of transportation, and at least three activities while you're there, using only the Internet. Make a list of all the information you discover, along with the time it took you to get it. Compare this to a reasonable estimate of how long it would take you to accomplish the same task without using the Internet.

21

Hour **22**

Education on the Internet

By now, everyone has heard of the great educational benefit of the Internet. Is it all hype? Most certainly not. In fact, as part of my work for Michigan State University, I have used the Internet as an integral part of various educational programs at all levels.

In this lesson, the following questions about education on the Internet will be answered:

- ☐ How can I get in touch with other teachers through the Internet?
- ☐ What are some specific K–12 resources on the Internet?
- ☐ What are some resources available for higher education institutions?
- ☐ Can you give me some examples of how one would find research and other academic information on the Internet?

You first are going to learn how you might connect with some other educators. From there, you will look at some resources geared specifically toward higher education professionals.

Educators on the Internet

Bob Matthews is an elementary mathematics and special education teacher at Green Hills School in Kalamazoo, Michigan. He is interested in distance education, math, and special education. If our hypothetical teacher wants to get in touch with other teachers and resources, what would he do? That's what you will find out.

JUST A MINUTE

> You might note that there is a pretty heavy emphasis on listservs in this section. Unfortunately, many K–12 teachers out there have very limited Internet access and often don't have access to the latest technology and computers. The K–12 resources you will see in this lesson try to take these factors into account.

Your Old Friend the Listserv

A vast number of K–12 teachers take advantage of the hundreds of educational listservs that are out there. They can locate listservs on many topics and can contact professionals and experts in their fields with the click of a mouse.

Bob is no different. He has decided that he would like to start off subscribing to three such listservs to see what will happen. Because he has read this book, he is going to start out at the Catalist Web site at `http://segate.sunet.se/lists/LIST_Q.html` (which was reviewed at length in Lesson 8, "Communicating with the World: Using Mailing Lists").

First, he is interested in distance education, so he would like to see if there are any listservs out there to help him. When he types in `distance education` in the search field at Catalist, he sees that there are indeed some listservs in which he's interested (see Figure 22.1).

22

Figure 22.1.

Catalist finds 16 distance education listservs, some of which look very promising.

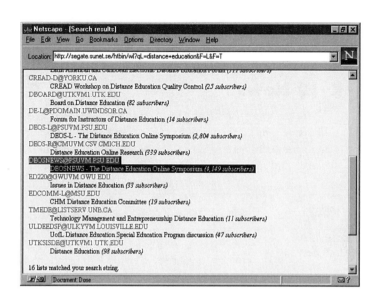

JUST A MINUTE

Pay attention to how many subscribers there are on these listservs. Lists with a lot of subscribers will have a lot of information but might be hard to keep current with all the mail they generate. Lists with a low number of subscribers might be easy to keep up with but might have little traffic.

After reading the information on how to subscribe to that list, Bob returns to the search page to search for a mathematics listserv. Because he doesn't really know where to begin, he searches for math,mathematics so that Catalist will find any listserv with either of these words in the title.

He is rewarded with 64 matches. Many of them are not really what he is looking for. However, two of them, the Methods of Teaching Mathematics at teachmat@listserv.uic.edu and the Mathematical, Logical, and Word Puzzles Discussion List at PUZZLE-L@LISTSERV.ACSU.BUFFALO.EDU, look particularly interesting.

Finally, he conducts a search for special education and finds the Special Education Discussion List at SPECED-L@UGA.CC.UGA.EDU among the several matches. After he has subscribed to these lists, he will probably monitor his e-mail for a few days to see what shows up, introduce himself to his new electronic colleagues, and begin gathering information.

K–12 News

There are other places Bob can go on the Internet to find other people who are interested in the same topics as he. After he starts WinVN, his newsreader, and brings up a list of all the newsgroups his news server carries, he is ready to find some relevant newsgroup. Maybe you'd like to find some newsgroups you are interested in, too.

TIME SAVER

Unlike Catalist searches for listservs, newsgroups won't have full "English" names. For example, don't look for a special education newsgroup. Instead, try special, education.special, or even sped or speced. Be creative in your search terms to find a newsgroup that's right for you.

To Do: Look for Interesting Newsgroups

1. By choosing Group|Find or clicking the Search toolbar button, search for distance. You will notice that WinVN locates the alt.education.distance newsgroup (see Figure 22.2).

2. With the group highlighted, choose Group|Subscribe Selected Groups.

3. Repeat the first two steps by conducting a search for math. Choose Group|Find Next (or press the F3 key) until you locate k12.ed.math.

4. Repeat the first two steps again, this time looking for special. If you repeat the search several times, you will find the group k12.ed.special.

You might notice that a few of the newsgroups you found were in the k12.* hierarchy. You might want to spend some time perusing the groups there. If you are a K–12 educator, you are sure to find a group that interests you.

Also, if you are interested in what educators in other countries are doing in education, just keep searching your newsgroups, and you'll come in contact with educators all over the world. If you continue your search for math, you will find math-related newsgroups in Canada, Germany, Taiwan, and other locales.

Figure 22.2.

WinVN can help you find a newsgroup on just about any educational topic, including Distance Education.

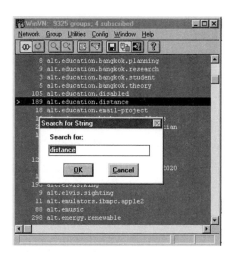

22

JUST A MINUTE

Although this section has focused on K–12 education, there are plenty of listservs and newsgroups available for those in post-secondary education as well. You can use the techniques learned in this section to search for just about any listserv or newsgroup.

K–12 on the Internet

It should be noted right away that, in essence, there really is little difference between finding educational resources and finding any other information on the Internet. World Wide Web and Gopher search engines are useful, as are many of the libraries and files available through Telnet and FTP.

Don't hesitate to use the same resources you would use for other purposes when you are looking for information on education. For example, an Excite search for k-12 +education produced over *two million* hits! The Internet is particularly useful to educators for many reasons, and you're going to look at these other resources in a little more detail now.

The World Is Your Classroom

One of the most exciting projects I ever worked on was a science project that was completed by two elementary schools in Michigan and Texas. For our project, the two schools took samples from nearby rivers and compared them. They took careful notes on indigenous vegetation, weather patterns, and other factors, all of which were gathered over the Internet.

They then used the Internet to compare their results and compose a final project. The power of collaboration like this can't be denied, but how would you start?

One of the first sites to look at would be the listing of K–12 Web servers located at The Texas Education NETwork (TENET) at `http://www-tenet.cc.utexas.edu/Pub/education/` `K_12states.html` (see Figure 22.3). From there, you can click any state's K–12 schools, school districts, or other resources.

Figure 22.3.

The U.S. is full of schools to collaborate with on projects of all types.

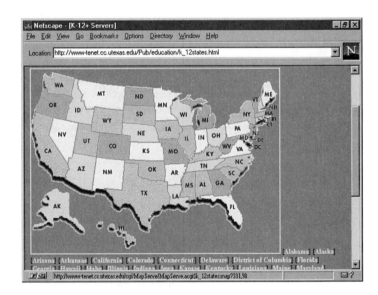

For example, suppose you are looking for an elementary school in Michigan with which to do a collaborative project.

22

To Do: Look for a School

1. From the state-by-state listing, click Michigan.
2. Next, click the School Districts link.
3. Now click Ingham Intermediate School District.
4. From there, click Ingham County Schools. You then could proceed to any school you like.
5. To finish the exercise, click Lansing.
6. Finally, scroll down and click Home Pages. After you do, you can e-mail or contact many staff and teachers in the Lansing School District.

CAUTION

> If you would like to collaborate on a project, have a very specific, well-designed project in mind. It is an undue burden (not to mention bad etiquette) to just start e-mailing teachers asking if they'd like to "work on some kind of project" with you.

Of course, you could click any state and follow many links to other schools and teachers throughout the nation. You might find that you can forge some lasting educational relationships with the help of the Internet.

The Computer Without the Internet

As shocking as it might seem, some teachers might want to use their classroom computers for reasons other than accessing the Internet. Many teachers want to make use of educational software. Although there is a lot of commercial software out there, it often is too expensive for teachers and school districts to purchase.

However, the Internet offers a wealth of educational software for all K–12 levels. But how do you find it?

You could go to http://www.shareware.com, and you'd probably eventually find quite a bit. However, Ziff-Davis already has compiled over 10,000 shareware titles for you in ZD Net Software Library, located at http://www.hotfiles.com/educate.html (see Figure 22.4).

Figure 22.4.

Browse by grade level or conduct a search for the software you want.

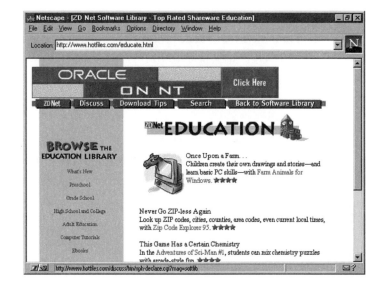

Suppose you were looking for some software to use in your high school chemistry class. Could you locate some? Let's find out.

To Do: Find Some Chemistry Software

1. Click the High School and College link to find higher-level programs.

2. Notice that there are two pages of high school and college shareware programs from which to choose. Scroll down to the bottom of the page and click the Next link.

3. Scroll down on the next page until you find the four-star-rated Periodic Table of the Elements (Cyber) v.2.1. Click its link.

4. You'll be taken to an information page on the Periodic Table software (see Figure 22.5). From here, you can simply click the Download button to put the software on your computer.

Figure 22.5.

This nifty piece of software will set you back only $5 if you decide to keep it.

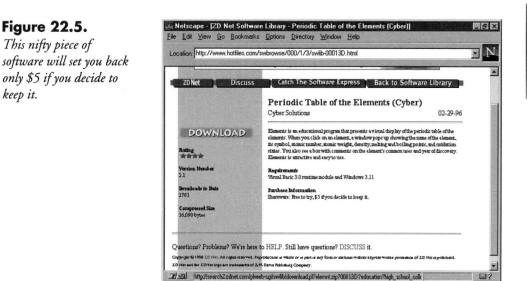

In addition to this piece of software, there were almost a dozen other chemistry and high school science programs available at this site. If you simply cannot find something for which you're looking, you can always conduct a search of the site.

There are many other ways in which you can use the Internet in your classroom. Collaboration and educational software use are just two of them. Feel free to explore some more on your own to discover even more uses.

Who's Who in Higher Education

The amount of higher education material out there is staggering. Literally hundreds of universities now are on the Web, giving users access to libraries, research, and other resources that only universities can offer.

When searching for anything, it's good to have a jumping-off point from which you can find your way to any university you want. This "jumping-off" place for higher education resources has got to be http://web.mit.edu/cdemello/www/geog.html. This page lists over 3,000 universities worldwide.

If you are interested in only U.S. universities, click the United States link to go to http://www.clas.ufl.edu/CLAS/american-universities.html. This page will take you to Web sites for hundreds of universities from Abilene Christian to Youngstown State.

JUST A MINUTE

If community colleges are more your speed, check out `http://www.mcli.dist.maricopa.edu/cgi-bin/search.html`. It has over 500 community colleges from which to choose.

Research, Research, Research

Knowing how to get to other universities and their resources is valuable, of course, but it's research that really drives higher education. Wouldn't it be wonderful if you could use the Internet to conduct some of that research?

Well, you can. Many journals and other research sources are already online, and more are joining them every day. Suppose you were a professor interested in 19th-century literature doing research on Edgar Allan Poe; where would you go?

An outstanding starting point would be the Washington and Lee University's Libraries and Research Web page at `http://liberty.uc.wlu.edu/~dgrefe/various/libres.html` (see Figure 22.6). You would see jumping-off points for a variety of different research resources.

Figure 22.6.

Periodicals, libraries, electronic journals, reference sources, mailing lists, and more. You'd better bookmark this one!

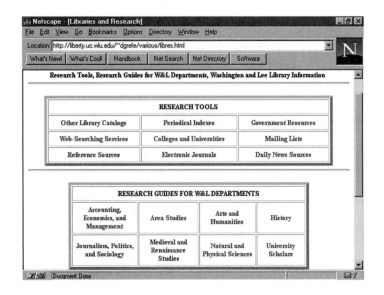

Although the second section of this page says that the listed resources are for Washington and Lee departments, these resources are generally available for anyone interested in the related topics. You will note that there is a section on the Arts and Humanities; you'll return to them later.

First, you might want to try your hand at some of the general resources.

To Do: Look for Some Periodical Information

1. Click the Periodical Indexes link.

2. Go to UnCover. By the way, you might want to spend some time exploring UnCover more in-depth on your own time. It is an excellent resource in and of itself.

3. Scroll down and click Search the UnCover Databases.

4. Next, click Search UnCover Now.

5. From the search page, type Poe on line 2 and press Enter.

6. At the time of this search, there were 151 articles about Poe. I found one article titled "The Violence of Melancholy: Poe against Himself," published in the Fall 1996 *American Literary History* periodical (see Figure 22.7).

Figure 22.7.

There is a wealth of information about Edgar Allan Poe being written even today.

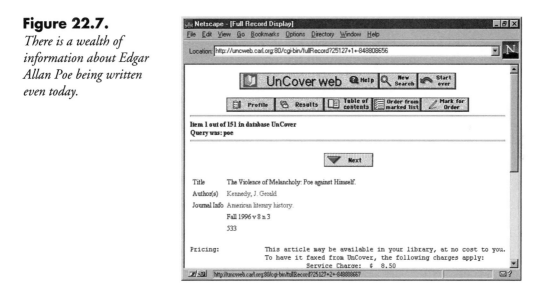

If you go back to the Libraries and Research page, you might want to explore a few of the other general resources available. In particular to our topic, following these paths will take you to even more information:

☐ **Electronic Journals | Philosophy and Literature | Search | edgar AND poe** will find a lot of related articles available through Project Muse, which is a pay for service database.

☐ **Other Library Catalogs/Libweb/Keyword Search/search for Humanities/Getty Research Institute/Iris on the Web/General Keywords/edgar poe** will find 33 resources, including a particularly interesting book on Poe written in 1908.

☐ **Reference Sources | Argus Clearinghouse | Humanities | Search | edgar and poe/Edgar Allen Poe/hypertext** will take you to a Web page that points to entire Web sites devoted to Edgar Allen Poe.

Before you're finished at Washington and Lee, take a look at one of the departmental links available.

To Do: Link Up with the Department

1. Click Arts and Humanities.

2. Next, click English and then select the Literary Resources and Guides option.

3. Now choose Literary Resources on the Net, and click the American category on the resulting page.

4. The next page shows a large number of links all related to American Literary resources. Scroll down and click Nineteenth-Century, and on the next page, find the 19th-Century link and click it.

5. Finally, scroll down the page until you find the entire section dedicated to Edgar Allan Poe pictured in Figure 22.8.

Before you go on, it is important to remember once again that, even though you chose to explore a 19th-century American author, you could have just as easily searched for information on modern quantum mechanics theory or the latest writings on supply-side economics. The topic really is irrelevant; the process is not.

22

Figure 22.8.

This mysterious 19th-century bard seems to have followers everywhere.

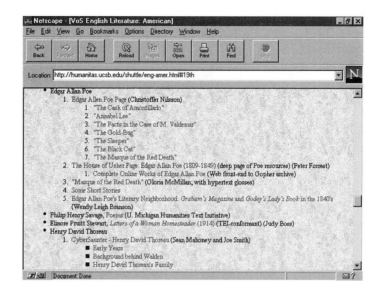

22

Summary

This lesson gave you some examples of what can be found on the Internet for educators at all levels. You learned how to find listservs and newsgroups to talk to colleagues and find information. As an added bonus, you found out how you can find educational software that you can actually use.

In addition, you are now able to find any university in the world through the Internet. Finally, with the help of Washington and Lee University, you can now look for research information on just about any topic.

Q&A

Q I'm really surprised you didn't mention ERIC. Isn't it accessible on the Internet?

A It sure is! Go to http://www.askeric.org for information on education. Visit its virtual library, ask one of its staff a hard-to-answer question through its Question and Answer service, or search its ERIC database. I didn't cover it because it is very easy to use and lots of books cover it. I wanted to give you some more in-depth coverage of resources that might be just as useful, but possibly harder to find and use.

Q **It sounds like you could probably write a whole book on education and the Internet. Does one already exist?**

A Yes. *Education on the Internet* by Jill Ellsworth (Sams Publishing, ISBN: 0-672-30595-X) is still available. Even though it is now more than two years old, it still contains a lot of useful information.

Workshop

The following workshop helps solidify the skills that you learned in this lesson.

Quiz

Take the following quiz to see how much you've learned.

Questions

1. When searching for a mathematics education newsgroup, what term would most likely find a newsgroup for you?

    (a) `math`

    (b) `mathematics`

    (c) `math education`

2. Which of the following would not be a likely way to use the Internet for most K–12 teachers in their instruction?

    (a) Location and use of educational software

    (b) Collaboration with other schools or educators

    (c) Real-time video collaboration with other students around the world

3. True or False: After you have a good starting point for doing research, the topic on which you are trying to find information really isn't that important.

22

Answers

1. (a)

2. (c) The TV commercials look nice, but most schools simply aren't ready to take advantage of this technology yet.

3. True. The method, not the specific subject, is the important thing when doing research on the Internet.

Activities

For K–12 teachers:

Using the methods you learned in this chapter, find at least one listserv and one newsgroup related to what you teach. Using a project that you already use for your class, see if you can turn it into a collaborative project and locate a school or teacher to share it with.

For post-secondary educators:

Pick a topic on which you currently need information and, using the techniques and sites you learned about in this lesson, find at least five resources on the Internet to help you.

Hour 23

Taking Care of Business Using the Internet

Whether you are starting up your own business or looking for the latest stock report, the Net has got something to offer. Business, advertising, and other free-market forces have in large part been responsible for the incredible recent growth of the Internet, so it should be no surprise that these elements play such an important role on the Net today.

This lesson will answer the following questions about business on the Internet:

☐ What information is out there for those running a business out of their home?

☐ Can I get up-to-date financial information on the Internet?

☐ What are some of the ways in which I can use non-Web sources of information for business?

☐ Are there resources to find employment on the Internet?

As with the other lessons in this section, there is far too much information on this topic to cover completely in a few short pages. However, this lesson should give you an excellent foundation for finding those business resources that exist on the Internet that are of interest to you.

The Entrepreneurial Internet

The fastest-growing sector of the business market is in small and home-based businesses. Some financial experts even estimate that it won't be long before businesses employing fewer than 50 people make up the majority of employers in the United States. Regardless of whether these predictions are true, entrepreneurs will continue to need and use information to help them realize their part of the American Dream.

This portion of the lesson is going to take you through some of the resources available from the perspective of my Aunt Rea Prenure. Aunt Rea has been trying to start her own small business for a long time. Let's see what's out there for her.

Getting Started

Rea has been keenly interested in craft items all of her life, and so, even though she isn't sure exactly what she's going to do with crafts, she wants to see what she *can* do. One of her many talents is in inventing and designing new craft patterns and tools to help others enjoy their own crafts. Whatever she does, she knows she wants to make these available to others, so she first needs to find out all she can about copyrights, inventions, and other legal issues.

The first place she goes is to DaVinci's Inventor Homepage at `http://sulcus.berkeley.edu/invention` (see Figure 23.1). Scrolling down the page reveals many interesting links.

To Do: Explore DaVinci's Inventor Homepage

1. Click the `Inventor & Entrepreneur Associations & Organizations` link to find out about many organizations that help inventors get started and keep going.
2. Click the `Master List of Legal Resources` in DaVinci's Workshop for information on patent law and related issues.
3. Click the `Master List of Usenet Links` in DaVinci's Workshop to find out about newsgroups for inventors such as `alt.inventors`, `misc.int-property`, and `misc.entrepreneurs.moderated`.

23

Figure 23.1.

DaVinci's Inventor Homepage is a great place for the creative entrepreneur to start.

Next, she wants to find out about franchising opportunities, so she checks out the Franchise Opportunity Superstore at `http://branch.com/franchise/franord.htm`, where she can fill out an interactive form to receive franchise information.

CAUTION

It's business owner beware as well as buyer beware on the Internet. Keep in mind that many sites dealing directly with "helping" businesses are also selling something. As with anything else, make sure you get multiple references on a source before pursuing it.

She also visits FranInfo at `http://www.frannet.com`. At FranInfo, she can get a lot of information about franchises. One of the first things she does is click the Self Test #1 link to see if she actually is suited to franchise ownership (see Figure 23.2).

Figure 23.2.

Some people might need to find out if they're cut out to own a franchise.

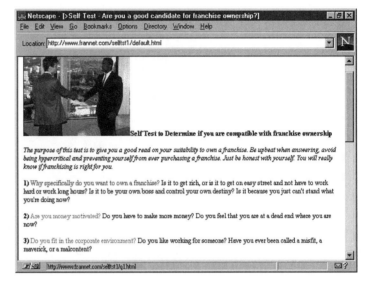

Going to the Next Level

Now that Rea has some beginning information, she's ready to move on. She has heard that there is information on starting, financing, and expanding a business, as well as local small business resources available at the Small Business Administration (SBA) Home Page (http://www.sbaonline.sba.gov). She was right. She even checks out the link on Women In Business available at SBA online.

For even more information, she goes to the Dun & Bradstreet Small Business Services page at http://www.dbisna.com/dbis/sbs/hsbs.htm. There, she can get the basics on business management and other practical information for keeping her business going.

The Long Haul

Of course, Rea has bookmarked in her Web browser the sites she has already checked out because they have excellent information for continuing a business as well as starting one. However, there are a couple of stops she wants to make before she's finished.

Her first stop is to check out the Internal Revenue Service (IRS) page at http://www.irs.ustreas.gov. While browsing America's "favorite" branch of the government, she can download forms or get valuable information, including tax information for businesses, at http://www.irs.ustreas.gov/prod/bus_info/.

Finally, she wants a little free advertising, so she is going to list her business with the Home Based Business Yellow Pages.

To Do: List Your Company in Online Yellow Pages

1. Point your browser at http://www.tab.com/Home.Business/yp.html.

2. Click the Submit Listing form link.

3. Fill out the form and click the Send Form button. You now are listed.

JUST A MINUTE

> You might be wondering about creating a Web page for your business. Well, most small businesses serve a local community and so choose to go with a local Internet company on which to advertise their business. Even a local Web page is accessible worldwide, but local companies generally have more visibility and name recognition for those clients they serve.

23

The Financial Market on the Web

In financial markets, seconds can mean money, so what better place is there to use the Internet? Wherever up-to-date market information is needed, the Internet certainly delivers. Get ready for a whirlwind tour of business that points you to some resources available for both beginners and experts.

CAUTION

> You might notice that none of the free Web sites listed in this section have up-to-the-minute stock figures during the trading day due to contractual considerations. However, after a market has closed, these sites are invaluable not just for listing closing numbers, but also for reporting on trends and other vital information.

More Than Just the News

In addition to delivering great worldwide coverage of the news, Cable News Network (CNN) now delivers up-to-the-minute financial news right to your desktop with CNNfn—the Financial Network. For those of you, like me, who don't know a lot about business, let's start out simple.

To Do: Browse the Financial Network

1. Point your browser to http://cnnfn.com.

2. Now scroll down to the bottom of the page and click the research it link.

3. Next, click the Reference Desk icon.

4. Click the Glossary of business terms.

5. Browse through the terms. For example, did you know that the Consumer Price Index (CPI) is the "measure of price changes in consumer goods and services used to identify periods of inflation or deflation"?

JUST A MINUTE

> Those interested in business or any kind of finance might want to bookmark this business glossary. If you think the computer field is full of jargon, wait until you tackle finance and business!

Many people who are interested in finance and business want to keep up with what's happening in all of the financial markets. CNNfn can help here, too. After returning to CNNfn's home page, click the Markets link and then click US Stock Markets. This will take you to a page that will look something like Figure 23.3.

Figure 23.3.

Bull or Bear? CNNfn tells you about gainers, losers, volumes, and other valuable information on all the major markets.

Netscape - [CNNfn - US Stock Markets]

File Edit View Go Bookmarks Options Directory Window Help

Location: http://cnnfn.com/markets/us_markets.html

Dow Jones Industrial Average Last updated: 16:05:00 ET, 1996/11/26	Level 6528.41 Change -19.38

NYSE Composite Last updated: 16:00:00 ET, 1996/11/26	Level 397.98 Change -0.88

Actives	Gainers	Losers	52-week high	52-week low	Volume alerts	High alerts	Low alerts

NASDAQ Composite Last updated: 16:42:00 ET, 1996/11/26	Level 1281.20 Change 0.83

Actives	Gainers	Losers	52-week high	52-week low	Volume alerts	High alerts	Low alerts

5% of 2K

From the Markets page, notice also that there is information on world stock markets, currencies, commodities, and more. In fact, just in case you are interested in how the Internet is doing in finance, from the Markets page (at http://ccnfn.com/markets/) click tech stocks and then Internet (see Figure 23.4).

23

Figure 23.4.

Hmmm, looks like the Internet didn't do so well on the stock market today.

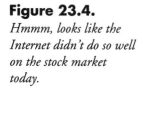

Before moving on, you should note just how much this Web site has to offer; you can do research, get the latest financial news, and look at resources related to your money. All this and more from CNNfn—a must-see Web site for the financially minded.

TIME SAVER

You might want to use CNNfn as your primary source of information on the New York Stock Exchange (NYSE). Although the Exchange does have a Web site at http://www.nyse.com, the site really doesn't have a lot to offer and isn't very up to date. On the day that I found NYSE's close for Tuesday on CNNfn, the Exchange's own Web site's numbers were more than a day behind.

The Next Hundred Years

Nasdaq recently ran a series of commercials claiming that it's the "stock market for the next 100 years." If Web sites are any indication, the company's commercials might just be right. If you are interested in progressive, cutting-edge stocks such as Microsoft, Novell, Oracle, Sun, Adobe, and Dell, Nasdaq is the place for you.

In addition to very current information, links to major companies' Web sites and more, Nasdaq's site offers a very comprehensive number of choices right from its front page (see Figure 23.5). Get multiple quotes, find out what stocks are most active, browse the Nasdaq Top 100 stocks, and more, all from the Nasdaq home page.

Figure 23.5.

Find out how the day's trading went, and a whole lot more, from Nasdaq's Web site.

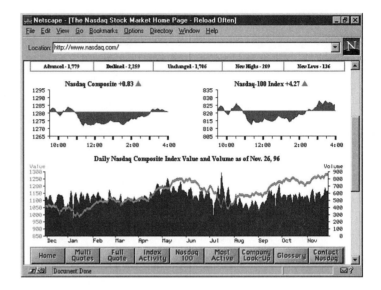

The following is a short list of some of Nasdaq's more useful features as accessed from its home page:

☐ Trends and Stock History: Click the Full Quote button, and then enter the code of the desired stock (for example, MSFT is Microsoft) and click Enter. Next, scroll down, click the radio button that indicates how many months of history you want to get on the stock, and click Get Graph. You will be taken to a page of detailed information on the stock you choose.

☐ Click the Contact Nasdaq button, and then click the FAQ link to get some answers to a few questions that are frequently asked about Nasdaq.

☐ To get a trading code for any company, click the Company Look-Up button. Next, type in the name of the company and click Enter to view the results.

Visit Wall Street

If you are one of those people who must have the most current information, perhaps you should visit *The Wall Street Journal's* Web site. For a fee, you can gain access to its Interactive Edition, which will give you 24-hour-a-day updates on financial markets, along with other news.

To Do: Visit *The Wall Street Journal* site

1. Point your browser to http://www.wsj.com.

2. Click the Learn More link to find out more about the Interactive Edition.

3. Next, click the Quick Tour icon and follow each link to get a complete picture of what the Interactive Edition is all about (see Figure 23.6).

Figure 23.6.

The WSJ Interactive Edition certainly has a lot to offer.

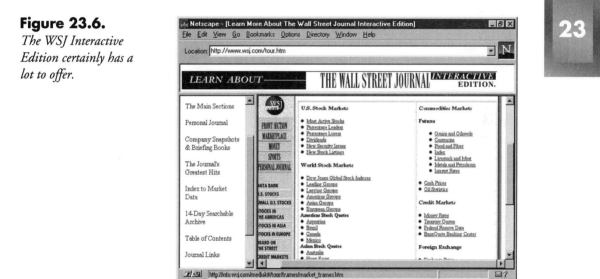

It won't take long to realize that there really is nothing to *The Wall Street Journal* Web site unless you subscribe, because every area is restricted. It offers an e-mail link as well as a toll-free number on its front page to enable you to subscribe. As of the time of this writing, the subscription price was $49 a year.

TIME SAVER

> You might want to keep an eye out for special offers. For example, at the time of this writing, *The Wall Street Journal* was offering several months free for using the latest edition of Internet Explorer. These types of offers are common on the Internet.

Get a Job

Who would ever think of looking for a job on the Internet? Well, you would, of course. Job searching and location services are popping up all over the Internet and offer yet another viable avenue of pursuit for those seeking employment.

JUST A MINUTE

Even though the types of job offerings on the Net are changing, you might find that there still are an awful lot of technical and computer-related jobs available on the Internet. However, this is already changing, and as more non-technical people get on the Net, it will change even more.

Searching for the Search

Because there are so many resources for job locators out there, you might want to first spend some time with your good old Web search engine to build a list of bookmarks that suit your needs.

For example, an Excite search for `employment +search` produced over 100,000 hits, many of which led to actual job locator sites. Another page you will want to bookmark is

```
http://www.yahoo.com/Business_and_Economy/Companies/Career_and_Job_Search_
Services/Resume_and_Job_Banks/Job_Banks/
```

This Yahoo! directory has links to dozens of online resumé and job-location sites on the Internet. You'll want to spend some time to see which one best suits you. You'll look at a couple as test cases in the following section.

America's Job Bank

For the sites you are going to look at, assume that you are looking for a job as a freelance writer, a fairly common "supplemental" and primary job for many in the U.S. today (myself included).

To Do: Find a Job Online

1. Point your browser to `http://www.ajb.dni.us/`.
2. Click the `Job Search Index` link.
3. Next, click the `Keyword Search` option (although you can use any of the other options, as well).

23

4. Now type writer in the Keyword Phrase: field. You can also restrict your search by state if you want.

5. Click the View Jobs Now button to see your jobs displayed. You probably will also want to view the jobs in groups of 100 or more to reduce the amount of paging you will have to conduct.

6. You now can place an X in the boxes of those jobs in which you are interested and then click the View Jobs button. If you want, you can sort the resulting list of jobs by salary, state, city, and other criteria. A typical job listing will look something like Figure 23.7.

Figure 23.7.

This is a typical job listing with America's Job Bank.

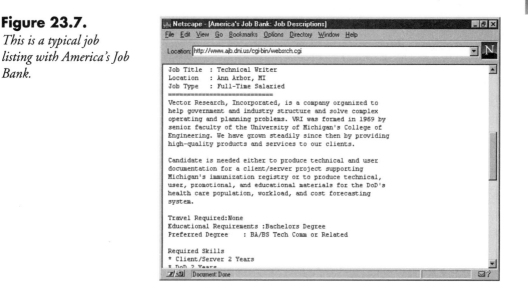

7. When you've found a job in which you are interested, scroll down and click the How To Apply button to find out how to apply for the job.

JobBank USA

Now look for that same job at another site called JobBank USA.

To Do: Try Another Online Job Resource

1. Point your browser to http://www.jobbankusa.com/.

2. Click the Find A Job link.

3. Next, click the Search For Jobs link.

4. Now type writer in the Keyword: field. You can fill in any of the other fields you want, but only this one is required.

5. A list of all matching available jobs will be listed. Click one to view it (see Figure 23.8). Contact information for each job is provided at the bottom of each job's page.

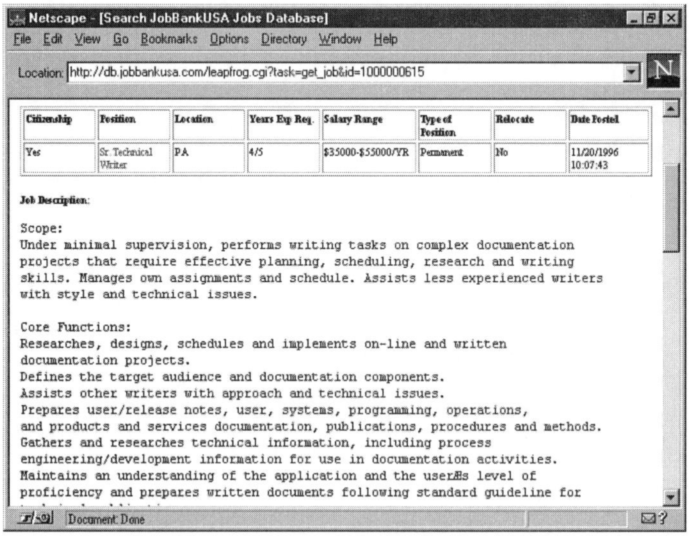

Figure 23.8.

JobBank doesn't have quite the selection of America's Job Bank, but there still are a few good-paying jobs here.

Job Potpourri

Many people would like to have a little help in how to go about finding a job. There is a definite need to brush up on important skills and techniques when you are looking for a job. There are, of course, sites out there to help with this, as well.

A very interesting as well as informative site is the Kaplan Career Center Web site at http://www.kaplan.com/career/. It offers interview simulation games, links, and an online Career Counselor and job search software.

From this page, click Links to get information on just about everything you'll need to know when getting a job. Use this page, as well as the Yahoo! job categories, to find places to submit your resumé, refine your techniques, and more. Break a leg!

Summary

This lesson showed you some of the resources available for business on the Internet. You first discovered all of the resources out there for those looking to start a business for themselves. In addition, you found out that there are many ways on the Net in which to find someone else to work for, as well.

You also know how people keep up with financial and business markets on the Internet by looking at Nasdaq, CNNfn, and other online market resources.

Workshop

The following workshop helps solidify the skills that you learned in this lesson.

Q&A

Q Is the Web the only place to get business information?

A No, but it certainly is the easiest. In arenas such as business, where current information is at a premium, however, the Web really is the best place to go. The best non-Web resources for business on the Internet is Usenet. Use your newsreader to search for `biz`, `jobs`, `employ`, and other keywords to find appropriate newsgroups.

Q I have a disability and am seeking employment. Is there anywhere for me?

A The business community is just starting to see the value of disabled workers. One site to which you might want to go is The Open Door Employment and Disability Network at `http://www.mrs.mjc.state.mi.us/`. This site is run by a Michigan state agency dedicated to helping persons with disabilities find employment. You might find some valuable information there.

Q I'm looking for temporary employment; how can I find it?

A Many temporary agencies are now online, as well. A few are Manpower at `http://www.manpower.com`, Adia at `http://www.adia.com`, and Olsten at `http://www.olsten.com`.

Quiz

Take the following quiz to see how much you've learned.

Questions

1. Which Web Site probably won't help a small business owner?

   (a) Small Business Association On-Line

   (b) IRS On-Line

   (c) The Nasdaq Web Site

2. It is possible to get up-to-the-minute stock reports any time of the day.

   (a) True

   (b) False

3. Which job would you be least likely to find on the Internet?

   (a) Electrical Engineer

   (b) Technical Writer

   (c) Housekeeper

Answers

1. (c)

2. (b) Contractual obligations prevent this.

3. (c) Maybe some day.

Activity

Choose a company in which you are interested and, using the resources covered in this lesson, develop a "portfolio" of the company, such as stock history, financial performance, general news, and anything else you can find.

Hint: It would be a good idea to pick a large, national company.

Hour 24

The Internet Just for Fun

You've put in a lot of work over the preceding 23 lessons, so now it's time to have some fun. What you find in the following pages may have almost no useful value whatsoever. But that's okay! Sometimes you just have to let loose a little bit.

In this lesson, you can find answers to the following questions regarding business on the Internet:

- ☐ Can the Web make me laugh?
- ☐ What are some of the funniest Web sites?
- ☐ Can you show me some newsgroups to brighten my day?
- ☐ What's just plain bizarre on the Web?
- ☐ What would I do if I were looking for stuff on a particular funny topic?

I hope that you'll find some rhyme or reason to this lesson as you read on. But face it, the people who come up with most of the stuff you'll look at here have way too much time on their hands!

Make Me Laugh

The most time-honored source of laughter is the good, old, simple joke. One-liners, knock-knocks, and a hundred other kinds of jokes can keep us in stitches. Let's find some of them, shall we?

TIME SAVER

> A great place to start looking for joke-related Web sites is `http://www.yahoo.com/Entertainment/Humor_Jokes_and_Fun/Jokes/`. Here you can find dozens of links to joke sites of different kinds.

A Joke-a-Day

Some of the best joke sites are the ones that cycle their humor. In other words, these sites can display random jokes, a different joke every day, and the like. These sites can be interesting and fun. Let's take a look at a few of them now.

JUST A MINUTE

> Many of these pages contain joke archives and links to other joke sites. Look for these links, and you'll never be at a lack for humor.

- ☐ ALLWORLD's Joke of the Day at `http://allworld.net/allworld/jokes/awjokes.html` has a different joke for you every day. For example, did you know that Coca-Cola was originally translated into Chinese as "bite the wax tadpole"?

- ☐ arbor.com's Joke of the Day page has cheesy graphics but funny jokes. Check it out at `http://www.arbor.com/joke/`.

- ☐ Netcenter's Joke of the Day assures that you get at least one good joke every day. While visiting the page at `http://netcenter.com/daily.html`, you can discover that Groucho Marx said, "Outside of a Dog, a book is Man's Best Friend. Inside of a dog, it's too dark to read!"

- ☐ If you like puns, you can find some real groaners at the Pun of the Day site, which is shown in Figure 24.1. When you go to this site at `http://www.escape.ca/~pun/potd.htm`, you get puns that tell you "those interested only in board games at Christmas might just be chess nuts roasting by an open fire."

24

Figure 24.1.

Get a new pun every day, enter a contest, or find more joke pages here.

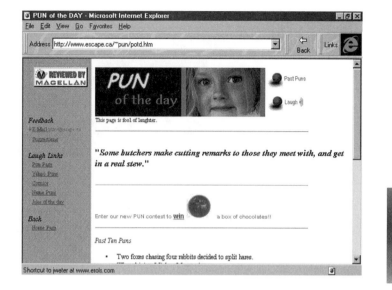

Topical Jokes

Many people like certain types of jokes. Blonde jokes, lawyer jokes, and light bulb jokes are among the more popular. If you have a fascination with a certain type of joke, the Internet has plenty for you, too:

☐ How many hippies does it take to screw in a light bulb? Three—one to change the light bulb and two to say "Oh, wow!" Get a new one of these classics every 10 seconds at `http://www.crc.ricoh.com:8080/~marcush/lightbulb/random.cgi`.

☐ Lawyer jokes have been around for years, as you can find at Nolo's Favorite Lawyer Jokes page at `http://www.nolo.com/jokes/jokes.html`. Can you believe that you can find over 20 categories of lawyer jokes?

☐ The redneck joke, near and dear to this redneck's heart, was made popular by the comic Jeff Foxworthy. To find this kind of joke, go to the Fort Ogden Outpost at `http://www.konnections.com/outpost/foredneck.html`, as shown in Figure 24.2. If you've been on TV more than five times describing the sound of a tornado, you might be a redneck.

☐ Musician jokes? Being a musician myself, I didn't think anyone would take the time to write jokes about us, but sure enough, Spence's Music Jokes at `http://www.primenet.com/~luckycat/musjokes.htm` has done it. How do you get an electric guitarist to turn down? Put sheet music in front of him!

Figure 24.2.

Are you a redneck? Find out here!

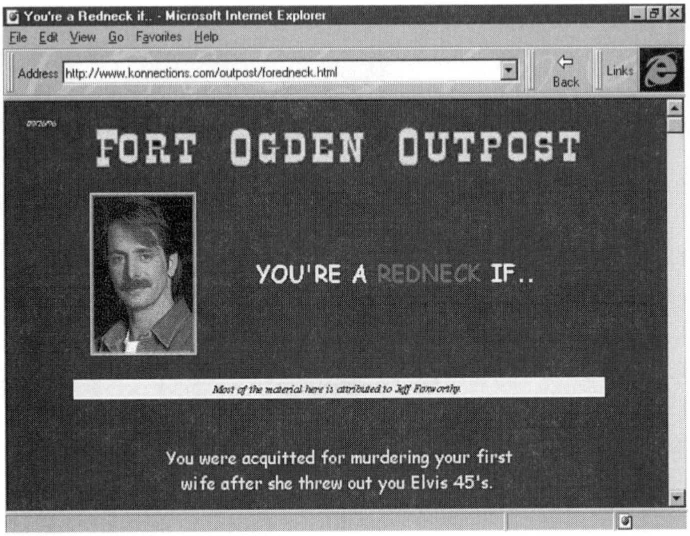

They Said It

Most people who follow comedy also follow the comedians who create the humor. Several sites cover jokes and material by particular comedians:

- ☐ Find out more about the host of *The Tonight Show* at Nicolai's Jay Leno Tribute Page at `http://www2.dk-online.dk/users/Nicolai_Ascanius_Jorgensen/leno.htm`. Find out everything there is to know about the "guy with the jaw."

- ☐ Opposite Jay is David Letterman, who is famous for his Top Ten lists. You can see all the lists and more by going to `http://www.cbs.com/lateshow/`, as shown in Figure 24.3. While there, you can find that the top sign you have a bad airline pilot is when he "keeps referring to the control tower as 'Mommy.'"

TIME SAVER

If you're interested in more comedians, go to `http://www.yahoo.com/Business_and_Economy/Companies/Entertainment/Comedy/Comedians/`. Oh, yeah, they're out there.

24

Figure 24.3.
Peruse the Top Ten lists, take a look at Dave, and get more Late Show information.

A Quick Tour of the Bizarre

Some things defy explanation or definition. These things you might call "bizarre." Next, let's visit the world of the bizarre and truly strange. If you're looking for something truly off-the-wall, begin with the sites listed in the following sections. To peruse more on your own, you might want to visit http://www.yahoo.com/Entertainment/Humor_Jokes_and_Fun/Bizarre/.

CAUTION

> On the Net, "bizarre" can also mean extremely offensive or off-color, so choose your spots carefully.

Websites-R-Us

One of the strangest experiences you will ever have is a visit to the Roadkills-R-Us Web site of Miles O'Neal. Every page causes you to either laugh or scratch your head as you wonder what you're missing, as you can see in Figure 24.4. But, hey, Miles does a better job of explaining his site than I could: "Roadkills-R-Us was formed on Usenet in 1988. It was formed in, and exists solely in cyberspace, as do its products. Dedicated to recycling as far up the food chain as possible, RRU (TM) is known throughout the inner solar system for its fine food and other products made from roadkill." Though Miles is the president of the company, he has capable help from the likes of Suzi Styrofoam and Gladys Gloria Glasshead.

Figure 24.4.

The RRU Web site at
`http://www.rru.com`
takes you to a virtual
world of virtual insanity.

From the RRU home page, you can go to the RRU News Flush, find out how much different types of roadkill cost these days, or find out about the Death Country, Jazz Rap, Tejano Punk Muzak, Barfy Manilow RRU jammin band. Whatever you do, check your sanity at the door.

Only Those Worthy

The Wacky Ninja home page is another shrine of the bizarre. With an apparent fixation on Twinkies and kitty litter, this one keeps you wondering if actual human beings really think up this stuff.

To Do: Learning About Twinkies

1. Point your browser to `http://www.owlnet.rice.edu/~gouge/index.html`.
2. Click the `T.W.I.N.K.I.E. Experiment` link to go to a particularly strange page, which is shown in Figure 24.5.
3. Click any of the fun and wacky Twinkie experiments listed at the bottom of the page. My favorite is the `Maximum Density Text`.
4. Try the experiment yourself if you have a Twinkie around. You may find out that a Twinkie is 68 percent air, for example, and only 32 percent "Twinkie stuff."

24

Figure 24.5.

If you like Twinkies, you'll love this site.

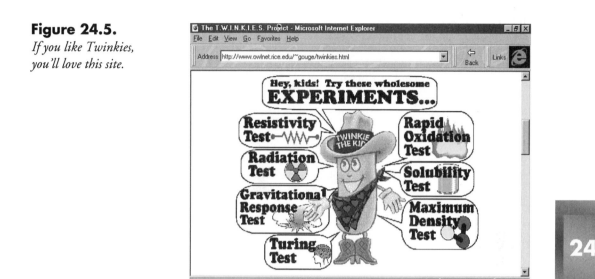

It'll Crack You Up

Somewhere between Joke of the Day and Mind-Numbing Strangeness is the CrackedWEB, as shown in Figure 24.6. Every week offers a new story of satire, wit, or weirdness. View their previous stories, order the CrackedWEB book, and more by going to http://www.starsend.com/ Cracked/cracked.HTM. STAR DWARVES and more are yours for the taking.

Figure 24.6.

This Old Haunted House comprises this week's entry on the CrackedWEB.

Humorous and Bizarre News

The Web isn't the only place to find weird stuff. Usenet offers its share of wackiness as well. Remember, the standard disclaimers apply—because many of these groups are unmoderated, "bizarre" can sometimes degenerate to "disgusting" very quickly. If you start out with the groups recommended here, you should be pretty safe.

JUST A MINUTE

Want the weirdness to come to you? Why not try the Weird News listserv? To subscribe, send e-mail to LISTSERV@BROWNVM.BROWN.EDU with no Subject: and the line SUBSCRIBE TREPAN-L in the body of your message.

Plenty of yucks and strangeness are to be had on a daily basis on Usenet. The following are a few of the best:

- [ ] The creme de la creme of funny newsgroups is rec.humor.funny. This moderated group generally has good jokes. Off-color humor is encrypted in ROT-13. You must decode these jokes before you can read them.

- [ ] The alt.comedy.* hierarchy has some great groups covering vaudeville to the Stooges.

- [ ] The alt.comics.* hierarchy has groups on Dilbert, Peanuts, and more.

- [ ] aus.jokes gives you a sense of humor from the Land Down Under. This group isn't moderated, so read carefully.

- [ ] The longest Usenet newsgroup name goes to (drumroll, please) alt.tv.lost-in-space.danger.will-robinson.danger.danger.danger. Believe it or not, some people actually post to this group. Of course, for a little more traffic, you might want to look at alt.tv.seinfeld or alt.tv.beakmans-world.

- [ ] You might also want to scan the alt.fan.* hierarchy. Several comedians and strange people are listed in this cluster of groups.

In Search of the Holy Grail

Arguably the best comedy troupe of modern times is Monty Python's Flying Circus. This comedy troupe (no, Monty Python isn't a person) was lead by John Cleese and Graham Chapman. Their television show aired on the BBC from 1969 to 1974, but they are probably most famous for movies such as *Monty Python and the Holy Grail.* Even if you've never heard of them, check out the rest of this section—you might find yourself hooked.

The FAQs About Monty Python

If you already know everything there is to know about Monty Python, you may want to skip the next couple of paragraphs. Even if you're very familiar with them, you might learn something here anyway.

You can access the Monty Python Frequently Asked Questions file from one of several locations:

- ☐ E-mail: Send e-mail to either John Kolesar at `kolesar@clark.net` or Bonni Hall at `bonni@prairienet.org`.

- ☐ FTP: If you point your browser to `ftp://ftp.uu.net/usenet/news.answers/monty-python`, you can see or download the full-text version of the Monty Python FAQ.

- ☐ Usenet: The FAQ is posted to the `alt.fan.monty-python` newsgroup every two weeks. Look for it.

- ☐ WWW: The FAQ is also posted at `http://www.clark.net/pub/kolesar/FAQ/FAQINDEX.html`.

JUST A MINUTE

The Monty Python FAQ is invaluable. It gives lots of information that is valuable not just to Python fans, but also to those looking for similar information on other groups and copyrighted materials, as you can see in Figure 24.7. Take a few moments to "have a go at it."

Figure 24.7.

This interactive FAQ is priceless to any Python surfer.

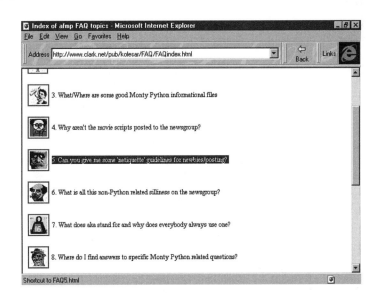

The Official Monty Python Homepage

The Official Python Homepage, shown in Figure 24.8, is a jolly good stroll through the wacky world of the Flying Circus. You can find pointers and links to everything you ever wanted to know about Monty Python on this site. It is located at `http://www.pythonline.com/afmp/`.

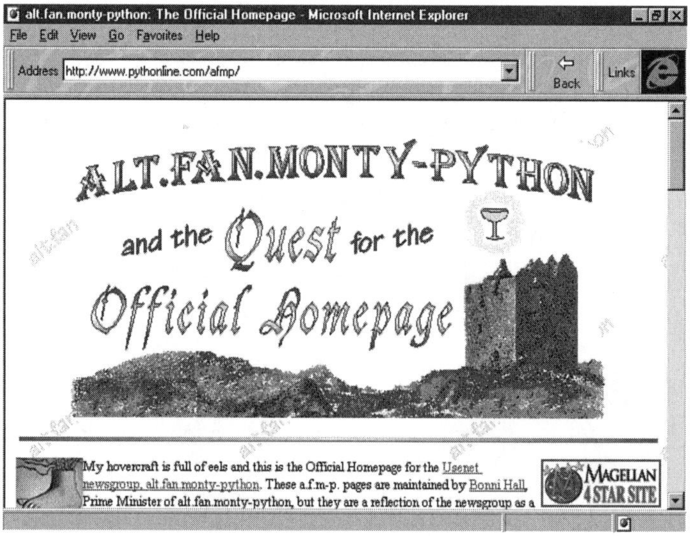

Figure 24.8.

The Holy Grail for Python followers everywhere.

If you want to see (or rather read) what all the fuss is about, follow the next set of steps from the AFMP Homepage.

To Do: Searching for the Holy Grail

1. Click the `alt.fan.monty-python Internet Resources Page` link. You can find a lot of stuff here.
2. Click the `Archive Sites` link.
3. Go to `Lord DarkWolfe's FTP Site` and then click `Movies`.
4. Click the `holy.grail.screenplay` to see the cult comedy classic in all its glory. If you've never seen the movie, just read a few pages of the script, and you'll want to.

Other Monty Python Pages

Several other sites are available for Python addicts. One of the best is the Monty Python's Flying Circus page. Get music chord charts, do full-text searches, or download audio files of some of their zaniest skits.

24

To Do: Playing with Monty Python

1. Point your browser to `http://bau2.uibk.ac.at/sg/python/monty.html`.

2. Click the `Sounds` link.

3. Click any one of the sound files displayed. Depending on how you've configured your browser, you can save the file to play later or have a plug-in play it for you right away.

The Monty Python Newsgroups

Most of this Monty Python silliness, of course, springs from the newsgroups `alt.fan.monty-python` and `alt.fan.monty-python.silliness`. If you're into Python for the long haul, subscribe to these groups. They're designed mainly for discussion, silliness, and mayhem, so you shouldn't expect to download files from these groups. But believe me, the conversation is entertaining enough!

Before this final lesson ends, just remember that most of these resources were located by searching. Whether you're searching the Web, FTP, Catalist, or newsgroups, the key is in finding the information. Give a man an Internet resource, and he'll surf for a day; teach him how to find Internet resources, and he'll surf for the rest of his life.

24

Summary

In this wacky lesson, you learned how to conduct density experiments on Twinkies and calculate the per pound cost of various flavors of roadkill. You now know if you're a redneck, and you probably know more light bulb jokes than your 10 closest friends.

You also learned more than you probably ever wanted to know about Monty Python's Flying Circus. Most importantly, though, you once again realized how important it is to be able to locate resources on the Internet. So, now, it's time; venture forth, use ye the Internet, and may your travels be fruitful.

Workshop

The following workshop helps solidify the skills that you learned in this lesson.

Q&A

Q You seem to have an awful lot of warnings in this lesson. Are they really necessary?

A In my opinion, yes. Any time you ask people for bizarre and funny material without regulation of the content, you're asking for trouble. You would probably be truly shocked by some of the material that's on the Internet, so you can never be too safe.

Quiz

Take the following quiz to see how much you've learned.

Questions

1. How many PR people does it take to change a light bulb?

    (a) One—they're very good at spinning things.

    (b) Two—one to find out if the people want it screwed in and one to screw it in.

    (c) I don't know, but I'll get back to you on that.

2. What were the conclusions of the Twinkie Oxidization Test?

    (a) Because they're 68 percent air, they already *are* oxidized!

    (b) No oxidization occurs with lard and flour.

    (c) Twinkies actually burn quite nicely after they are dried out.

3. This whole lesson was silly!

    (a) True

    (b) False

Answers

1. (c) According to the Random Light Bulb Joke page. I came up with (a) and (b) myself.

2. (c) See `http://www.owlnet.rice.edu/~gouge/twinkie.docs/oxidation.html` for confirmation of these results.

3. (a) Are you kidding?

Activity

See the most bizarre or funny resource you can find in under 15 minutes. If it's really funny, send it to me—I like a good joke.

24

Part

VII

Appendixes

Appendix A

Hot Sites

Many of the sites in this appendix appear elsewhere in the book. This simply represents a quick reference of sites that you might find most useful or entertaining.

Computer and Internet Related Sites

These sites take you to some of the major producers of computers, computer systems, and related hardware and software.

Computer Systems

IBM

http://www.ibm.com

Apple Computer

http://www.apple.com

Sun Microsystems, Inc.

http://www.sun.com

Digital Equipment Corporation (DEC)

http://www.dec.com

Compaq

http://www.compaq.com

Gateway 2000

http://www.gateway2000.com

Dell

http://www.dell.com

Toshiba

http://www.toshiba.com

Printers

Hewlett-Packard

http://www.hp.com

Brother

http://www.brother.com

Canon

http://www.canon.com

Modems

US Robotics

http://www.usr.com

Hayes

http://www.hayes.com

Practical Peripherals

http://www.practinet.com

Microcom

http://www.microcom.com

Zoom

http://www.zoom.com

Global Village

http://www.globalvillage.com

A

A

Major Software Corporations

Microsoft

http://www.microsoft.com

Novell

http://www.novell.com

Claris

http://www.claris.com

Adobe Systems Incorporated

http://www.adobe.com

Quarterdeck

http://www.quarterdeck.com

Internet Sites

This section contains Internet-related World Wide Web sites.

Browsers and Plug-Ins

Netscape Communications

http://www.netscape.com

Netscape Navigator plug-ins

http://www.netscape.com/comprod/mirror/navcomponents_download.html

Microsoft Internet Explorer

http://www.microsoft.com/ie/

Using Navigator plug-ins in Microsoft Internet Explorer

http://www.microsoft.com/ie/challenge/comparison/plug.htm

NCSA Mosaic

http://www.ncsa.uiuc.edu/SDG/Software/Mosaic/

Search Engines

Excite

http://www.excite.com

Yahoo!

http://www.yahoo.com

Infoseek

http://www.infoseek.com/

AltaVista

http://www.altavista.digital.com/

Magellan

http://www.mckinley.com/

Lycos

http://www.lycos.com/

Open Text

http://www.opentext.com/

WebCrawler

http://www.webcrawler.com/

MetaCrawler—Searches by geographic region

http://metacrawler.cs.washington.edu

shareware.com—Searches for shareware

http://www.shareware.com/

Catalist—Searches for listservs

http://segate.sunet.se/lists/listref.html

People Finders

Four11

http://www.four11.com/

InfoSpace

http://www.infospace.com

WhoWhere?

http://www.whowhere.com

America Directory Assistance

http://www.lookupusa.com/lookupusa/adp/peopsrch.htm

A

Government Sites

The following are a few of the more popular governmental sites on the Web:

The White House

http://www.whitehouse.gov

The U.S. Senate

http://www.senate.gov

The U.S. House of Representatives

http://www.house.gov

Library of Congress

http://lcweb.loc.gov/

FedWorld

http://www.fedworld.gov

Broadcast Media

This list of sites covers everything from network TV to cable to the movies.

Network TV

ABC

http://www.abc.com

CBS

http://www.cbs.com

NBC

http://www.nbc.com

Fox

http://www.foxworld.com

Cable TV

Cinemax

http://www.cinemax.com

HBO

http://www.hbo.com

The Disney Channel

`http://www.disney.com/DisneyChannel/`

ESPN

`http://www.espn.com`

Movie Studios

MCA/Universal

`http://www.mca.com`

Metro Goldwyn Mayer

`http://www.mgmua.com`

Paramount Pictures

`http://www.paramount.com`

Sony Pictures

`http://www.spe.sony.com/Pictures/SonyMovies/index.html`

20th Century Fox

`http://www.tcfhe.com`

Walt Disney Studios

`http://www.disney.com/DisneyPictures/`

Warner Brothers

`http://www.movies.warnerbros.com/`

A

Appendix B

Shareware Products for Windows

Just about every shareware program you need for optimal use of the Internet on your PC-compatible computer is contained in this appendix.

E-Mail Clients

We recommend using Eudora Light, but we have listed several other clients, as well. For more discussion of what e-mail clients can do, refer to Part II, "E-Mail: The Great Communicator."

Eudora Light—Shareware version of Eudora Pro

`ftp://ftp.qualcomm.com/eudora/windows/light/eudor154.exe`

Pegasus Mail—A Windows-based e-mail client

`ftp://oak.oakland.edu/pub/simtelnet/win3/email/winpm242.exe`

Pronto Lite—An award-winning standalone e-mail client

`ftp://oak.oakland.edu/pub/simtelnet/win3/email/plite.zip`

News Clients

We recommend WinVN as a stable, easy-to-use news reader. FreeAgent and NewsXpress also are good news readers. For more details on what news readers can do, refer to Lesson 9, "Basic Journalism: Introduction to Newsgroups," and Lesson 10, "Getting the Scoop: Using Newsgroups."

WinVN for Windows 95—The premiere news reader for Windows

```
ftp://oak.oakland.edu/pub/simtelnet/win95/news/wv32i998.zip
```

WinVN for Windows 3.1—The 16-bit version of WinVN

```
ftp://oak.oakland.edu/pub/simtelnet/win3/news/wv16i998.zip
```

NewsXpress for Windows 95—Another good news reader

```
ftp://wuarchive.wustl.edu/systems/ibmpc/win95/netutil/newsx86.zip
```

NewsXpress for Windows 3.1—The 16-bit version of NewsXpress (beta version only)

```
ftp://ftp.download.com/pub/win3/internet/nx20b2.zip
```

Free Agent—The shareware version of this excellent news reader

```
ftp://ftp.coast.net/Coast/win3/winsock/fagent10.zip
```

Web Browsers

Browser versions change almost constantly. These links enable you to download the most current version of your favorite browser with easy-to-follow directions.

Netscape Navigator—Still the most popular browser around

```
http://www.netscape.com/comprod/mirror/client_download.html
```

Microsoft Internet Explorer—Gives Netscape a run for its money

```
http://www.microsoft.com/ie/download/
```

NCSA Mosaic—The original Web browser

```
http://www.ncsa.uiuc.edu/SDG/Software/Mosaic/
```

B

FTP Clients

FTP clients can help you download files from the Internet easily and add more flexibility to FTP than Web browsers offer. There really are no other clients that compare to WS_FTP. For more on what FTP can do for you, refer to Lesson 17, "Getting Files with FTP."

WS_FTP—This program enables you to install either the 16- or 32-bit version on your computer.

```
ftp://oak.oakland.edu/pub/simtelnet/win95/inet/ws_ftp32.zip
```

B

Gopher Clients

Web browsers do an excellent job with Gopher, but if you want a little extra functionality, you might want to pick up one of these. For more information on Gopher, refer to Lesson 18, "Gopher Even More."

WSGopher—An excellent Gopher client

```
ftp://wuarchive.wustl.edu/systems/ibmpc/win3/winsock/wsg-11.exe
```

Hampson's Gopher—This one has been around a long time and works very well.

```
ftp://wuarchive.wustl.edu/systems/ibmpc/win3/winsock/hgoph24.zip
```

Telnet Clients

These clients help you access online libraries and other resources that aren't available through the Web or Gopher. There are quite a few Telnet clients out there. In fact, there is a built-in Telnet client with Windows 95 that works very well. We've included a couple of the best shareware Telnet clients here. For more information on Telnet, you might want to look at Lesson 19, "Telnet to the Internet."

Yawtel—Yet another Windows Telnet client, and a good one

```
ftp://wuarchive.wustl.edu/systems/ibmpc/win3/winsock/yawtel09.zip
```

EWAN (emulator without a good name)—This is also a very effective Telnet client.

```
http://www.yahoo.com
```

QWS3270—This client gives you access to those sites that require TN3270 emulation. They're rare, but this is a handy program to have around.

```
ftp://ftp.ccs.queensu.ca/pub/msdos/tcpip/qws3270.zip
```

File Compression Utility

Many of the files in cyberspace are compressed in order to save space. In order to use them, you have to be able to decompress them. For this job, there's really only one utility to get:

WinZip—The premiere compression utility for Windows. Get an evaluation copy for either Windows 3.1 or 95.

`http://www.winzip.com/ddc.htm`

Plug-Ins

To enjoy some of the "snappier" features of the Web, you might want to grab a few of these. Refer to Lesson 11, "Chatting Live on the Internet," and Lesson 12, "Internet Phone and Video," for more information on these exciting products.

Plug-Ins

This list consists of some of the plug-ins we feel are definitely worth the time to download.

Real Audio—Real Audio in real time

`http://www.realaudio.com/products/player/download.html`

Shockwave—Another great utility to make the Web come alive

`http://www.macromedia.com/shockwave/download/index.cgi`

Bubbleviewer—Brings "visual splendor" to your PC running Windows 3.1

`http://www.omniview.com/viewers/win/win31.html`

Bubbleviewer plug-in for Windows 95

`http://www.omniview.com/viewers/win/win95plug.html`

Live 3D—Take a walk through the Web side.

`http://home.netscape.com/comprod/products/navigator/`
`live3d/download_live3d.html`

B

FutureSplash—Delivers interactive buttons, drawings, and animations to the Web

`http://www.futurewave.com/downloadfs.htm`

To directly download the Windows 3.1 version, go to

`ftp://ftp.futurewave.com/plugin/win/splash16.exe`

For the Windows 95 version, go to

`ftp://ftp.futurewave.com/plugin/win/splash32.exe`

Key View—View dozens of different file types right in Netscape's window!

`http://www.ftp.com/cgi/key.cgi`

Jutvision—View 3-D worlds without losing perspective.

`http://www.visdyn.com/downloadplug.html`

B

Internet Phones

Although VocalTec's product has been highly favored in many reviews, here are some others you might want to check out.

Internet Phone 3.2 from VocalTec for Windows 3.1

`http://www.vocaltech.com/down1.htm#release3`

Internet Phone 4 from VocalTec for Windows 95

`http://www.vocaltech.com/iphone4/ip4_dnld.htm`

Netspeak Corporation's WebPhone

`http://connect.netspeak.com/getwphn2.htm`

DigiPhone from Third Planet Publishing

`http://www.planeteers.com/download/pctrial.htm`

TeleVox from Voxware (for Windows 95 only)

`http://www.voxware.com`

FreeTel

`http://www.freetel.com`

Popular FTP Sites

Here are a few of the popular FTP sites that contain Windows 3.1 and Windows 95 software:

`ftp://ftp.cdrom.com`

`ftp://oak.oakland.edu`

`ftp://wuarchive.wustl.edu`

`ftp://mirrors.aol.com`

B

Appendix C

Shareware Products for the Macintosh

This appendix lists every shareware program you need for optimal Internet use with your Macintosh.

E-mail Clients

For the Macintosh, Eudora is really the only full-blown shareware e-mail client available. For more discussion of what e-mail clients can do, refer to Part II, "E-Mail: The Great Communicator."

Eudora Light—The shareware version of Eudora Pro. This directory contains versions for both PowerPC and non-PowerPC Macs.

News Clients

I recommend Newswatcher as a stable, easy-to-use newsreader. The News is also a decent newsreader. For more details on what newsreaders can do, refer to Lessons 9, "Basic Journalism: Introduction to Newsgroups," and 10, "Getting the Scoop: Using Newsgroups."

Newswatcher—The premiere news reader for Macintosh.

`ftp://mirror.apple.com/mirrors/Info-Mac.Archive/comm/inet/ya-newswatcher-240.hqx`

The News—A news reader with a slightly different approach.

`ftp://mirror.apple.com/mirrors/Info-Mac.Archive/comm/inet/the-news-24.hqx`

Web Browsers

Browser versions change almost constantly. These links enable you to download the most current version of your favorite browser with easy-to-follow directions.

Netscape Navigator—Still the most popular browser around.

`http://www.netscape.com/comprod/mirror/client_download.html`

Internet Explorer—Gives Netscape a run for its money.

`http://www.microsoft.com/ie/download/`

NCSA Mosaic—The original Web browser.

`http://www.ncsa.uiuc.edu/SDG/Software/Mosaic/`

FTP Clients

FTP clients can help you easily download files from the Internet and add more flexibility to FTP than Web browsers offer. There are two main FTP clients for Macintosh: Anarchie and Fetch. They are both very good. For more on what FTP can do for you, refer to Lesson 17, "Getting Files with FTP."

Anarchie—Lets you FTP files and search Archie databases with one application.

`ftp://ftp.download.com/pub/mac/internet/anarc201.sit.hqx`

Fetch—The first, and still very powerful, FTP client for the Macintosh.

`ftp://mirror.apple.com/mirrors/Info-Mac.Archive/comm/inet/fetch-301.hqx`

Gopher Clients

Web browsers do an excellent job with Gopher, but if you want a little extra, you might want to pick up TurboGopher. For more on Gopher, refer to Lesson 18, "Gopher Even More."

TurboGopher—THE Gopher client for Macintosh.

`ftp://mirror.apple.com/mirrors/Info-Mac.Archive/comm/inet/turbo-gopher-203.hqx`

Telnet Clients

These clients help you access online libraries and other resources that aren't available through the Web or Gopher. A few Telnet clients are available for the Macintosh, although NCSA's Telnet is by far the best. I've included a couple of the best shareware Telnet clients here. For more information on Telnet, look at Lesson 19, "Telnet to the Internet."

NCSA Telnet—The best.

```
ftp://mirror.apple.com/mirrors/Info-Mac.Archive/comm/inet/ncsa-telnet-27b4.hqx
```

TN3270—This client gives you access to those sites that require TN3270 emulation. They're rare, but this is a handy one to have around.

```
ftp://mirror.apple.com/mirrors/Info-Mac.Archive/comm/inet/tn3270-25b2.hqx
```

File Compression Utility

A lot of those files out there in cyberspace come compressed in order to save space. In order to use them, you have to be able to *un*compress them. For this job, there's really only one utility to get:

StuffIt Expander—The best compression utility for Macintosh. Also available in a commercial version. There is, however, a chicken-and-egg problem in that you need a decompression program to decompress a compressed program, but StuffIt Expander usually comes compressed. (For Netscape 3 users, this is no problem, as StuffIt Expander comes included with Netscape 3.) To solve this problem, you should go to Aladdin's StuffIt Expander Web page for help:

```
http://www.aladdinsys.com/consumer/expander2.html
```

Other Compression Utilities—If you are interested in handling files compressed with non-Macintosh compression, you might check out some of the utilities in the following directory:

```
ftp://mirrors.aol.com/pub/info-mac/cmp/
```

Plug-Ins

To enjoy some of the "snappier" features of the Web, you might want to grab a few of these. Refer to Lessons 11, "Chatting Live on the Internet," and 12, "Internet Phone and Video," for more information on these exciting products.

Real Audio—Real audio in real time.

```
http://www.realaudio.com/products/player/download.html
```

Shockwave—Another great utility to make the Web come alive.

`http://www.macromedia.com/shockwave/download/index.cgi`

Bubbleviewer Plug-In for PowerMacs—Get a warped—spherical—view of the Web.

`http://www.omniview.com/viewers/mac/macppcplug.html`

Bubbleviewer For 68K Macs—360 degrees of Web site freedom.

`http://www.omniview.com/viewers/mac/mac68k.html`

Live 3D—Take a walk through a Web site.

`http://home.netscape.com/comprod/products/navigator/live3d/download_live3d.html`

FutureSplash for PowerMacs—Interactive buttons and animations galore.

`http://www.futurewave.com/fssetup/plugin/futuresplashpm.hqx`

FutureSplash for 68K Macs—Enables animations and activity on your Web site.

`http://www.futurewave.com/fssetup/plugin/futuresplash68k.hqx`

Internet Phones

Although VocalTec's product has been highly favored in many reveiws, here are some others you might want to check out.

Internet Phone 3.0.1 from VocalTec For PowerMac—The leader in Internet phones.

`http://www.vocaltech.com/mac/web/mac_dnld.htm`

DigiPhone from Third Planet Publishing—A good beginner phone.

`http://www.planeteers.com/download/mactrial.htm`

Popular FTP Sites

The following are popular FTP sites that contain Macintosh software:

`ftp://wuarchive.wustl.edu`

`ftp://mirrors.aol.com`

`ftp://mac.archive.umich.edu`

`ftp://sumex-aim.stanford.edu`

C

Glossary

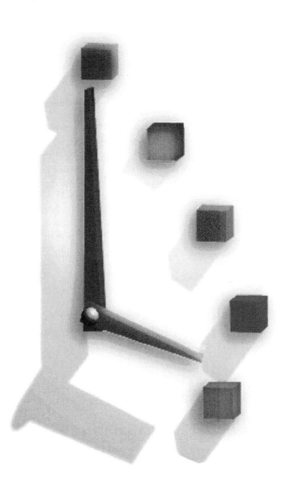

ActiveX. Microsoft's answer to Netscape's plug-ins. ActiveX components act like plug-ins but claim to be more dynamic because they can be downloaded along with the page that uses them.

alias. Also called a *nickname*, an alias is a shortcut that represents a real e-mail address.

Archie. A search engine designed specifically to find files and information on FTP sites.

backbone. Nothing more than a major cable that carries network traffic.

BBS. An abbreviation for *bulletin board system*. Bulletin board systems contain information specific to the organizations that sponsor them. They are often similar to freenets, except that they rarely offer any type of Internet access.

Big Seven Hierarchies. Newsgroup hierarchies that were established years ago and are still in effect today. They comprise what's known as the Big 7 newsgroup hierarchies. These seven hierarchies contain a majority of all newsgroup traffic: comp, soc, rec, sci, talk, news, and misc.

binary. Any non-text file, such as a picture or shareware program. Special utilities usually are required to decode these files.

bookmark. A way that a Web browser can keep a permanent record of Internet sites. Internet Explorer refers to bookmarks as *Favorites*.

Boolean operators. These operators are designed to put conditions on a search. The most common Boolean operators are AND, OR, and AND NOT.

browser. A software program that requests, interprets, and presents World Wide Web documents. Frequently used browsers include Internet Explorer, Netscape Navigator, Lynx, and Mosaic.

CC. The Carbon Copy message header. This field contains the e-mail addresses of additional message recipients.

CERN. The European Laboratory for Particle Physics and the birthplace of the World Wide Web.

client. All the computers and software that make up the Internet are either *clients* (which receive and translate data) or *servers* (which provide and translate data). Thus, client software allows you to get information from the Internet.

codec. Short for *compression/decompression*, a mathematical algorithm responsible for encoding an analog signal into digital form. It also decodes a received digital signal back into an analog signal.

command-line environment. In this environment, you type text on a line, the server responds with text, you type in another command, and so on. These interfaces often require special commands and keystroke combinations to perform special functions.

cross-posting. A method by which you can post a single article to multiple newsgroups.

digital data. Data is made up of a series of 0s and 1s that are grouped in unique sequences. Each sequence of 0s and 1s can mean an infinite number of commands to the computers translating them into what you see on your screen.

domain name. The name given to any computer registered on the World Wide Web as an official provider of information and files. Domain Names are usually two or more terms separated by periods. A couple of examples are `aol.com` or `www.msu.edu`.

download. Transferring a file from a host computer to your computer, usually using FTP.

dropouts. The sudden loss of a digital signal, consequently cutting off the person who is speaking using an Internet phone application. Dropouts are usually caused by incorrect audio settings.

e-mail address. Consists of a user ID, followed by an @ sign and a domain name. For instance: `tom@candlestick.com`.

e-text. This term stands for *electronic text*. E-text is becoming a popular way to put textbooks, noncopyrighted books, and other literature on the Internet.

emoticons. Short for *emotional icons*. These character combinations are one way of trying to get across a little emotion in what you say. For instance, `:)` is a smile.

encoding. Sometimes referred to as *encryption*. A method for turning binary data into textual data for transmission over the Internet. Binhex (used on Macintosh computers and the Eudora e-mail client), UUDecode (used by UNIX and some other e-mail clients), and MIME (used on the Web and by a few other e-mail clients) are standard encoding schemes.

FAQ. Stands for *Frequently Asked Questions*. Many times, newcomers to a newsgroup will ask questions that the old-timers have heard over and over again. FAQs are written and posted periodically to reduce the number of redundant questions.

filter. Simply a way that an e-mail client looks at e-mail message header information in order to determine what to do with the message. A filter might be defined to put all messages from a certain sender into a particular location.

flame. An Internet message that often uses profanity or otherwise berates and belittles the recipient.

frames. A feature available on the World Wide Web that presents text, links, graphics, and other media in separate portions of the browser display. Some sections remain unchanging, while others serve as an exhibit of linked documents.

freenets. Organizations that offer limited bulletin board system-like access onto the Internet, although some freenets offer no Internet access at all.

FTP. An abbreviation for *File Transfer Protocol.* FTP is a set of rules for transferring files on the Internet.

full-duplex. Referring to a type of sound card, a full-duplex card allows two users to speak simultaneously while using an Internet phone application.

Global Online Directory (GOLD). A server that maintains the status of all the current users who are using VocalTec's Internet Phone application.

Gopher. Developed at the University of Minnesota, a system whereby many types of information can be displayed and accessed in a simple, menu-based structure.

Gopherspace. The term used to describe the portion of the Internet that contains Gopher sites.

half-duplex. Referring to a type of sound card, a half-duplex card allows only one user to speak at a time while using an Internet phone application.

hits. When conducting an Internet search on the Web, each result of a particular search is called a hit.

home page. Frequently, this term refers to the cover of a particular Web site. The home page is the main, or first, page displayed for an organization's or person's World Wide Web site.

HTML. An abbreviation for *HyperText Markup Language.* HTML is the coding language for the World Wide Web that informs browsers how to display a document's text, links, graphics, and other media. This language forms the foundation for all Web pages.

ICE. The Excite search engine uses *Intelligent Concept Extraction* (ICE) to search more than 50 million fully indexed Web pages. The ICE method allows for highly accurate searches based on real language searches, as well as more standard search types.

image map. A feature available on the World Wide Web that allows users to click on various locations in a graphic image to link to different documents.

include marks. These > characters, which are found in e-mail messages and newsgroup postings, are the quotation marks of the Internet. When reading or replying to an e-mail message, an include mark indicates a line of text that belonged to a previous message.

Integrated Services Digital Network (ISDN). Currently the fastest connection capable using existing phone lines. ISDN allows users to connect at speeds of 128KB per second. The ISDN line is capable of transmitting voice and data simultaneously.

Internet phone. An application that transmits a user's speech across a network (in this case, the Internet) to another user's machine.

Internet Relay Chat (IRC). A very large network of servers that allow users to communicate in real time to one another via the keyboard.

Internet Service Provider (ISP). An organization or company that provides users access to the Internet.

IP Address. An address used by Internet Protocol (IP) to identify each computer on the Internet. This number consists of four numbers between 0 and 255, each separated by a period. A typical IP address might be 35.8.7.92.

link. Short for *hypertext link*. A link provides a path that connects a user from one part of a World Wide Web document to another part of the same document, a different document, or another resource.

listserv. An e-mail address that is configured to forward every message it receives to the e-mail addresses of those who have subscribed to it. You can think of it as an electronic interactive newspaper.

local/remote. These terms are often used in reference to FTP. A local machine is your computer. A remote machine is simply a server to which you connect via means of a modem or network connection.

lurking. Reading a newsgroup without posting to it.

mailbox. A place where your e-mail client stores mail.

mailing list. See *listserv*.

Megahertz. One hertz represents a single cycle of current in a circuit. A Megahertz represents 1,000 cycles. PC speed is usually gauged in Megahertz per second, so a 66 Megahertz processor can complete 66,000 cycles in one second.

message headers. The part of an e-mail message (or newsgroup posting) that contains basic information such as sender, receiver, and subject. Message headers act much like the information on the envelope of a letter.

micropayments. A method by which companies can keep an "electronic charge account" for customers. Micropayments offer an affordable way to charge anywhere from one cent to one-hundredth of a cent as payment for services or products offered over the Internet.

modem. A device that allows your computer to talk to other computers using your phone line. Modems range in speeds of 9.6 to 33.6 KB per second.

moderated listserv. Just as a debate has a moderator to make sure both sides stick to the rules, so too do some listservs have a human moderator who makes sure the rules of the listserv are being followed. These listservs are called *moderated listservs*.

moderator. Anyone who moderates, or filters, the content on a listserv or newsgroup.

Mosaic. The first Web browser, written by Marc Andreessen.

Multi-User Dungeon (MUD). A game on the Internet very similar to IRC. Users solve puzzles, find clues, and interact with other players in hopes of mastering the game.

newsgroups. Topical areas of Usenet that operate much like bulletin boards for the discussion of topics regarding recreation, society, culture, business and—of course—computers. Currently, there are more than 12,000 newsgroups available.

.newsrc file. A file that contains information about your newsgroups, such as which groups you're subscribed to and how many articles (both read and unread) are in each group you subscribe to.

NNTP Server. NNTP stands for *Network News Transfer Protocol*. An NNTP server transfers news to your client using the language of Usenet.

node. Generally the computer (or computers) at each routing station on the Internet.

noise. Sooner or later, you'll hear the term *signal-to-noise ratio*. This is merely a way of describing how much useful material (signal) compared to useless material (noise) is contained on a given newsgroup.

operator. Anything that modifies a term or equation. In the equation $2 + 2 = 4$, the plus sign is an operator. When searching on the Web, you can often use special symbols or words to build a search "equation" that is often more effective than searching for a single word or phrase.

packet. A single sequence of digital data. As each packet of data is sent through the various networks, it has a distinct digital marker.

plug-in. A small file that increases the capabilities of a Web browser. Plug-ins enable browsers to display file types beyond images and text.

POP. An abbreviation for *Post Office Protocol*, which is the technical name for the way some e-mail servers deliver your mail.

post. What a message to a Usenet newsgroup is called. When you submit messages (also called articles) to newsgroups, you are said to be *posting*.

protocol. A set of rules. On the Internet, this translates into the set of rules computers use to communicate across networks.

search engine. A computer program that indexes a database and then allows people to search it for relevant information available on the Internet.

server. Any computer that delivers—serves—information and data.

signature. A small text file that contains information your e-mail or newsgroup client automatically attaches to the bottom of every message you send.

SMTP. An abbreviation for *Simple Mail Transport Protocol,* which is another technical name for the way e-mail messages are sent.

spam. Any mass-mailed material meant for self-promotion, advertisement, or pure silliness. Spam, or electronic junk mail, is probably one of the most offensive aspects of the Internet.

streaming audio/video. The capability for multimedia to begin playback as the file is being downloaded.

T1 line. A connection capable of transferring data at 1,544,000 bits per second. A T1 is the fastest connection commonly used to connect networks to the Internet.

T3 line. A connection capable of carrying 45 million bits per second. Commonly used in video conferencing and telecommunications where high bandwidth is needed. A T3 is capable of carrying full-screen, full-motion video.

Tables. A feature available on the World Wide Web that presents document text, links, graphics, and other media in row and column format. Table borders may be visible in some documents and invisible in others.

TCP/IP. An abbreviation for *Transmission Control Protocol/Internet Protocol.*

Telnet. A method of establishing a direct terminal connection to an Internet host computer. VT100 and TN3270 are popular Telnet protocols.

thread. A series of newsgroup articles all dealing with the same topic. Someone replies to an article, and then someone else replies to the reply, and so on.

traffic. A term used to describe how much activity there is on either a listserv or a newsgroup.

UNIX. A very powerful and portable operating system that is the foundational operating language of the Internet. UNIX is not an acronym for anything.

upload. Transferring a file to a host computer from your computer, usually using FTP.

UPS. An abbreviation for Uninterruptable Power Supply. A backup battery supply that allows you to safely shut down your machine as the result of a sudden power loss.

URL. An abbreviation for *Uniform Resource Locator*. A URL (pronounced "You-Are-El" or "Earl") serves as identification for all Internet documents.

Usenet. The name is modeled after Usenix, the UNIX users' conference series. It was supposed to mean *UNIX Users Network*, because all the early sites were UNIX machines, and many of the early discussions were about the UNIX operating system.

UserID. Every person with an e-mail address has a user identification of some sort. This is usually something very simple, like johndoe, but could be quite a bit more enigmatic.

Veronica. An acronym for the *Very Easy Rodent-Oriented Net-Wide Index to Computerized Archives*. This is a search engine designed to search Gopherspace.

Web Phone. See *Internet Phone*.

Web Site. A collection of World Wide Web documents, usually consisting of a home page and several related pages. You might think of a Web site as an interactive electronic book.

Webmaster. The individual responsible for maintaining and updating the content of a World Wide Web document. Webmasters are the creative force behind the World Wide Web.

INDEX

G

Galacticom bulletin board system, 251
Gateway 2000 site, 332
GIF (Graphics Interchange Format) files, 192
Global Village modems site, 332
GOLD servers (Global Online Directory), 151
GOLD window, 154
Gopher, 233-234
  clients, 344
  E-texts, 241-242
  links, 236
  locating people, 261
  Minnesota site, 235
  navigating, 236-237
  searches with Veronica, 261-263
  structure, 237
  Telnet, 238
  weather, 240
Gopher Jewels, 239
government sites, 335
Graphical User Interface (GUI) for IRC clients, 132
graphics hyperlinks, 165
Group Listing window (newsgroups), 122-123
GUI (Graphical User Interface) for IRC clients, 132

H

Hayes modems site, 332
HBO Web site, 335
headers
  e-mail messages, 56-58
  filters, 86

headphones (Web phone), 149
helper applications, 177, 193
Hewlett-Packard site, 332
higher education, 295-298
history of the Web, 28-29
history files, 167-169
home pages, 30
Hot Bot site (Inktomi), 212
hotlists, 31
HTML (HyperText Markup Language), 30
humor, 318-320
  bizarre, 321-324
  CrackedWEB, 323
  Monty Python, 324-327
  newsgroups, 324
  Twinkie experiment, 322
hyperlinks, 164-165
  cursor, 165
  Gopher, 236
  image maps, 165
hypertext links, 30
HyperText Markup Language (HTML), 30

I

IBM computers site, 331
ICE (Intelligent Concept Extraction), 210
ichat (IRC client), 137-138
icons, 61-62
images
  image maps, 30, 165
  interactivity, 35
In-Box Direct (Netscape), 180
include mark (>)
  in e-mail, 71
  in newsgroups, 126

Information Super-highway, 4
Infoseek search engine, 334
InfoSpace search engine, 334
  locating people, 258-259
Inktomi's Hot Bot site, 212
installation
  plug-ins, 193-194
  RealAudio Player, 196-197
  Shockwave, 198-199
Intelligent Concept Extraction (ICE), 210
interactive images, 35
Internal Revenue Service (IRS) page, 306
international resources, 279-283
Internet
  overview, 4-12, 16-17
  phone system comparison, 4-8
Internet Explorer
  ActiveX, 185
  configuration, 249
  favorites, 171-172, 181
  features, 181-183
  future plans, 183
  Netscape comparison, 175-183, 186-187
  Web site, 333
Internet phone, 147-157, 178
  applications, 156-157
  calls
    answering, 152
    placing, 154
    receiving, 155
  connection, 149-150
  controls/displays, 152-154
  directories, 153

You'll find thousands of shareware files and over 1600 computer books designed for both technowizards and technophobes. You can browse through 700 sample chapters, get the latest news on the Net, and find just about anything using our

We're open 24-hours a day, 365 days a year.

You don't need a card.

We don't charge fines.

And you can be as **LOUD** as you want.

MACMILLAN COMPUTER PUBLISHING USA

A VIACOM COMPANY

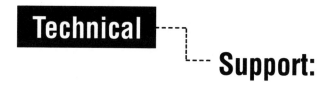

Support:

If you cannot get the CD/Disk to install properly, or you need assistance with a particular situation in the book, please feel free to check out the Knowledge Base on our Web site at **http://www.superlibrary.com/general/support**. We have answers to our most Frequently Asked Questions listed there. If you do not find your specific question answered, please contact Macmillan Technical Support at **(317) 581-3833**. We can also be reached by email at **support@mcp.com**.

Teach Yourself Microsoft Office 97 in 24 Hours

— *Greg Perry*

An estimated 22 million people use Microsoft Office, and with the new features of Office 97, much of that market will want the upgrade. To address that market, Sams has published a mass-market version of its best-selling *Teach Yourself* series. *Teach Yourself Microsoft Office 97 in 24 Hours* shows readers how to use the most widely requested features of Office. This entry-level title includes many illustrations, screen shots, and a step-by-step plan for learning Office 97. Teaches how to use each Office product and how to use the products together. Readers learn how to create documents in Word that include hypertext links to files created with one of the other Office products. Covers Office 97.

Price: $19.99 USA/$28.95 CDN   User Level: New - Casual - Accomplished
ISBN: 0-672-31009-0   450 pp.   Integrated Software/Suites

Teach Yourself Access 97 in 24 Hours

— *Timm Buchanan & David Nielsen*

As organizations and end users continue to upgrade to NT Workstation and Windows 95, a surge in 32-bit productivity applications, including Microsoft Office 97, is expected. Using an easy-to-follow approach, this book teaches the fundamentals of a key component in the Microsoft Office 97 package: Access 97. Readers will learn how to use and manipulate existing databases, create databases with wizards, and build databases from scratch in 24 one-hour lessons. Covers Microsoft Access 97.

Price: $19.99 USA/$28.95 CDN   User Level: New - Casual
ISBN: 0-672-31027-9   400 pp.   Databases

Teach Yourself Access 97 in 14 Days, Fourth Edition

— *Paul Cassel*

Through the examples, workshop sessions, and Q&A sections in this book, users will master the most important features of Access. In just two weeks they'll be able to develop their own databases and create stunning forms and reports. Updated for Access 97. Covers Wizards, tables, data types, validation, forms, queries, artificial fields, macros, and more. Readers learn how to program with Access Basic and Access lingo. Covers Access.

Price: $29.99 USA/$42.95 CDN   User Level: New - Casual
ISBN: 0-672-30969-6   700 pp.   Databases

Access 97 Unleashed, Second Edition

— *Dwayne Gifford, et al.*

Access, one of Microsoft's database managers for Windows, has become one of the most accepted standards of database management for personal computers. The *Unleashed* format for this book allows current and new users to quickly and easily find the information they need on the new features. It also serves as a complete reference for database programmers new to Access. Readers learn advanced techniques for working with tables, queries, forms, and data. Shows how to program Access and how to integrate the database with the Internet. CD-ROM includes Access utilities and applications and an electronic Access Reference Library. Covers Access.

$49.99 USA/$70.95 CDN   User Level: Accomplished - Expert
ISBN: 0-672-30983-1   1,100 pp.   Databases

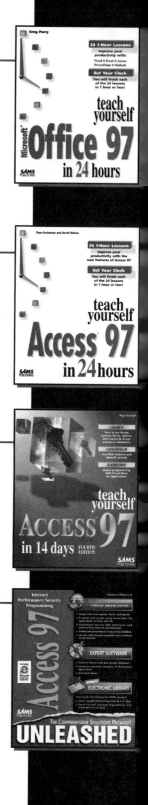

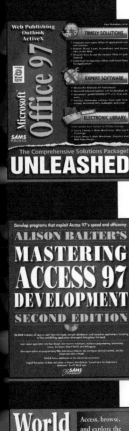

Microsoft Office 97 Unleashed, Second Edition

— Paul McFedries & Sue Charlesworth

Microsoft has brought the Web to its Office suite of products. Hyperlinking, Office Assistants, and Active Document Support let users publish documents to the Web or an intranet site. It also completely integrates with Microsoft FrontPage, making it possible to point and click a Web page into existence. This book details each of the Office products—Excel, Access, Powerpoint, Word, and Outlook—and shows the estimated 22 million registered users how to create presentations and Web documents. Shows how to extend Office to work on a network. Describes the various Office Solution Kits and how to use them. CD-ROM includes powerful utilities and two best-selling books in HTML format.

Price: $39.99 USA/$56.95 CDN   User Level: Accomplished - Expert
ISBN: 0-672-31010-4   1,200 pp.   Integrated Software/Suites

Alison Balter's Mastering Access 97 Development, Second Premier Edition

— Alison Balter

One of the premier corporate database applications, Access is a powerful application that can be programmed and customized. This book shows users how to develop both simple and complex applications for Access 97. Demonstrates how to create tables, forms, queries, reports, and objects. Teaches how to program Access applications for a client/server environment. CD-ROM includes source code, reusable functions, forms, and reports. Covers Access 97.

Price: $49.99 USA/ $70.95 CDN   User Level: Accomplished - Expert
ISBN: 0-672-30999-8   1,100 pp.   Databases

The World Wide Web 1997 Unleashed

— John December

This book has unleashed the latest Web topics previously known only to the field experts. It is designed to be the only book readers will need from their initial logon to the Web to creating their own Web pages. Takes the reader on an updated tour of the Web—highlighting sites and outlining browsing techniques. Includes Sams.net *Web 1,000 Directory*—the "yellow pages" of the Internet. CD-ROM contains everything from starter software to advanced Web site development tools. Covers the World Wide Web.

Price: $49.99 USA/$70.95 CDN   User Level: All User Levels
ISBN: 1-57521-184-X   1,300 pp.   Internet—General/WWW Applications

Teach Yourself Web Publishing with Microsoft Office 97 in a Week

— Michael Larson

As the number-one selling office suite in the business world with more than 22 million users, Microsoft Office is taking the market by storm. Using a clear, step-by-step approach and practical examples, users will learn how to effectively use components of Microsoft Office to publish attractive, well-designed documents for the World Wide Web or an intranet. Focuses on the Web publishing features of the latest versions of Microsoft Word, Excel, Access, and PowerPoint. Explains the basics of Internet/intranet technology, the Microsoft Internet Explorer browser, and HTML. CD-ROM is loaded with Microsoft Internet Explorer 3.0 and an extensive selection of additional graphics, templates, scripts, ActiveX controls, and multimedia clips to enhance Web pages. Covers Microsoft Office 97.

Price: $39.99 USA/$56.95 CDN   User Level: New - Casual - Accomplished
ISBN: 1-57521-232-3   500 pp.   Integrated Software/Suites

Add to Your Sams.net Library Today
with the Best Books for Internet Technologies

ISBN	Quantity	Description of Item	Unit Cost	Total Cost
0-672-31009-0		Teach Yourself Microsoft Office 97 in 24 Hours	$19.99	
0-672-31027-9		Teach Yourself Access 97 in 24 Hours	$19.99	
0-672-30969-6		Teach Yourself Access 97 in 14 Days, Fourth Edition	$29.99	
0-672-30983-1		Access 97 Unleashed, Second Edition (Book/CD-ROM)	$49.99	
0-672-31010-4		Microsoft Office 97 Unleashed, Second Edition (Book/CD-ROM)	$39.99	
0-672-30999-8		Alison Balter's Mastering Access 97 Development, Second Premier Edition (Book/CD-ROM)	$49.99	
1-57521-184-X		The World Wide Web 1997 Unleashed (Book/CD-ROM)	$49.99	
1-57521-232-3		Teach Yourself Web Publishing with Microsoft Office 97 in a Week (Book/CD-ROM)	$39.99	
		Shipping and Handling: See information below.		
		TOTAL		

Shipping and Handling: $4.00 for the first book, and $1.75 for each additional book. If you need to have it NOW, we can ship product to you in 24 hours for an additional charge of approximately $18.00, and you will receive your item overnight or in two days. Overseas shipping and handling adds $2.00. Prices subject to change. Call between 9:00 a.m. and 5:00 p.m. EST for availability and pricing information on latest editions.

201 W. 103rd Street, Indianapolis, Indiana 46290

1-800-428-5331 — Orders   1-800-835-3202 — FAX   1-800-858-7674 — Customer Service

Book ISBN 1-57521-236-6